Fitness Education for Children

A Team Approach

Stephen J. Virgilio, PhD
Adelphi University, Garden City,

Human Kinetics

Library of Congress Cataloging-in-Publication Data

Virgilio, Stephen J.
    Fitness education for children : a team approach / Stephen J.
        Virgilio.
            p.   cm.
        Includes bibliographical references (p.) and index.
        ISBN 0-87322-723-9
        1. Physical fitness for children--Study and teaching--United
States.   2. Physical education for children--Study and teaching-
-United States.   3. Curriculum planning--United States.   4. Teaching
teams--United States.   I. Title.
    GV443.V54   1997
    372.86'044--DC21   96-39567
                                                              CIP

ISBN: 0-87322-723-9

Photos courtesy of Stephen J. Virgilio. Figure 7.3 adapted, by permission, from Gerald S. Berenson, *The Heart Smart Gazette*, Vol. 1, No. 9, May 1986. Figure 7.8 adapted, by permission, from Jeanne Lyons, Incorporated Village of East Williston, NY, 1986. Figure 9.3 courtesy of the American Heart Association.

Acquisitions Editors: Rick Frey and Scott Wikgren; **Developmental Editor:** Julia Anderson; **Assistant Editors:** Jacqueline Eaton Blakley and Sandra Merz Bott; **Editorial Assistants:** Amy Carnes and Laura Majersky; **Copyeditor:** Bonnie Pettifor; **Proofreader:** Sarah Wiseman; **Indexer:** Diana Witt; **Graphic Designer:** Stuart Cartwright; **Graphic Artist:** Francine Hamerski; **Cover Designer:** Jack Davis; **Photographer (cover):** F-Stock/Thia Konig; **Illustrators:** Roberto Sabas, Tom Janowski, and Beth Young; **Printer:** United Graphics

Printed in the United States of America   10   9   8   7   6   5   4   3   2   1

Human Kinetics
Web site: http://www.humankinetics.com/

United States: Human Kinetics
P.O. Box 5076
Champaign, IL 61825-5076
1-800-747-4457
e-mail: humank@hkusa.com

Canada: Human Kinetics, Box 24040
Windsor, ON N8Y 4Y9
1-800-465-7301 (in Canada only)
e-mail: humank@hkcanada.com

Europe: Human Kinetics, P.O. Box IW14
Leeds LS16 6TR, United Kingdom
(44) 1132 781708
e-mail: humank@hkeurope.com

Australia: Human Kinetics
57A Price Avenue
Lower Mitcham, South Australia 5062
(08) 277 1555
e-mail: humank@hkaustralia.com

New Zealand: Human Kinetics
P.O. Box 105-231, Auckland 1
(09) 523 3462
e-mail: humank@hknewz.com

*To my sons, Stephen and Joseph,
the true inspiration for my work*

CONTENTS

Preface   ix

Acknowledgments   xi

Part I   Foundations of Fitness Education   1

Chapter 1   A New Perspective in Elementary Physical Education   3
How Physical Activity Affects Health and Mortality   4

Healthy People 2000   5

Surgeon General's Report on Physical Activity and Health   6

Components of Health-Related Physical Fitness   6

Sport-Related Physical Fitness   8

What Is Fitness Education?   9

Summary   10

Chapter 2   A Team Approach to Fitness Education   11
Mixed Messages   11

A Multidisciplinary Team Approach   12

Health Assessment   13

Authentic Assessment   17

Summary   17

Chapter 3   Behavioral Change and Motivational Strategies   19
Rainbow to Youth Fitness and Active Lifestyles   19

What Motivates Children to Move?   21

Types of Motivation   22

Motivational Strategies   23

Summary   26

Chapter 4   Teaching Strategies   27
Traditional Models of Teaching   27

A Humanistic Approach to Teaching Fitness   28

The Spectrum of Teaching Styles   29

Class Structure   38

Summary   38

Chapter 5   Principles of Health-Related Physical Fitness   **39**
Core Principles of Health-Related Physical Fitness   39
Stages of a Physical Activity Session   42
Components of Health-Related Physical Fitness   42
Summary   46

Chapter 6   Fitness Education for Children With Physical Disabilities   **47**
Individualized Education Plan   47
Guidelines for Inclusion   48
Obesity   49
Asthma   51
Spinal Cord Impairments   52
Mental Retardation   56
Summary   58

Chapter 7   Getting Parents and Your Community Involved   **59**
Establishing a Plan of Action   59
Communication   60
Parent Education   68
Parent Participation During School Hours   69
Home-Based Activities   69
Community Involvement   74
Summary   77

Part II   Planning and Teaching Fitness Education   **79**

Chapter 8   Planning for Fitness   **81**
Sample Yearly Plan for Developmental Level III   81
Sample Lesson Plans   83
Fitness Education Lessons   83
Fitness Integration Lessons   89
Summary   95

Chapter 9   Teaching Health-Related Physical Fitness Concepts   **97**
Strategies for Teaching Fitness Concepts   97
Scope and Sequence   99
Developmental Level I Fitness Concepts: Fitness Is Fun   101
Developmental Level II Fitness Concepts: The Best I Can Be   103
Developmental Level III Fitness Concepts: Let's Get Heart Smart   108
Summary   114

Chapter 10   Collaborating With the Classroom Teacher   **115**
Collaborating With the Classroom Teacher   115
Communication Strategies   116

Thematic Units: An Approach to Integrated Learning   117
Cardiovascular Health: A Thematic Unit   118
Health-Related Physical Fitness Classroom Activities   125
Developmental Level I Classroom Activities   129
Developmental Level II Classroom Activities   132
Developmental Level III Classroom Activities   138
Summary   141

Part III   Fitness Activities   143

Chapter 11   Developmental Exercises   145
Cardiorespiratory Endurance   145
Muscular Strength and Muscular Endurance   147
Flexibility   161
Exercises to Avoid   166
Summary   168

Chapter 12   Active Games   169
Characteristics of Developmental Games   169
Promoting Physical Activity Through Active Games   171
Developmental Level I Games   171
Developmental Level II Games   173
Developmental Level III Games   175
Summary   178

Chapter 13   Dance and Rhythmic Activities   179
Safety Precautions   179
Planning Developmentally Appropriate Activities   180
Developmental Level I Dance and Rhythmic Activities   180
Developmental Level II Dance and Rhythmic Activities   182
Developmental Level III Dance and Rhythmic Activities   184
Summary   190

Chapter 14   School-Wide Events   193
Fitness Field Day   194
Fit for Life Family Night   197
Geography Run   197
School Health Fair   198
Early Bird Stretch and Afternoon Perk-Up   198
Jump Rope for Heart, Hoops for Heart, and Step for Heart   198
ACES: All Children Exercising Simultaneously   199
Recess Workouts   199
Fitness Clubs   199

Principal Walks   199

Holiday Classics   199

Summary   200

Appendix A: Sample Personal Fitness Education Portfolio   201

Appendix B: Additional Resources   213

References   217

Index   221

About the Author   227

What can be done about childhood obesity and the sedentary lifestyles of the youth in this country? How can parents and teachers reverse these negative trends and develop a stronger, healthier nation for the 21st century? Elementary physical educators throughout the country are concerned about answering these questions, and now you have the resource to help: *Fitness Education for Children: A Team Approach.*

Physical educators have always been concerned with the health and physical development of our youth. Certainly, hundreds of professional books and manuals that illustrate exercises and describe fitness tests have been published. Unfortunately, these books support a narrow, shortsighted view of children's health. As educators, we must recognize that merely asking our students to run, do push-ups, and maneuver through an obstacle course is *not enough* if we expect them to develop lifetime patterns of health and physical activity. As a profession, we can—and must—do better.

I have written this book to bridge the gap between research, which clearly documents the benefits of physical activity, and practice, the way physical education is taught in schools. This resource provides you—whether you're an experienced teacher or a teacher-in-training—with a comprehensive model for elementary school fitness education to help you reform your program to meet the health challenges of the 21st century.

In *Fitness Education for Children: A Team Approach* the undergraduate student studying to become a physical educator will find the necessary philosophy, strategies, and pedagogical models to incorporate fitness education into a well-balanced elementary school physical education curriculum. The experienced physical educator will find this book a refreshing change from the traditional "activities books," which usually leave you looking elsewhere, as you strive to modify your current program to emphasize health-related physical fitness and increase activity levels.

Specifically, I'll go beyond the typical fitness games and activities found in other books and include

- sample physical activity lesson plans for different developmental levels,
- contemporary teaching techniques,
- creative activities for teaching fitness concepts,
- strategies for involving parents and community members,
- fitness games,
- rhythmic activities,
- developmentally appropriate exercises,
- fitness education strategies for children with disabilities, and
- reproducible instructional materials.

The practical, easy-to-use format of this book will help you implement fitness education throughout your physical education curriculum immediately—both in and out of the school setting.

The term "fitness education" conveys my belief that a comprehensive approach is the best way to teach fitness. A comprehensive, quality physical education program integrates developmentally appropriate physical activities, concepts, and values relevant to leading healthy lives throughout a child's experiences in the home, school, and community. Specifically, fitness education should help students learn cognitive information about physical fitness concepts, involve them in learning experiences that help them apply fitness information, and lead them to value an active, healthy lifestyle.

But you can't do it alone: Fitness education must be a team effort at the elementary school level. For many years, physical educators have been planning and teaching in isolation with little or no connection to the faculty or school curriculum. This isolation has made it very difficult to reach professional program goals, especially when classes are scheduled for only one or two days per week. I'll address this issue and present strategies to help you implement a team approach at your school. We'll discuss how to include school administrators, classroom teachers, homeroom parents, school lunch personnel, parents, the PTA, health service professionals, and the community. Through a team approach, you'll enlist the people your students value the most in their lives to help reinforce to them that physical activity has benefits in all aspects of their lives. Furthermore, this multidisciplinary team approach will allow you to expand your program goals because it creates more opportunities for your students to develop healthy long-term physical activity attitudes and practices.

Should you change your physical education curriculum completely? Probably not. Unlike those activity books on your shelf, a unique feature of this book is that it shows you how to promote healthy, active lifestyles in school-aged children *within* a balanced program of physical education. How? By emphasizing the health-related benefits of physical fitness: cardiorespiratory endurance, muscular strength, muscular endurance, flexibility, and body composition. I'll show you how to personalize your approach by focusing on individual and developmental needs rather than on fitness activities or measurements. I don't, for example, recommend emphasizing fitness testing, thereby categorizing children for awards and grades. Instead, we'll discuss how fitness scores provide you and your students with information to set goals and to individualize programs. Indeed, studies show that your students will be much happier and progress more smoothly when your program emphasizes support and cooperation for improvement rather than competition. Physical activity should be fun and enjoyable for every child—not only the "physically gifted." To this end, I have designed the activities in this resource to include all children, giving everyone the opportunity to succeed.

This book is divided into three major sections. In Part I, "Foundations of Fitness Education," I'll describe a new perspective on fitness education and discuss the need for creative teaching approaches in schools, behavioral change and motivational strategies, the components of fitness, fitness education for children with physical disabilities, and parent and community involvement. Part II, "Planning and Teaching Fitness Education," includes teaching strategies, sample lesson plans, how to teach fitness concepts, and ways to collaborate with the classroom teacher. Part III, "Fitness Activities," offers you a number of practical, developmentally appropriate exercises, active games, dance and rhythmic

activities, and school-wide events to incorporate into your physical education program.

How do you know what activities and concepts are appropriate for each class? In school systems throughout the country, children are grouped by their age and grade level rather than their true developmental level. Likewise, for too many years physical educators have been planning learning activities by grade level alone. Yet within each grade level, a wide range of mental, physical, and social-emotional development exists. The children in any one class may be performing at a number of developmental levels, making it difficult for you to select activities for your classes. How do you take into consideration the many relevant facets of childhood development—individual abilities, physical characteristics, and past experiences—in order to plan an appropriate lesson and ensure success? To make it easier for you to plan your program and individual lessons, I have organized the health-related physical fitness concepts and activities into three developmental levels:

Developmental level I	Kindergarten and first grade
Developmental level II	Second and third grade
Developmental level III	Fourth through sixth grade

Keep in mind, however, that within any given grade level you may still have children participating at different levels of development. This supports the rationale for a more personalized approach to your fitness education program that emphasizes choice, decision making, and self-directed learning. Use the activities within each level as guides to help you establish the appropriate developmental progression for your school.

Teaching is tough! At the same time, the need for quality elementary physical education programs has never been greater. This innovative fitness education resource will complement an existing curriculum or help you plan a balanced curriculum of motor skills, physical education knowledge, physical activity and physical fitness, and personal and social development, freeing you to concentrate on the challenging task of interacting with and guiding children throughout the most important years of their lives.

ACKNOWLEDGMENTS

I would like to express my heartfelt gratitude to my wife, colleague, and best friend, Irene. We've come a long way since Woodbridge Elementary School in Tampa, Florida. Special thanks for her assistance in developing the thematic unit in chapter 10 and for her unwavering support, patience, and love throughout my career.

I would like to thank Gerald S. Berenson, MD, the director of the Bogalusa Heart Study and the Heart Smart Program. I am truly grateful for his insightful guidance and encouragement during the early stages of my career. He taught me the value of and need for research and intervention in schools, which remain our best chance for a healthier future generation. The work of the Heart Smart team will continue to live through the spirit and contents of this book.

Thank you to the students I have taught at the University of New Orleans and Adelphi University; you have been a constant source of motivation. Special thanks to Sharon Zotara for her organizational skills and Amy Coopersmith for her assistance with the rhythmic activity content.

I would like to extend my deepest appreciation to the professionals at Human Kinetics. Rick Frey and Scott Wikgren believed in this project from the start. Their vision for a new and improved physical education is reflected in this book. Special thanks to Julia Anderson for her editorial contributions. It was a pleasure to work with such a kind person and superb professional. Additional thanks to Jacqueline Blakley for taking the reins of the project in its later stages and seeing it through to completion. Her sense of humor and ready laughter helped to remind me of the true purpose of this book. I am indebted to her for the attention to detail she so skillfully brought to this project.

Finally, this book would not have been possible without the love and confidence of my parents, Mary and Joseph, who always supported my passion for physical activity; and my brothers, Joseph and Nicholas, for always being there.

FOUNDATIONS OF FITNESS EDUCATION

PART I

A New Perspective in Elementary Physical Education

CHAPTER 1

> *Where there is an open mind,*
> *there will always be a frontier.*
> —Charles F. Kettering

Children are this country's most treasured possessions. They are the key to future generations leading healthy, productive lives.

Unfortunately, many children today eat foods high in fat, sodium, and sugar and are more likely to be obese than their counterparts in the past. Furthermore, they are less physically active than were children in past generations. To reverse these trends will take teamwork by parents, teachers, politicians, health care professionals, and community members to help our nation's youth modify their health habits so they can meet the demands of the next century. As an educator, you must consider reforming and supplementing your current physical education curriculum to help attain this goal. This book offers you a vision—a look at teaching physical education—that promotes active and healthful lifestyles. Indeed, a strong fitness education program at the elementary school level is our best opportunity to reverse the downward trends in the general health of our nation's youth.

Ironically, children are usually the most active segment of our population. Most children love to play, run, jump, hop, and skip. Yet in upper elementary grades and continuing through middle and high school, children tend to become less active, thereby gaining excess weight. What happens?

As children reach about 10 years of age, they discover various interests and hobbies that may pull them away from physical activity. Moreover, they resist being labeled a "child," and so they may stop playing active childhood games. Too often, parents and teachers convey the message that physical activity must have a purpose, such as joining a team to compete or taking karate lessons to become a black belt. Children who are not very athletic may become inactive if they feel incompetent and unsupported. We must stop treating 10-year-olds as miniature adult athletes and start letting them develop as children who need to move freely and express their physical selves.

Some improvements have occurred in recent decades. According to the U.S. Department of Health and Human Services (1991a), we now average 10.1 infant deaths per 1,000 live births, a record low rate representing a 65 percent decline since 1950. Thanks to the widespread use of vaccines, such childhood diseases as mumps, measles, and rubella are rare. Seat belts, infant car seats, new vehicle designs, and lower speed limits have significantly reduced the number of children who die on the road (U.S. Dept. of Health and Human Services 1991b). But what about nutrition, physical fitness, and exercise habits? Unfortunately, they have not shown substantial gains over the last two decades.

When students in middle schools are asked why they stopped participating in physical activity and sports, most say, "I didn't care for the competition," and "It wasn't fun anymore." In contrast to the thinking in programs that foster these negative attitudes, my fitness education philosophy is based on four simple principles:

1. Physical activity is for everybody: All children have the right to the healthful benefits of exercise, games, dance, and sport.

2. We can develop positive attitudes toward physical activity by building on children's innate desires to move and express their feelings.

3. The health benefits of physical activity should be a major concern.

4. Children are entitled to enjoy daily physical activity in school, at home, or in the community in a safe, supportive environment.

Apply these principles to your physical education curriculum to encourage your students to value physical activity throughout their lives.

How Physical Activity Affects Health and Mortality

We know that among adults even moderate levels of exercise will result in a lower risk of death (Blair et al. 1989). For example, rates for death from cancer are substantially lower in physically active men and women. Active people also develop less coronary heart disease (CHD) than their inactive counterparts, and when they do develop CHD, it occurs at a later age and tends to be less severe (Berlin and Colditz 1990). To heighten public awareness of the need for physical activity, the American Heart Association announced on July 1, 1992, that an inactive lifestyle is the fourth major risk factor for heart disease after cigarette smoking, high blood pressure, and elevated cholesterol levels.

Despite significant reductions in heart disease mortality rates during the last decade, CHD remains the major cause of death, disability, and disease in the United States. Did you know that cardiovascular disease begins in childhood?

For more than 20 years, a team of doctors, nurses, and researchers have studied more than 14,000 children in Bogalusa, Louisiana, compiling The Bogalusa Heart Study (Berenson 1986), the world's largest data bank of heart disease risk factors in children. They found that

- adolescent Caucasian boys experienced a dramatic rise in LDL to HDL (bad to good) cholesterol ratios from childhood to adolescence, which may predispose them to developing heart disease early in life;

- kidney factors predispose African American children to high blood pressure;

- cardiovascular risk factors are interrelated in most children, as they are in adults (e.g., obesity and high blood pressure);

- more than 50 percent of children consume too much salt, fat, and sugar;

- overweight children are more likely to become overweight adults;

- sedentary children are more likely to become sedentary adults;

- most school-aged children possess one or more CHD risk factors; and

- families with a history of heart disease have children with higher risk factors.

More recently, a summary statement was released by the Centers for Disease Control and Prevention and the American College of Sports Medicine. Based on scientific evidence, they concluded that every adult should be engaged in physical activity most days of the week, preferably every day, for 30 minutes (Centers for Disease Control and Prevention and American College of Sports Medicine 1993). You should move continuously, either doing the same activity the entire 30 minutes or in segments of at least 10 minutes. Activities that encourage gross motor movements, such as running, jumping rope, manipulative activities (for example, throwing a baseball), and active games are the most beneficial (Pate et al. 1995). How intensely should you exercise? Warm up with low-intensity exercise, then devote most of your workout to moderate to vigorous physical activity (sometimes referred to as MVPA) (Simons-Morton 1994). MVPA is activity that requires repeated weight transfer such as jogging, rope jumping, and dancing. Children should engage in 30 to 60 minutes of MVPA each day (Corbin, Pangrazi, and Welk 1994). It's best to encourage children to be physically active at least one hour per day because evidence indicates that they'll become less active as they age. In other words, start high and hope that they will be more likely to exercise at least 30 minutes a day as adults.

What does all this research mean to you? It simply means that if you know what to look for, you can identify young children who are likely to develop health-related problems as adults. Not surprisingly, activity improves overall health, helping to prevent serious diseases. As an elementary school physical educator, you can have a positive influence on the lifestyle choices made by children, thereby impacting their entire lives. What an exciting time to be an elementary physical education specialist!

Healthy People 2000

In 1991, the U.S. challenged the citizens of this country with *Healthy People 2000*, a document setting lifesaving health-related goals for the year 2000. Not only does this project seek to prevent death, it also seeks to reduce suffering, illness, and disability. The U.S. Department of Health and Human Services is committed to attaining three broad goals:

1. Increase the span of a healthy life for Americans.
2. Reduce health disparities among Americans.
3. Facilitate access to preventive services for all Americans.

The report set several major objectives that are specifically related to physical activity patterns, school nutrition, and physical education classes, including the following:

- Increase to at least 30 percent the proportion of people aged 6 and older who engage regularly, preferably daily, in light to moderate physical activity for at least 30 minutes per day.

- Increase to at least 20 percent the proportion of people aged 18 and older and to 75 percent the proportion of children and adolescents aged 6 to 17 who engage in vigorous physical activity that promotes the development and maintenance of cardiorespiratory fitness 3 or more days per week for 20 or more minutes per occasion.

- Reduce to no more than 15 percent the proportion of people aged 6 and older who engage in no leisure-time physical activity.

- Increase to at least 40 percent the proportion of people aged 6 and older who regularly perform physical activities that enhance and maintain muscular strength, muscular endurance, and flexibility.

- Increase to at least 50 percent the proportion of overweight people aged 12 and older who have adopted sound dietary practices combined with regular exercise to attain an appropriate body weight.

- Increase to at least 50 percent the proportion of children and adolescents in 1st through 12th grade who participate in daily school physical education.

- Increase to at least 50 percent the proportion of school physical education class time that students spend being physically active; preferably engaged in lifetime physical activity.

- Increase to at least 90 percent the proportion of school lunch and breakfast services and child care food services with menus that are consistent with the nutrition principles in the Dietary Guidelines for Americans.

- Increase to at least 75 percent the proportion of the nation's schools that provide nutrition education from preschool through 12th grade, preferably as part of quality school health education.

In 1995, the U.S. Department of Health and Human Services published an updated review of the progress made toward the goals of *Healthy People 2000*. Although no data was available on children relative to the physical activity objectives, the percentage of students engaged in daily school physical education and the proportion of school physical education time that students spend physically active are continuing to decline (U.S. Department of Health and Human Services 1995).

Support for regular physical activity and nutrition education is widespread. Physicians, researchers, politicians, educators, and parents all agree that an active, healthy lifestyle is critical to the physical, mental, and social development of the growing child. Certainly, as an elementary physical educator, it's imperative that you play a major role in developing positive attitudes in children toward physical activity.

Surgeon General's Report on Physical Activity and Health

This report, sponsored by the U.S. Department of Health and Human Services (1996), brings together for the first time what has been learned about physical activity and health in decades of research. The major findings report that:

- People who are inactive can improve their health and well-being by becoming even moderately active on a regular basis.

- Physical activity need not be strenuous to achieve health benefits.

- Greater health benefits can be achieved by increasing the frequency, intensity, and duration of physical activity.

The report also recommends that each community should provide a quality K-12 school physical education program taught by a certified specialist, preferably daily. According to acting Surgeon General Audrey F. Manley, MD, "Physical inactivity is a serious nationwide public health problem, but active and healthful lifestyles are well within the grasp of everyone." Among young people aged 12 to 21, almost 50 percent are not vigorously active on a regular basis. Female adolescents are much less physically active than males and activity levels of both females and males significantly decline with age during adolescence. This report serves as a national alert as well as a call to action for parents, communities, and schools to unite to meet this public health challenge.

To order the full report, call the Centers for Disease Control's Nutrition and Physical Activity Information Line at 1-800-CDC-4NRG.

Components of Health-Related Physical Fitness

Health-related physical fitness prevents diseases (e.g., heart disease) and promotes future health (e.g., weight control). Components include cardiorespiratory endurance (CRE), muscular strength, muscular endurance, flexibility, and body composition (figure 1.1), which work together to provide the proper balance of physical development throughout life. The health-related components of physical fitness should be the focus of your class rather than sport-related components.

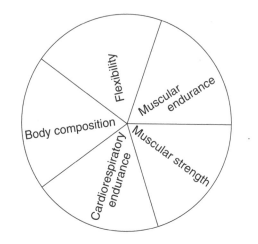

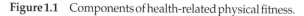

Figure 1.1   Components of health-related physical fitness.

Cardiorespiratory Endurance

Cardiorespiratory endurance is the ability to participate in large muscle physical activity for relatively long periods of time at moderate to vigorous levels of intensity. It is the capacity of the heart, blood vessels, and lungs to deliver nutrients and oxygen to the tissues to provide the energy you need for endurance exercise. Jogging, dancing, and swimming are three popular activities that build cardiorespiratory endurance (see figure 1.2).

Figure 1.2   Jogging for cardiorespiratory endurance.

Muscular Strength

Muscular strength is the capacity of a muscle or muscle group to exert maximum force against a resistance. Dynamic strength is the force exerted by a muscle group as a body part moves. You use dynamic strength when you do push-ups and pull-ups (see figure 1.3a). Static strength is the force exerted against an immovable object. You use static strength when you do a hand push (see figure 1.3b).

Muscular Endurance

Muscular endurance is the capacity of a muscle or group of muscles to exert force over a period of time against a submaximal resistance. Games and sports that require leg and arm movements for an extended period of time require muscular endurance. For example, you can throw a softball repeatedly to build muscular endurance in your arms (see figure 1.4a), or do as many curl-ups as possible to build muscular endurance in your abdominal muscles (see figure 1.4b).

a   b

Figure 1.3 Pull-up for dynamic strength (a) and hand push for static strength (b).

a   b

Figure 1.4 Repeatedly throwing a softball (a) or doing curl-ups (b) can help build muscular endurance.

Flexibility

Flexibility is the ability to move joints in an unrestricted fashion through the full range of motion in order to bend, stretch, twist, and turn. Properly stretching muscles, ligaments, and tendons promotes good body alignment as well as reduces stress in the neck and back area. The seated hamstring stretch and other stretching exercises require and develop flexibility (see figure 1.5).

Body Composition

Body composition is the ratio of body fat to lean body tissue. Teach children the dangers of excessive body fat and the role exercise plays in controlling body weight (see figure 1.6). When you talk about nutrition, discuss body composition as well.

Sport-Related Physical Fitness

Sport-related physical fitness (sometimes referred to as skill-related) includes agility, speed, power, balance, and coordination. While these components are not absolutely necessary for maintaining physical health, it is still important to include them in your physical education program so that your students can apply them to games, sports, and recreational activities.

Agility

Agility, often called "quickness," is the ability to quickly change direction or body position accurately while moving through space. Agility is essential in certain sports, such as basketball and soccer.

Speed

Speed is the ability of the body to perform a movement in the shortest possible time—essential in most sport-related activities and movement skills—including track, basketball, baseball, and soccer.

Power

Power is the product of strength and speed. Activities that require power, such as the standing broad jump and shot putting, should be practiced with explosive movements in short periods of time.

Balance

Balance is the ability to maintain equilibrium and body position whether moving or stationary. Tumbling, gymnastics, balance beam activities, in-line skating, and snow and water skiing demand a high degree of balancing ability.

Figure 1.5 Seated hamstring stretch for flexibility.

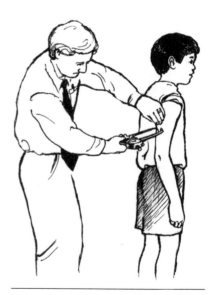

Figure 1.6 Teacher measuring triceps skinfold with calipers.

Coordination

Coordination is the ability to integrate a number of motor skills into a smooth, efficient motor pattern—vital in most sport-related activities. Contrary to popular opinion, nearly everyone can develop and improve their coordination with proper instruction and adequate practice time. Hitting a softball, shooting a basketball, or juggling are examples of advanced motor skills that require a high degree of coordination.

What Is Fitness Education?

Fitness education is a comprehensive, multidisciplinary approach to help children acquire the knowledge, attitudes, beliefs, and behaviors for the promotion of long-term active, healthy lifestyles within a quality physical education program. In order for this approach to work, the school, home, and community must share the responsibility of promoting healthful habits in your students.

But start with your own program, making it the foundation on which the other influences in your students' lives can build. Your overall physical education program should include a balance of health-related physical fitness, motor skills, content knowledge, and personal and social development activities. According to the National Association of Sport and Physical Education (NASPE), a physically educated person

- demonstrates competency in many movement forms and proficiency in a few movement forms;
- applies movement concepts and principles to the learning and development of motor skills;
- exhibits a physically active lifestyle;
- achieves and maintains a health-enhancing level of physical fitness;
- demonstrates responsible personal and social behavior in physical activity settings;
- demonstrates understanding of and respect for differences among people in physical activity settings; and
- understands that physical activity provides opportunities for enjoyment, challenge, self-expression, and socal interaction (NASPE 1995).

In this book, I'll show you how fitness education can complement and enhance your overall elementary physical education program.

Characteristics of a Quality Fitness Education Program

As you plan the fitness education component of your program, consider that physical educators in quality programs usually do the following:

- Plan, communicate, and cooperate with classroom teachers, administrators, health service professionals, school lunch personnel, and parents.
- Choose noncompetitive, developmentally appropriate fitness activities, including a wide variety of exercises and movement experiences for general body development.
- Make sure children will be physically active 30 minutes per day, four to five days of the week.
- Teach children the benefits of an active lifestyle and of staying active throughout their lives.
- Design activities to include every child regardless of physical abilities.
- Emphasize rewards, not awards, using incentives, positive reinforcement, and intrinsic value to motivate children rather than giving awards for particular levels of fitness.
- Encourage children to accept responsibility for their own fitness progress by teaching them how to monitor themselves and by giving them opportunities to make decisions related to their own health and fitness goals.
- Make fitness activities fun, allowing children to enjoy fitness activities with friends, family, or alone in a safe, supportive environment.
- Integrate fitness education throughout the school year and throughout other classroom subject areas.
- Teach fitness activities using a wide variety of teaching strategies, recognizing that how children learn about physical fitness will have a lasting impact on their feelings about physical activity.
- Model positive exercise behaviors, remembering that actions speak louder than words.

How do you include every important aspect of a quality fitness education program? I'll give you tips and suggestions throughout this book.

Physical Education Reform

It's important to provide children with a balanced curriculum: movement education, motor skills, rhythms, dance, gymnastics, tumbling, games, sports, *and* fitness education. Each component is critical to developing an active, healthy lifestyle. Thus, over the last five years, in response to society's shifting demands and expectations and to recent research, physical educators have moved from emphasizing sports and skills to emphasizing health and fitness through a well-rounded curriculum. This shift is necessary to prepare to meet health demands in the future. Make promoting healthy lifestyles one of your primary goals (see figure 1.7), integrating fitness education throughout each unit of your curriculum. Remind children continually that the general purpose of learning motor skills and participating in sports is to stay physically active and to develop lifetime skills—not to compete or earn awards. To join the reform movement, you need not throw out your current physical education program—simply modify it to meet the demands of a changing society.

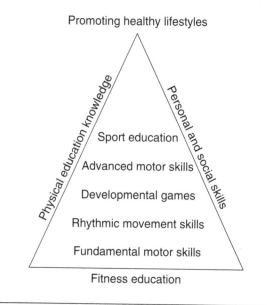

Figure 1.7   A balanced elementary physical education curriculum.

Summary

We must modify the traditional elementary physical education curriculum to promote active, healthful lifestyles. To get started, advocate fitness education throughout your curriculum. Work together with home and community to promote long-term positive health behaviors in school-aged children.

Not only should you integrate fitness education community-wide, you should also integrate fitness education throughout your physical education curriculum, thereby helping to create a quality, balanced program. Teach fitness skills alongside movement skills, sports, games, dance, and gymnastics, showing relationships among the various content areas. Finally, through your own attitudes, actions, and instruction, teach children that the general purpose of physical education is not to create elite athletes for future competition but to establish positive physical activity attitudes, beliefs, and behaviors for a lifetime of health and enjoyment.

A Team Approach to Fitness Education

Two stonecutters were asked what they were doing. The first said, "I'm cutting this stone into blocks." The second replied, "I'm on a team that's building a cathedral."

Over 97 percent of the children in this country 5 through 12 years of age attend private or public elementary schools. This creates tremendous opportunities to develop positive, healthy habits in school-aged children for the 21st century.

Unfortunately, many children may not be getting enough physical education to foster a significant change. According to the National Children and Youth Fitness Study II (Ross and Pate 1987), only about 36 percent of first through fourth graders, less than 19 percent of fifth graders, and about 27 percent of sixth graders had daily classes in physical education. The average for all children ages 6 through 18 was about three times per week. Many students only have physical education one or two days per week: about 37 percent of first through fourth graders, about 48 percent of fifth graders, and 42 percent of sixth graders. The studies also found that the average class period was about 33 minutes for first through fourth and about 90 minutes per week for fifth and sixth graders. This is clearly not enough time to develop long-term positive health behaviors in children let alone reach the standards for elementary physical education set forth by the American Alliance for Health, Physical Education, Recreation and Dance (Council on Physical Education for Children 1992).

Mixed Messages

Yet, time allotted for physical activity may not be your only problem. For many years, elementary schools have given children mixed messages about the importance of health and physical activity. Do these mixed messages sound familiar?

- Physical Education is often only a part-time subject for students, meeting two or three times per week in the elementary school curriculum.

- Classroom teachers often tell children that they may attend "P.E." only if they finish their classroom assignments.

- Classroom teachers often take away physical education for misbehavior.

- Physical educators often include fitness activities without teaching the knowledge, value, content, or importance of physical activity.

- Many administrators and teachers regard physical activity merely as a chance to "let off steam" or give children a break from class.

- Teachers and parents often provide snacks and treats that are loaded with empty calories (e.g., cake, candy, soda).

- School fund-raising campaigns often include the selling of candy or cookies.
- The average school lunch contains high amounts of sodium, fat, and sugar.

Make it your goal as a physical educator to sort out these mixed messages by providing a cohesive educational plan that will impact the entire home, community, and school environments. You can accomplish this by using a multidisciplinary team approach.

A Multidisciplinary Team Approach

The responsibility for developing health-related fitness education and positive eating habits should not lie entirely with you, the physical educator. To achieve your program goals, begin to incorporate a multidisciplinary team approach, enlisting the help of many professionals, resources, and parents in both the school and local communities. For example, the Heart Smart Program developed a comprehensive cardiovascular health and physical activity model for school-aged children in New Orleans, Louisiana (Downey et al. 1987). This model modified and built upon existing educational components, such as school health assessment, the classroom curriculum, the school lunch program, school health services, parent and community involvement, and school-wide events and included a fitness education curriculum called "Superkids-Superfit" that was integrated into a traditional physical education program (Virgilio and Berenson 1988). We need more elementary school programs that model the Heart Smart approach if we are going to accomplish health goals for the year 2000 and beyond.

Lobby for this kind of multidisciplinary support to reach your goals for healthier children in the 21st century. Indeed, everyone who serves and cares for your students should reinforce the need for healthful and physically active lifestyles. This holistic, united approach helps children see the benefits of a healthy lifestyle in a more relevant, meaningful way in every aspect of their lives (Virgilio et al. 1993).

In this book, I'll provide you with a number of strategies and practical activities to implement a multidisciplinary approach to encouraging healthy and active lifestyles that includes the classroom curriculum, the school lunch program, school health services, parent and community involvement, and, of course, physical education (see figure 2.1). Let's take a brief look at each of these five areas.

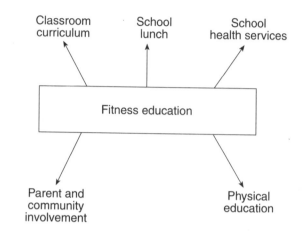

Figure 2.1   Multidisciplinary model.

Classroom Curriculum

Enlist the help of the classroom teacher. First, educate them about the benefits of physical activity and proper nutrition.

- Distribute brochures and articles about exercise and general health.
- Arrange to have guest speakers at faculty meetings.
- Establish a school staff wellness room that includes videotapes, exercise equipment, spring water cooler, cookbooks, reading materials, and magazines.
- Teach an exercise class for staff members after school, one or two days per week.

Second, give classroom teachers ideas for new and creative activities. Show them ways to integrate health-related fitness and nutrition into other subject areas, such as math, science, and reading. In addition, help create thematic units in which students study various aspects of a topic. For example, cover cardiovascular health from a fitness perspective at the same time the students are learning about the cardiovascular system in science class. (See chapter 10 for more information on working with the classroom teacher.)

School Lunch

The school lunch program and school parties give children opportunities to practice making healthy choices. To improve the fare available at school, establish a health committee, involving homeroom parents, the school nurse, a classroom teacher, a member of the school lunch staff, a consultant such as a university professor, as well as yourself. Ask the question, "How can we reduce fat, sodium, and sugar in our school lunches?" In addition, create and label "heart smart" choices on the menu so children can make their own decisions about what they are eating. Educate parents about the importance of healthy snacks and about how the school is trying to help children develop positive eating habits. Encourage parents and classroom teachers to make sure that all parties include heart smart choices, such as frozen yogurt, fruit, bottled water, and low-fat cookies.

School Health Services

Make professionals such as the school nurse, guidance counselor, and psychologist your allies. As a representative of the medical profession, the school nurse adds credibility to the notion of prevention. The counselor and psychologist can help you understand human behavior by outlining techniques to help change health attitudes.

Parent and Community Involvement

As the most important aspect of a child's life, the family must participate in teaching, modeling, and reinforcing a healthy lifestyle. You can engage the support of parents and community by educating them through newsletters, workshops, PTA demonstrations, and health fairs; by involving them as volunteers, teacher aides, and committee members; and by including them in home-based activities, such as family exercise, homework helpers, and family contracts. (See also chapter 7.)

Physical Education

Physical education is a pivotal component of the multidisciplinary approach. Plan a year-long curriculum that teaches the knowledge, skills, and behaviors that encourage and reinforce active lifestyles by integrating health-related fitness concepts and activities into each module to constantly remind students of the need for physical activity. (See also chapter 8).

The multidisciplinary approach is a team effort in which various professionals, parents, and the community promote healthy and active lifestyles in children to accomplish the many goals of health and physical education in elementary schools.

Health Assessment

General health and physical fitness screening is a school-wide responsibility, but how do you undertake a comprehensive screening program? Once again, use a team approach and establish a school-wide health committee in your school, including teachers, parents, health care professionals, university faculty, and community members. You may be able to enlist the help of volunteer professionals or students from a local medical school, university, or wellness institute to help you establish baseline health evaluations for the children at your school. The team may choose to measure

- height,
- weight,
- blood pressure,
- vision,
- hearing,
- posture,
- cholesterol, and
- health-related physical fitness.

Hard work? Certainly—but well worth it. You may even identify children who are at-risk for heart disease or other health-related problems. If you lack support, screen only the third and fifth graders each year and monitor their progress by keeping a file on a data disk.

Health-Related Physical Fitness Testing

For many years physical educators viewed fitness testing as an end in itself. The goal was simply to increase the number of curl-ups—or whatever—children did in one minute. The typical pre-post test measures, which many teachers used, may have indicated marked improvement by the end of the school year, yet researchers are convinced that a large percentage of those increases may be attributed to genetics and natural growth and development (Bouchard et al. 1990). Unfortunately, when you emphasize fitness testing, children get the message that they should only exercise to get an award or to compete against their classmates. In contrast, a quality fitness education program emphasizes education, prevention, and intervention with health-related physical fitness testing playing a minor, yet valuable, role. I encourage you to use physical fitness testing as a tool to help children monitor their own progress and plan individual goals. In addition, use the physical data to help you plan how to help your students improve their performances in the different components of health-related fitness (Virgilio 1996). A quality fitness education program includes authentic assessments in addition to standardized fitness test results to help evaluate an individual student's progress. Student participation, effort, knowledge, and personal feelings can also indicate progress.

Review the following guidelines as you plan ways to include fitness testing in your physical education program.

1. Test for a purpose. Know why you are testing. What are your major objectives? How will you use the data?

2. Test to teach. Perform each assessment component in association with a health-related fitness concept. For example, teach children the health benefits of performing curl-ups: Stronger abdominal muscles keep the internal organs intact, reduce stress on the low back, and develop trunk stability, strength, and muscular endurance.

3. Focus on individual progress. Base your standards on students' personal goals and improvement rather than on established national test standards.

4. Create a humanistic environment. Keep testing as private and confidential as possible. Never announce or post class fitness scores or embarrass students. For example, never gather 25 students around the flexibility box to watch each student perform.

5. Limit testing time. If you are spending eight class periods both in the fall and spring testing, you are squandering too much class time! If necessary reduce the number of items on the fitness test, or request extra class periods from the principal to complete the assessments.

6. Allow students time to prepare for the tests. Provide exercise classes and time to practice actual test items. Teach safety precautions and training principles as well.

7. Allow students to test themselves. Encouraging them to monitor their own progress and accept the responsibility for their personal development will help them develop long-term values.

8. Communicate test results. Help students interpret the meaning of their fitness scores. Communicate your testing philosophy and the results to parents. Consider a computer-assisted report card system (Cooper Institute for Aerobics Research 1992).

9. Offer feedback. After sharing test results with students, recommend strategies, activities, and specific exercises to help them improve. For example, give a student at the 20th percentile in flexibility a set of stretches to practice seven days per week both at home and in school.

10. Reward effort and achievement. Be certain that goals are attainable for all students. Children who improve their scores, complete a program, or demonstrate increased physical activity levels should be rewarded as well as the students who achieve desirable levels of fitness.

Youth Fitness Tests

Let's look now at several common fitness test items described in *The Prudential Fitnessgram Test Administration Manual* (Cooper Institute for Aerobics Research 1992). As you read, think about which ones you'd like to include in your program. (For more information in the area of fitness assessment see also Safrit and Pemberton [1994] and AAHPERD's Physical Best recognition system.) Keep in mind that measuring fitness components is only one aspect of a complete assessment approach in a quality fitness education program.

Cardiorespiratory Endurance

These two basic tests measure cardiorespiratory endurance.

ONE-MILE RUN-WALK

Have students run for one mile as fast as possible. Permit walking and jogging if a student cannot run the entire distance. Do not time students in kindergarten through third grade. **Equipment:** One-mile running course, 1 stopwatch (for teacher), and 1 scorecard and pencil per student.

THE PACER (PROGRESSIVE AEROBIC CARDIOVASCULAR ENDURANCE RUN)

Have several students run as long as possible back and forth between two lines marked 20 meters apart at a specified pace that gets faster every minute. Have students attempt to reach the opposite line before they hear a beep (programmed on the Fitnessgram cassette tape). Allow slower students to catch up with the pace until they have missed two beeps. Stop them after they are twice (not necessarily in succession) unable to reach the line. Direct those students to the cool-down area to walk and stretch. A student's score is the total number of laps completed beating the beeps. **Equipment:** A safe, 20-meter running area, 1 PACER cassette tape (Fitnessgram), 1 tape player, 1 tape measure, 4 cones, and 1 scorecard and pencil per student.

Body Composition

Skinfold measurements are a simple, yet reliable, way to measure body composition. You will need skinfold calipers as well as some training and practice to do this assessment. A good resource for this training is the *Practical Body Composition Kit*, which includes a guidebook, instructional video, software, and skinfold calipers. The kit can be ordered from Human Kinetics (800-747-4457).

SKINFOLD MEASUREMENTS

Measure the triceps and calf skinfolds to determine percent body fat. These sites are recommended because they are easily measured and are highly correlated with total body fat. The triceps skinfold is measured on the back of the arm over the triceps muscle of the right arm midway between the elbow and the acromion process of the scapula. The calf skinfold is measured on the inside of the right leg at the level of maximal girth. **Equipment:** Skinfold calipers and 1 scorecard and pencil per student.

Abdominal Strength and Endurance

How well a student can perform curl-ups is a good measure of abdominal strength and endurance.

CURL-UP TEST

Have students complete as many curl-ups as possible at a specified pace of about 20 curl-ups per minute (up to a maximum of 75 total). The student curls up, slowly sliding the fingers across a measur-

ing strip on the mat under the knees. When the fingertips reach the other side of the measuring strip, the student curls back down. Organize students into groups of three. Tape measuring strip securely to the mat. One performs the curl-ups, another places her hands under the head of the student doing curl-ups, and the third stands to the side and acts as a counter (see figure 2.2). **Equipment:** Gym mats, 1 scorecard and pencil per student, 1 cardboard measuring strip (30 inches long by 4.5 inches wide) per 3 students.

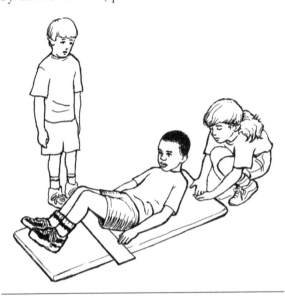

Figure 2.2   Curl-ups in group of three students.

Upper Body Strength

Use one of these three tests to assess upper body strength.

PUSH-UP TEST

Have students complete as many push-ups (to an elbow angle of 90 degrees) as possible at a rhythmic pace of 20 push-ups per minute to a prerecorded cadence (see figure 2.3a and b). **Equipment:** Cassette tape of cadence, tape player, 1 scorecard and pencil per student.

PULL-UP TEST

Have students complete as many pull-ups as possible. (Only use this test with students who can pull up at least once.) **Equipment:** Horizontal bar at a height at which the student's feet clear the floor or ground when hanging with the arms extended and 1 scorecard and pencil per student.

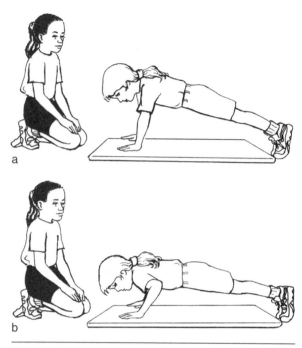

Figure 2.3 (a) Push-up starting position; (b) down position.

FLEXED-ARM HANG TEST

Have students hang with the chin above the bar as long as possible. **Equipment:** Horizontal bar at a height that the student's feet clear the floor or ground when hanging with the arms extended and 1 scorecard and pencil per student.

Flexibility

Use one or both of these two tests to measure flexibility.

BACK-SAVER SIT-AND-REACH

Have students sit and reach a maximum distance first on the right side of the body and then on the left (see figure 2.4). By reaching on one side of the body at a time, students should be encouraged not to hyperextend. **Equipment:** 3 back-saver sit-and-reach boxes for the class and 1 scorecard and pencil per student. If you design your own box, be sure to use a sturdy box about 12 inches high. Place a measuring scale on top of the box with the 9-inch mark even with the near edge of the box. The zero end of the ruler is nearest the student.

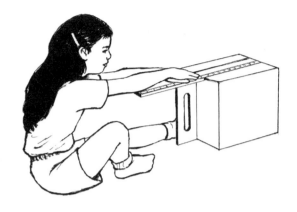

Figure 2.4 Back-saver sit-and-reach for the left side.

SHOULDER STRETCH

Have students try to touch their fingertips together behind their backs by reaching over the shoulder and under the elbow. To test left shoulder, student reaches with left hand over left shoulder and down the back as if to pull up a zipper. At the same time, student places the right hand behind the back and reaches up, trying to touch the fingers of the left hand (see figure 2.5). If the student is able to touch fingertips, she passes. Then test the right shoulder by reversing hand positions.

Figure 2.5 Shoulder stretch on the left side.

Authentic Assessment

If standardized tests are only part of a complete assessment approach, what can you do to make sure you have enough data to guide your students properly and modify your future lessons? Authentic assessment requires both teachers and students to engage in an ongoing process of evaluation, including self-evaluation (Vacca and Vacca 1996). You must become as actively involved in class as your students by providing feedback, monitoring progress, and making checklists. Simply put, the better you understand your students' performances, the better you will be able to plan instruction that will help them progress. Authentic assessment is an informal approach through which you can gather and interpret useful information about students' feelings, attitudes, knowledge, physical activity levels, likes and dislikes, individual goals, personal choices, and health-related fitness levels. Ideally, students will learn to see assessments as realistic and meaningful tasks to improve their personal fitness levels, perhaps developing and maintaining their own physical activity programs because of the guidance they receive.

Have students use personal fitness education portfolios (see sample in appendix A) to assist them in collecting, organizing, and analyzing their physical activity progress throughout the school year. The portfolios are individual booklets used to help both the student and the teacher understand the factors that affect health-related physical fitness. If you choose, have students also use their portfolios as reflective logs of their attitudes, feelings, and opinions about physical activity. Additional samples of authentic assessment you may wish to include in student portfolios are checklists for students to use (chapter 4), family fitness contracts (chapter 7), and nutrition logs (chapter 10). Students should keep their fitness education portfolios in the regular classroom and use them throughout the school year to help integrate various learning experiences in the classroom as well as in physical education class (see chapter 10).

Summary

The elementary school environment is ideal for establishing healthy lifestyles in our nation's youth. To accomplish this ambitious goal, use a multidisciplinary team effort such as the Heart Smart program. Enlist the support of classroom teachers, lunchroom personnel, the school nurse, special service teachers, administrators, parents, and the community to help children adopt healthy attitudes and behaviors to help reach the national health goals established by the U.S. Department of Health and Human Services in *Healthy People 2000*.

Behavioral Change and Motivational Strategies

They can do all because they think they can.

—Virgil

If children inherently like to move and enjoy active play, why are they becoming so unfit? Why are children getting heavier and physical activity levels dropping lower?

One answer may be that we need a behavioral change plan and new motivational strategies in physical education classes. Traditionally, the physical education curriculum included a number of fitness-related activities, such as obstacle courses, active games, jogging, exercises, and aerobic dance, to increase activity levels. Teachers presented these activities to meet the short-term needs of a particular class period, sport purpose, or fitness test.

Even now, most teachers neglect to build into their curriculum behavioral skills that will help children

value physical activity for a lifetime. In other words, you must motivate your students to maintain their interest in physical fitness so that they will develop an appreciation for physical activity as a way of life. Otherwise, doing all the developmentally appropriate fitness activities in the world will fail to teach children positive long-term lifestyle habits (see figure 3.1).

Rainbow to Youth Fitness and Active Lifestyles

Corbin (1987) developed the "Stairway to Lifetime Fitness" in which he established sequenced

Developmental activities and concepts — **Motivational strategies and behavior plan** — **Fitness levels and active lifestyles**

Figure 3.1 Behavior plan: the missing link.

steps to help students increase their fitness levels and improve test performances. This model approach created an awareness of the need to develop fitness behaviors in a developmentally appropriate sequence. For our purposes, I have developed the "Rainbow to Youth Fitness and Active Lifestyles" (figure 3.2). My model also incorporates a developmentally appropriate sequence through which you can establish healthy physical activity patterns in children by following a progression from "fitness fun," the first level for young children, to the final stage, "active lifestyle."

Do children naturally go from depending on you to provide fitness fun to independent active lifestyles overnight? Of course not, but by gradually increasing students' opportunities to make choices and to monitor themselves, you'll be helping them reach the pot of gold at the end of the rainbow: active, healthy lifestyles. Use the Rainbow to Youth Fitness and Active Lifestyles to guide your planning as you strive to shape positive fitness behaviors.

Fitness Fun

Young children are naturally active. They love to play and express themselves through movement. Take advantage of this to promote fitness fun. Keep in mind that if children think an activity is fun and enjoyable, they will repeat it over and over again. In

this stage, children who perceive the movement environment as safe, supportive, interactive, and exciting will develop a positive attitude toward a variety of physical activities.

Practice

Children are naturally creatures of habit. In order to develop positive physical activity habits, engage children in physical activity daily. Try to create a school environment that gives children frequent chances for physical activity. Recess, free play, before-school programs, intramurals, and fitness breaks are all good opportunities for children to move. Encourage parents to be active with their children and try to promote community opportunities such as parks or recreation centers to enhance physical activity outside of school. But don't stop at this stage, assuming that ample physical activity levels will meet your program goals. Children merely participating in physical activity without sufficient knowledge and support will not develop lasting values or behaviors.

Knowledge

Knowledge is the key to teaching children to value physical activity and healthy lifestyles long-term. Children need to understand why they are exercising

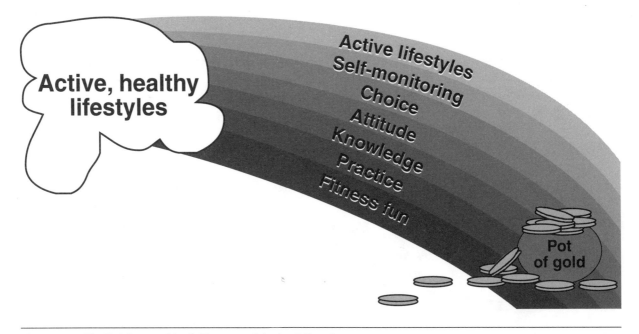

Figure 3.2   The Rainbow to Youth Fitness and Active Lifestyles.

and how to perform the activities correctly. They are more likely to participate in physical activity when they understand how and why their bodies respond to exercise. Include a sequence of planned health-related fitness concepts throughout the elementary school physical education experience. Work with classroom teachers, parents, and special service professionals such as the school nurse, lunch director, or counselor to reinforce these concepts outside of the gym. (See also chapter 10.)

Attitude

Your role as the teacher is especially critical when it comes to developing positive attitudes. Once children have experienced physical activity in a supportive environment, engaged in practice, and established a foundation of knowledge, they can begin to develop positive attitudes toward physical activity based on these experiences. Use the motivational strategies that I'll describe later in this chapter to build upon children's natural inclination to enjoy movement. And remember, use a multidisciplinary team approach to design your physical education program so that your students experience a cohesive home, community, and school environment united in support of positive behavioral changes (Bandura 1986).

Choice

Would you want to do the same activity over and over? Try not to hamper children's naturally positive attitudes toward movement by failing to provide variety. While children do enjoy repeating activities that they enjoy, a wide variety of physical activities will generate fresh interest when boredom threatens. Choice gives your students a chance to discover what they enjoy the most, and, over time, they'll learn to make their own selections based on their personal preferences. Therefore, allow children to select from various activities and exercises and to choose the amount of time they will spend on each choice whenever possible.

Yet choice needs to go beyond the variety you provide. This is the time to teach children how to set personal goals and make effective choices to reach their goals. By establishing goals, students will discover the need for self-direction and meaning in their physical development. Students must have practice thinking independently and making choices based on their individual needs in order to eventually lead physically active lives independently. Empower your students to take charge of their physical selves. (See also chapter 4.)

Self-Monitoring

As children move closer to independence, be more flexible in your teaching approach. Allow fourth, fifth, and sixth graders to be responsible for maintaining their personal fitness education portfolios (see appendix A). Children at this stage should be able to plan, self-evaluate, and track their activity patterns. Self-monitoring will allow children to set goals for achieving their personal bests and make decisions regarding their activity preferences. If you lead your students through the Rainbow to Youth Fitness and Active Lifestyles, this stage is reachable for many school-age children in the final year of level III.

Active Lifestyles

Students who have reached this stage exhibit a genuine commitment to physical activity. They are motivated to participate, eager to improve, happy to volunteer to help others, open to learning new activities, persistent in their efforts to reach goals, able to work independently, and are happy and relaxed in the learning environment. While they will continue to need support and reinforcement for their choices throughout middle school and high school, they have a firm foundation that will almost certainly lead to a lifetime of health and fitness.

What Motivates Children to Move?

The word "motivation" comes from the Latin word *movere*, which means "to move." We can think of motivation as something that directs, sparks, or maintains behavior: It's what gets students moving and keeps them going. For many years we taught children under the assumption that they had similar motivations as adults to exercise.

But children are not miniature adults! Adults engage in physical activity to enhance their appearances, develop physical attributions for their health, and to prevent disease. Children are physically active because they enjoy play, need to interact with their peers, wish to develop physical competence, and need to express themselves through various movement forms (figure 3.3). Let's examine each of these aspects closely.

Play and Fun

Children view play as an important ingredient in their lives. When an activity is nonthreatening, success-oriented, and exciting, children become very motivated. The desire to play is inherent in all human beings and is a necessary developmental stage in childhood.

Social Interaction

Children need the opportunity to relate to other children through active play. In a supportive movement environment, children develop a sense of belonging and acceptance, which helps bond them to their peers. The feelings of security experienced through group play may both enhance the sense of self-esteem and the ability to form positive relationships with others.

Physical Competence

Children have a strong desire to develop competence in physical skills. The challenge inherent in mastering physical skills motivates children to continue physical activity. The perception children have of their abilities may be determined by the amount of time, effort, and value placed on a specific activity. When children receive support and encouragement from the important people in their lives, they gain the confidence they need to develop active lifestyles and continue in a chosen physical activity.

Self-Expression

Not surprisingly, children naturally express themselves through active movement. Physical activity is often the vehicle for children to express their feelings and emotions to friends, parents, and teachers. Unlike teenagers and adults, children are not as able to verbalize their feelings or discuss differences of opinion. This usually results in more physical expressions of feelings, such as, happiness, anger, frustration, or excitement.

Types of Motivation

Motivation takes two general forms. *Extrinsic* motivation involves factors outside of the individual, unrelated to the task being performed. *Intrinsic* motivation is an individual's internal desire to perform a particular task (Ormrod 1995). Intrinsic motivation promotes long-term behav-

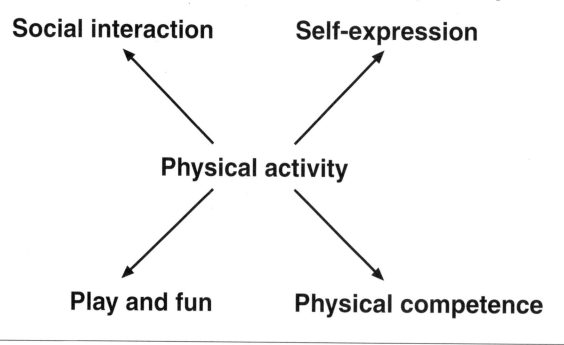

Figure 3.3 Why are children physically active?

ioral change more effectively. Indeed, students who learn to rely on intrinsic motivation are more likely to develop a long-term commitment to an active lifestyle. To enhance intrinsic motivation, empower students to develop the self-confidence to believe that they are capable of accomplishing certain tasks, the self-esteem to believe that they are worthy of good health, and the self-efficacy to believe that they are in control of their own destinies.

For many years physical educators have provided children with poor and inappropriate motivation, turning them off to exercise, rather than turning them on. The following are examples of inappropriate practices and conditions:

- Boring, repetitive, drill-like fitness activities (e.g., running laps each class)
- Group exercising
- Inflexible standards
- Using fitness testing along with an award system
- Competition
- Traditional curriculum offerings each year (e.g., soccer, softball, volleyball)
- Low levels of activity in class
- Continual use of direct teaching techniques
- Poor equipment and sterile, dingy facilities
- Unmotivated teachers

Would you be motivated to exercise in this type of environment?

Motivational Strategies

What can you do to foster intrinsic motivation throughout your physical education program? Read on!

Teach Basic Skills

Teach your students basic skills, such as how to jog and how to do curl-ups. When you take the time to instruct your students on the proper form and techniques, they will assume you really care about improving their physical development. Moreover, show a personal interest in each student by providing individual skill feedback in a positive, supportive way.

Choose Success-Oriented Activities

When children feel successful, they'll repeat an activity and gain the confidence to advance to more difficult activities. To motivate students, design activities at the appropriate developmental level that include challenges that students can achieve through practice. For example, students should have activity choices, such as the regular push-up, open stance push-up, or wall push-up to meet their physical needs and ensure some degree of success.

Have Fun, Fun, Fun

I can't emphasize this point enough: Children should laugh, sing, play, and interact while engaged in physical activity. See how fast they tune into your class objectives when they are having fun and enjoying the lesson. For example, develop arm strength and endurance using the parachute by making waves or pretending popcorn is popping (use playballs; see chapter 11). Children will have enormous fun while developing muscular strength and endurance.

Add Creative Equipment

Add new and exciting equipment to add spark your classes. Many times physical educators use the same equipment year in and year out and children become bored and tired of the same old thing. Add unusual items such as rubberized exercise toners (figure 3.4), heavy jump ropes, or heart rate monitors to renew interest in physical activity.

Figure 3.4   Upper body exercise using rubberized exercise toner.

Create a Colorful Environment

Decorate the gym with colorful posters, exercise charts, and bulletin boards. Schedule a monthly theme. For example, February can be "Heart Smart Month." Have different grades and their parents take turns decorating each month. To really add pizzazz, organize a "Sport Art Show" for which you display everyone's project in the gym.

Provide Incentives

Students need support and encouragement for their hard work in your classes. Occasionally provide children with positive, healthy incentives for active participation. Exercise bands, free choice of an activity, or frozen yogurt certificates all make good incentives to help motivate students (see figure 3.5).

Be a Role Model

Provide your classes with a positive role model. Keep trim, exercise with your classes, eat healthy foods at lunch, keep nutritious snacks on your desk, and talk to your students about your after-school activities such as volleyball leagues, jogging, hiking trips, and so on. Looking good always counts, too! Dress professionally in sharp-looking warm-ups and T-shirts with the message, "Physical education is the best health insurance."

Accentuate the Positive

Of course, positive reinforcement strengthens existing habits as well as encourages student progress. Practice using the gestures and words of encouragement I have listed in table 3.1.

Organize a Health Club

Use the intramural sports model but modify it for health-related fitness. Then, designate a club workout area. Students who join the club can work on their individual goals or participate in a group physical activity of their choice, exercising before school, during recess, or after school. Your job is to plan group activities and help participants plan their individual programs. T-shirts with the club name may motivate more students to participate.

Table 3.1	Gestures and Words of Encouragement	
Words	**Gestures**
Wow!	Laugh with student
Great Job!	Smile
Nice Going!	Hug
Yes!	Raise eyebrows in delight
I'm proud of you for your effort!	
Good for you!	Nod head
Way to go!	Give thumbs up
All right!	Give high five
Terrific!	Shake hands
Thank you for cooperating!	Pat back
	Wave
Much better!	Put hand on shoulder
Looking good!	Raise both arms (touchdown signal)
Beautiful!	Stare with smile and nod head
Keep up the good work!	
Wonderful!	Silent cheer with fists raised
I'm impressed!	
Very creative!	

Encourage Self-Direction

Allowing fourth, fifth, and sixth grade students the opportunity to manage their own personal fitness education portfolios motivates them as well. Portfolios should include each student's personal fitness scores, daily logs, individual program, contracts, graphs, and other learning activities (see appendix A).

Use Authentic Assessments

Use authentic assessments throughout the year to give students ongoing information about their progress. This way, they can see what they need to improve before you do final evaluations at the end of the school year. After all, everyone appreciates

Figure 3.5 Physical activity incentive.

having a chance to improve. Moreover, seeing incremental improvement is motivating in itself. It also helps students set realistic, yet challenging, goals.

Involve Parents

Students will gain additional support and reinforcement when they know their parents are interested and involved in physical activity. Through a newsletter sent to parents and suggested home-based activities the family can become more physically active. (See also chapter 7.)

Hold Special Events

Remember, special school-wide or community events can bring needed attention to your program goals. For example, in the Geography Run students calculate the walking and jogging miles they have done both in and out of school and report them to you. You, in turn, plot the school's total mileage on a large U.S. map, updating your school's run from New York to California each week. Encourage the school lunch program and classroom teachers to help integrate learning experiences around this event. (See also chapters 7, 10, and 14.)

Form Cooperative Learning Groups

Cooperative learning can enhance self-confidence and security in physical activity. For example, Group Hoops is an activity in which six students hold hands to form a circle, with a hoop threaded through one pair of grasped hands. Then the students pass the hoop around the circle counterclockwise without releasing their hands. You can vary the hoop size based on the developmental level of the class and size of the students. Encourage the children to cooperate to complete the task—not to race against other groups.

Invite Guest Speakers

Schedule guest speakers from the community who may have expertise to share with the class (e.g., marathon runner, body builder, fitness instructor, physical education professor, health care professional). Include speakers from a variety of ethnic and racial backgrounds so students can identify with these role models.

Organize Big Buddies

Arrange for each first grader to have a fifth or sixth grade big buddy by scheduling classes in which students can occasionally be together. Make the older student responsible for teaching the younger student certain concepts and exercises. Big buddies can also be pen pals and academic tutors to the first graders.

Vary Your Teaching Strategies

Children learn differently, so use a variety of teaching strategies, such as small groups, independent activities, and partner workouts to meet the individual needs and interests of your students. (See also chapter 4.)

Summary

Fitness education includes much more than providing children with highly active games and exercises. The contemporary approach to a quality physical education program includes a plan for long-term behavioral change and motivational strategies to encourage children to be physically active throughout their lives. Work with your colleagues, students' parents, administration, and community to create a supportive, healthy school environment. Plan learning experiences according to a child's motivation to move and emphasize the intrinsic value of physical activity as you guide children to follow the rainbow to the pot of gold—an active, healthy lifestyle!

Teaching Strategies

This chapter is dedicated to the memory of a friend and colleague, Muska Mosston.

> *Education is what survives when what has been learned has been forgotten.*
>
> —B.F. Skinner

Both physical educators and society at large have been concerned about childhood fitness in the United States for over 80 years. As we have discussed, physical educators have tended to emphasize tracking national fitness testing over developing positive fitness behaviors. Recently, as physical educators, we have debated major issues such as the award system, measuring body composition, and which specific test items to use. For many years we have been teaching children about physical activity through national fitness testing programs, which may be the very reason why past generations have become discouraged and unmotivated about physical activity.

Enough is enough! It's time to change our teaching methods and generate intrinsic interest in physical activity with updated approaches.

Traditional Models of Teaching

Traditional models of teaching fitness education have proven unsuccessful. Do you recognize these methods from the past? Unfortunately, they may still be alive and well in your district.

Military Style

This approach uses direct commands to get children to exercise. The military-style physical educator organizes children in squad formation to perform exercises in unison and uses physical activity as punishment for not conforming to class procedures. This approach is unsuccessful because it does not allow for individual differences. Moreover, it forces children to exercise on command without a true understanding of the value of physical activity. Indeed, many children feel threatened by this approach. Certainly, it fails to lead to long-term positive physical activity behaviors.

Pretest and Posttest Design

In this approach, the physical educator begins the school year with a fitness pretest and ends the year with a posttest. To prepare children, the teacher usually gives a few lessons about the proper techniques of exercising that are related to the tests. Otherwise, she rarely teaches health-related physical fitness or incorporates it into her traditional unit plans. This approach has proven unsuccessful because it makes children view fitness as something that is evaluated simply to separate the fit from the unfit. Improving fitness scores and receiving awards are the only motivators in this approach.

Five-Minute Warm-Up

In this model, class starts with five minutes of calisthenics and a short run, usually while the teacher is taking attendance. This approach leads to repetitious and inappropriate exercises. Students exercise like robots, usually resulting in boredom and poor exercise techniques. Rarely are fitness concepts presented in this approach; therefore, students never learn the reasons why they are exercising. Also, teachers usually give very little attention to this stage of the class, so students eventually see exercise as unimportant. (See also chapters 5 and 9.)

Fitness Unit Approach

In this approach, the physical educator designs a four- to six-week fitness unit as a separate component of the yearly curriculum. If taught as a completely separate unit, children tend to view fitness as an isolated subject rather than as an ongoing activity important in their daily lives. It is, however, an important strategy to present a fitness unit in September to kick off your fitness program for the school year.

Games and Sports Model

This approach uses games that require little organization and team sports as a means to teach the value of exercise concepts and increase physical activity levels. Due to class size, time constraints, and limited player responsibilities, games are often short in duration and produce only moderate levels of physical activity for a minimal number of children. In game situations, for example, the most active participants are usually the most skilled and conditioned children, leaving a large percentage of children inactive—usually the children who have the greatest need to develop their skills and increase physical activity levels. This approach encourages games and team sports as an end in themselves. Instead, teach students how certain activities such as games and team sports are agents of health-related fitness and active lifestyles.

Fitness Concepts

This approach uses the premise that if children know how their bodies work and understand basic exercise principles, they will become active because they understand the value of and need for exercise. Yet, by itself, a strong academic approach is not enough; it is only one component of a quality fitness education program. Children need to experience fitness, interact with their peers through activity, and learn by doing. Thus, I advocate the multidisciplinary model throughout this book.

A Humanistic Approach to Teaching Fitness

Humanism is not so much a theory as it is a teaching approach. The humanistic physical educator values children rather than the activity, values fitness participation rather than fitness scores, and values student choice and responsibility rather than class control (Virgilio 1996). In these ways, a humanistic approach helps develop a quality fitness education program in the elementary school.

The Teacher's Role

According to Rodgers (1994), significant learning takes place when you adopt three basic attitudes toward students and their learning.

- **Be genuine**. Share your thoughts and feelings with students as openly and honestly as possible. When students are misbehaving, share your frustration and disappointment with them while also showing warmth, caring, and encouragement. If you make a mistake, admit it, apologize, and move on. If you can't answer a fitness question, say so and work together as a class to find the answer.

- **Value individuals**. Learn to value students for who they are—whatever their skills, thoughts, or feelings. Rodgers calls this an attitude of "unconditional positive regard," meaning an open, nonjudgmental, nondefensive approach to others. If, for example, a student is clowning around in your aerobic movement class, she has a real need for attention and respect. The student may feel a genuine fear of being rejected if she acts "normal." Recognize the needs behind the behavior.

- **Offer empathy**. Place yourself in your students' shoes as much as you can. Seek to understand their feelings and work to express this knowledge to the students in a concrete manner. Don't merely say, "I know how you're feeling," describe the feelings clearly and offer suggestions. This opens the way for a trusting student-teacher relationship. For example, if an overweight student is having trouble jogging in your class, speak to him privately about the frustration and anxiety he may be feeling and share a similar experience you may have had in math class when you were in school. Reaffirm that you accept him as a person and offer your support. With your assistance, it won't be long before the student will accept individual responsibility for planning fitness goals. Empathy has great power to set the stage for genuine learning and development.

Instructional Applications

Several ways exist to make fitness education more humanistic, or student-centered. Start with what students consider important. Students will relate better to an educational goal when it is associated with something relevant to their personal development. For example, teach first graders aerobic dance through cartoon characters, animation, and playacting. Use an exciting video, such as *Mousercise*, in which Disney's Mickey Mouse presents fitness activities.

Provide a variety of resources to meet the different needs of students, thereby enhancing the learning environment. For example, use books, handouts, exercise videos, charts, guest speakers, and special equipment (e.g., medicine balls, exercise bands) and videotape students doing activities.

Furthermore, don't always use class time for traditional instruction. Infuse variety into your program by letting students make more choices as to how they'll achieve their own and program goals (Hellison and Templin 1991). For example, have "Open Gym" now and then. Set up 10 to 15 fitness stations in the playing area. Let students choose any station in any sequence. If you plan enough variety and emphasize individual choice, students will avoid clustering at certain stations. And have "Practice Time" classes, giving students time to practice a dance fitness routine or to work on whatever aspects of fitness or movement skills they feel need extra attention.

Variety must not only come from using different resources and changing the way you use class time but also from varying your teaching strategies. But where do you start? Next, let's examine a number of practical, easy-to-use teaching methods based on Mosston and Ashworth's "Spectrum of Teaching Styles" in *Teaching Physical Education* (1994).

The Spectrum of Teaching Styles

It's essential to teach fitness using a variety of teaching styles because your preferred style may not be reaching every student. So stretch yourself and match your approach to different learning styles at different times. Your classes will be more interesting and accessible to all of your students and learning will increase accordingly.

Before selecting a particular teaching style for a particular lesson, however, you must decide what the learning objective is for the lesson, clearly identifying what students will learn. Regardless of the teaching approach, children learn more effectively when you clearly state the purpose for the activities. The learning objective should be something concrete that you can observe and assess to determine if learning has taken place. Furthermore, develop class objectives that speak to the three major aspects of learning: cognitive (knows), affective (values), and psychomotor (does) (Franck et al. 1991). The following is an example of learning objectives for level III:

- **Cognitive**: Students will be able to locate their biceps and identify one exercise to develop these muscles.
- **Affective**: Students will exercise independently after school, weekends, or during recess and report their activities in their fitness portfolios (see appendix A).
- **Psychomotor**: Students will walk or jog one mile at their own pace to the best of their abilities.

Keep in mind when selecting a teaching style that one method is not better than another. Indeed, each style has its advantages and disadvantages. The one you choose all depends on your objective. With experience, you'll be able to choose an appropriate style or mix of styles to elicit the outcome you desire. Certainly, effective teachers possess a wide repertoire of styles and techniques. Be innovative and use a variety of techniques to add excitement to the learning experience (Mosston and Ashworth 1994).

Command Style

This approach is highly teacher-centered. Students learn to do tasks accurately within a short period of time, directly under your control. You instruct students *en masse*, using the demonstration and explanation technique. In this style, use command signals for each movement for the learner to perform accordingly. The advantages of this approach are that it uses time efficiently, it develops listening skills, it increases safety, and it streamlines class management. The command style is useful when you are introducing a new activity or teaching certain types of lessons, such as swimming, mass exercises, or aerobic dance.

Practice Style

The practice style allows students to accept more personal responsibility for learning. As with the command style, you decide the learning objectives and class content when using the practice style. In contrast to the command style, however, you allow the learners to perform the task at their own pace. Add variety by having students complete tasks individually, in pairs, or in small groups. Have everyone work on the same task at once or have several different activities going on at the same time. One easy way to organize several activities at once is to incorporate the station approach with task cards to help with instruction. Task cards give students practice learning independently, making the practice style more student-centered than the command style. Each task card lists directions, giving the teacher more freedom to give feedback (see figure 4.1). Write tasks on large index cards or on posters placed around the gym. Use pictures, graphics, and color to make the task card more visually appealing. The major advantage of this style is that it frees you to give individual attention to students.

Reciprocal Style

In the reciprocal style, you still establish the learning objectives and class content, but the students take responsibility for teaching each other.

First, develop a "criteria checklist," a checklist that students will use as a reference to provide feedback for the fitness activity (see figure 4.2). Include a simple breakdown of the important skill components. Pictures may also be helpful. You may want to attach each checklist to a clipboard. Laminate the sheets and have students write on them with erasable overhead projector marking pens so you can wash the cards off and reuse them for years to come. Criteria checklists are especially effective when teaching specific movements of certain exercises. Large task cards may also be posted on the gym wall to help supplement and reinforce appropriate techniques.

In the reciprocal style, students work in pairs in a teaching-learning partnership, so the next step is to pair the students in your class at random. Talk to them about how important it is to be a teacher and how you need their help. Ask each pair to decide who will be the doer performing the activity first and who will be the observer, or teacher, first. The doer performs the physical activity according to your directions, and the observer gives feedback, using the checklist as an instructional resource. After several trials, have the students switch roles. Try not to interfere with the doer-observer relationship, thereby reducing the impact of this style. Your role as the teacher is to stay neutral and act as a facilitator. Therefore, the reciprocal teaching style is highly student-centered.

Self-Check Style

In the self-check style, more decisions are shifted to the learner to promote greater responsibility. The purpose of this approach is to encourage self-reliance and self-improvement and show students how to honestly and objectively assess their performance.

The self-check style allows a great deal of freedom for you and for the students. You can design the learning objectives and content activities yourself. Have all students work on the same task, or include a variety of activities. The criteria checklist (see figure 4.3 for another example) used in the reciprocal style may also be used here.

Ensure that you have already given several related lessons on the chosen skill or activity. This lays the foundation for safe and effective independent work. (Remember that exercises performed incorrectly may result in injury.) Then have students move throughout the play area performing the assigned tasks and stopping periodically to review the checklists to evaluate their performances. Students may either move on to another task or repeat the task to correct their performances. Circulate through the play area, allowing students to develop independently; provide feedback only when the activity is unsafe or for disciplinary reasons.

Name _____   Date _____

Class _____   Level III

Upper Body Strength

Practice each exercise as described below. Place a checkmark (✓) next to each completed task. Turn in your card when you are finished.

Exercise	Task	Completed	Comments
A. Regular or modified push-up	5 reps		
B. Bent-arm hang	Maximum hang time_____		
C. Horizontal ladder	Two crossings		
D. Cargo net climb	One round up and down		
E. Medicine ball catch	Ten individual catches and throws		

Figure 4.1   Individual task card for upper body strength.

Doer 1_____   Date _____

Doer 2 _____   Class _____

Level III

Jogging Criteria

Observer: Give the doer some pointers about their jogging form. Use the tips below to help you. Try to be friendly.

Doer: Jog at a moderate pace. When the teacher signals, slow down—then change roles.

	Doer 1		Doer 2	
	Yes	**No**	**Yes**	**No**
1. Runs tall, leans slightly forward				
2. Swings legs from hip, knees bent				
3. Lands on heels with weight rolling along the outside portion of foot to toes				
4. Points toes straight ahead, lands heel directly under knee				
5. Swings arms straight forward and backward, hands relaxed				
6. Breathes from stomach in an even rhythm				

Figure 4.2   Reciprocal style criteria checklist for jogging techniques.

Name _____   Date _____

Class _____   Level III

Self-Check: Flexibility

Directions: Follow the steps listed below. Practice each exercise five times on each leg. Check (✓) the box to the right after completion.

Hamstring stretch:	OK	Feels uncomfortable
1. Sit with left leg extended; bend right leg at the knee, place sole on the floor near the knee of the extended leg.		
2. Flex the foot of the extended leg, toes up, against a wall, box, or other support.		
3. Bend forward from the hips, keeping the lower back straight. The bent knee may rotate slightly outward.		
4. Relax and breathe normally. You should not feel pain!		
5. Hold the stretch for 15 seconds. Repeat with opposite leg.		

Figure 4.3   Self-check style: criteria checklist for flexibility.

This style allows individuals to set their own pace better than they can with a partner. Show respect for individual differences by allowing everyone ample time to complete tasks to their own satisfaction. With the self-check style, you can learn many interesting things about your students' affective, cognitive, and psychomotor development from observing their independent behavior.

An extension of self-checking is the personalized learning contract. Once you get to know your students, you may want to use this approach to allow greater independence and more accelerated individualized fitness development. You design the contracts ahead of time, basing the number of options you include on the learner's needs (see figure 4.4).

Inclusion Style

This approach emphasizes that everyone has the right to participate and be successful in class activities. For this style, you establish various levels of performance for each fitness activity. Then the learners select their entry levels based on their own preferences and physical abilities. Your role is to encourage learners to evaluate their own performances. Encourage students who are having trouble to stay at the same level of difficulty. The hard part—if you naturally lean toward the command style of teaching—is to allow students to choose their individual levels of activity. Keep in mind that this style gives students the right to choose to enjoy mastery of a particular level before moving on. Task cards at various stations can help implement this style, too (see figure 4.5). (See chapter 6 for ways to include students with disabilities.)

Guided Discovery and Problem Solving

Guided discovery and problem solving represent a significant change from the techniques discussed thus far. When using guided discovery and problem solving, you ask students to think differently about the subject matter. The process, or the learning itself, becomes more important than the final product, or achievement levels.

Guided Discovery

In guided discovery, you establish a predetermined answer to a problem. Then you plan a series of questions (Q) and anticipated responses (AR) that will lead the learner to the final answer. The response you should give (YR) is listed after the anticipated response.

Q: What are the largest muscles in your body?
AR: Legs.
YR: Right!

Q: What are the muscles in the back of the legs?
AR: Hamstrings.
YR: Excellent!

Q: Suppose your dad asked you to move a few boxes from the garage. How would you approach the box to pick it up?
AR: Bend the knees, keeping the back straight.
YR: OK!

Q: What body part should be used to get to a low position to reach down and pick up the box?
AR: Legs.
YR: Yes!

Q: So what muscles are used to do most of the work when we pick up anything?
AR: Leg muscles.
YR: Very good. Now let's practice.

Problem Solving

In the problem-solving style, the answers are unlimited. You still select the general subject matter content, posing a specific movement problem for the small group or individual to solve, which may have hundreds of potentially correct answers. You must be careful to establish class procedures and closely supervise the class for safety and organization. But once the students are involved in the problem, don't interfere, or you will detract from the learning process. An example of small group problem solving for level II may simply be to ask children to design a highly active game using four hoops, two jump ropes, and two 8.5-inch playballs. Possible interpretations are endless and are all correct.

Add a problem-solving aspect to the basic personalized learning contract by using an open-ended contract that allows the student to develop her own goals and to design activities to reach those goals (figure 4.6). (See also the family fitness contract in figure 7.5.)

Name _____   Date _____

Class _____   Level _____

I, _____, desire to improve my fitness level by agreeing to perform the following activities designed by _____, my physical education teacher.

I realize I must stay on-task and complete the program to the best of my ability.

This contract will begin _____ and will end on _____. I will perform the activities described below each class period.

Warm-up: Jog for 2 minutes.

Flexibility: Stretch with a friend for 5 minutes.

Muscular endurance: 15 curl-ups (total)
                        Jump rope, 30 turns
                        10 push-ups (total)
                        Obstacle course 2 times around

Sport activity—select one:
   Basketball: 2-on-2 game or individual practice
   Soccer: Goal kick practice
   Softball: Running bases or throwing against wall

If I successfully complete the above program I will be rewarded with a frozen yogurt certificate and a free P.E. period.

Sign _____   Sign _____
          Teacher   Student

Figure 4.4   Personalized learning contract.

Name _____   Date _____

Class _____   Level III

Push-ups: Upper Body Strength

Directions: Select any color push-up. Perform as many as you can. Record your score in the space provided to the right. When you master one color, try selecting another.

Repetitions

A. Blue: Straight back   _____

B. Green: Bent knees   _____

C. Red: Wide hands   _____

D. Tan: Push-up and hold   _____ **seconds**

E. Yellow: Chair push-up   _____

F. Brown: Wall push-up

Figure 4.5   Inclusion style task card for push-ups.

Name _____   Date _____

Class _____   Level _____

Physical Fitness Contract

I, _____, would like to improve _____ (fitness area). I understand I need additional work in this area of fitness. My long-term goal is _____.

I understand that I will be given class time to achieve this goal. I also promise to work on my goal outside of school at least three days per week. (Select two days: M Tu W Th F Sat Sun)

This contract will begin on _____ and will end on _____. I agree to inform my teacher each week about my progress and the specific activities used to achieve my goal.

If I achieve my goal, I will reward myself by _____.

Sign _____
            Student

Sign _____
            Teacher

Sign _____
         Parent or guardian

Figure 4.6 Open-ended student choice contract.

Computer Learning

Looking for a fun way to keep track of individual fitness scores and to reinforce the cognitive aspect of fitness development? Try computers. The Prudential Fitnessgram system (Cooper Institute for Aerobic Research 1992) is an example of a software program that provides a simple, easy-to-read printout of a student's fitness scores with recommendations for improvement. Are your muscle anatomy lessons dull and boring? Let Dino the Dinosaur add spice to them with *Dino*Fit*, a software package that teaches children about muscle anatomy (Dotson 1989). In addition to fun programs, have students use a simple computer spreadsheet to record their eating and exercise patterns (see daily log sheets in appendix A). Giving students opportunities to practice computer skills in physical education is another excellent way to employ the multidisciplinary approach, integrating your goals with classroom objectives. Indeed, you'll have to work with the classroom or computer lab teacher to determine what computer uses each particular class is ready for and to coordinate computer time.

Class Structure

Once you determine which style of teaching is right for a particular lesson, you are ready to organize the lesson. Structure your lesson plans into three parts: set induction, lesson focus, and closure.

Set Induction

Children feel more secure if they know what is going to happen before it happens. So explicitly set up each lesson. Review what the class accomplished in the last activity and then introduce what you've planned for this lesson. Orient the learners to what they'll be doing, how they'll be doing it, and why it is important (Rink 1993). Here is an example for level II: "Last week we learned how important exercise is for our hearts. Today we are going to learn how to take our heart rate, which we'll call 'HR,' and count how many times our heart beats before and after our basketball skills lesson. At the end of class, I'll give you a learning activity to do at home with your parents. Remember, you really have to take good care of your heart: It is the most important muscle in your body. Even Michael Jordan needs a strong heart to play basketball every day!"

Lesson Focus

Be sure to organize your class so that you give the primary focus of the lesson top priority. In other words, don't try to do everything in one class. If the focus of the lesson is teaching children to take their heart rates, then direct most of your time to this end. Add other related learning objectives to help facilitate and extend the primary focus of the lesson as time allows.

Closure

To close a lesson effectively, give a brief review of what the lesson attempted and accomplished. If appropriate, compliment the students' efforts, but don't criticize. Review what will be coming up in physical education, making them eager to attend the next lesson. If the lesson was very strenuous, use this time to have students cool down and relax before leaving. Here is an example of closure for level II: "OK, let's finish class. Please come over and sit by this tree. I thought we had a great class today. Everyone seemed interested in finding their HR and counting the number of heartbeats in one minute. Next week we are going to play a game called Circle Circulation and learn how the heart pumps blood throughout our bodies. Tonight when you are at home, show you parents how to take their HRs and have them calculate their one-minute resting HRs. Have a great day and remember to stay heart smart!"

Summary

Historically, traditional fitness education models and teaching strategies have proven unsuccessful in developing fitness levels and patterns of physical activity in children because they emphasized end results over process. But there are alternatives to traditional approaches to fitness education! Let's emphasize *how* we teach children physical activity so that they can use the same processes independently. Adopt a humanistic philosophy, which places each student's personal needs and abilities first, before planning a quality program of physical education. The "Spectrum of Teaching Styles" approach in Mosston and Ashworth (1994) offers you a number of creative choices from which to select an appropriate teaching style for each set of objectives.

Principles of Health-Related Physical Fitness

> *We are underexercised as a nation. We look instead of play. We ride instead of walk. Our existence deprives us of the minimum of physical activity essential for healthy living.*
>
> —John F. Kennedy

Let's briefly review basic exercise principles so you can properly plan health-related physical fitness instruction for your physical education program. As you reshape your physical education curriculum to educate children and develop positive values and behaviors relative to an active lifestyle, follow the guidelines in this chapter to help you teach safe, efficient, and developmentally appropriate physical activities. Tailor specific exercises to meet the individual needs and interests of children; however, keep in mind that children do not require a specific exercise prescription as adults do. Instead, children respond better to short periods of vigorous activity throughout the day than they do to one 30-minute intense workout. In fact, activity that is too intense may have an adverse effect on children's motivation to continue physical activity.

Core Principles of Health-Related Physical Fitness

To make it easy for both you and your students to remember the exercise principles and guidelines, use the acronym SPORT-FITT.

SPORT stands for

S - pecificity

P - rogression

O - verload

R - eversibility

T - rain and Maintain

FITT stands for

F - requency

I - ntensity

T - ime

T - ype

Sets and repetitions are common terms used in recommending exercises. Repetitions refers to the number of times a movement is repeated; sets refers to a number of repetitions to complete before resting. For example, if you did two sets of eight repetitions for arm curls, you would do eight arm curls, rest briefly, then do eight more.

Specificity

The principle of specificity simply means that only the muscles or body systems being worked benefit from the exercise. In other words, exercise the specific muscles you want to improve. For example, to improve their one-mile run times, children at level III should jog one to two miles, three or four days per week. This activity specifically develops muscular endurance in the legs and the cardiorespiratory system but does little for the arms, chest, and shoulders.

Progression

The principle of progression means that in order to improve, children should *gradually* increase their physical activity in a certain fitness component, especially during the first four to six weeks of exercising. The rate of progression depends on the individual; however, you can generally apply the "10-percent rule," increasing duration by no more than 10 percent per week. For example, if a child can comfortably jog 10 minutes per day, four days per week, he may jog for 11 minutes, four days the next week.

Overload

To improve any component of fitness, the body must work above the normal level: This is the principle of overload. You may overload any activity by increasing the intensity—repetitions, duration, or frequency—which I'll discuss further under "intensity" in the FITT section. Remember, though, that activity sessions need not be exhaustive or stressful to achieve health-related physical fitness. Fitness levels may be improved by slowly adding to the workload in a safe, comfortable manner.

Reversibility

Reversibility simply means, "Use it or lose it." Unfortunately, no one can store the benefits of fitness. Physical activity, therefore, must be a lifetime commitment. The achieved fitness level will be lost if it is not maintained through continuous activity.

Train and Maintain

Children who apply the exercise principles will train effectively and reach their physical bests. Once your students have acquired fitness, however, it's important to encourage them to maintain adequate activity levels and establish appropriate long- and short-term goals based on their individual needs.

FITT Guidelines

Using the FITT acronym helps both you and your students remember these exercise guidelines: frequency, intensity, time, and type.

Frequency

In general, children should exercise to improve most components of health-related physical fitness three to five times per week (Powers and Dodd 1996). Children should be physically active for at least 30 minutes most days of the week, preferably every day, to maintain the health benefits of exercise.

Intensity

Intensity is the physiological stress placed on the body during an exercise session. The method for gauging the intensity of exercise will vary based on the type of exercise performed. For example, checking the heart rate is a way of monitoring the body's stress during cardiorespiratory activity. By fourth grade, children should be able to take their resting and training heart rates to monitor their activity levels.

The two easiest places to locate the heart rate are at the radial artery and the carotid artery. To find the radial pulse, bend the wrist slightly downward and place the index and middle finger on the thumb side of the wrist (see figure 5.1). To find the carotid pulse, slide the index and middle fingers into the groove along the throat (see figure 5.2). Count the number of beats for 10 seconds and multiply by six to calculate the number of beats in one minute, or count for 6 seconds and add a zero to the number.

To monitor physical stress during cardiorespiratory fitness, it's also helpful to calculate the target heart rate zone (THRZ), ensuring a safe and efficient exercise session. Here is an example for a 10-year-old child.

1. Subtract age from 220 to obtain a maximum heart rate (MHR) of 210: $220 - 10 = 210$.

2. Multiply MHR by .70 to find 70 percent of MHR: $210 \times 0.70 = 147$ beats per minute.

3. Multiply MHR by .80 to find 80 percent of MHR: $210 \times 0.80 = 168$ beats per minute.

Figure 5.1 Radial pulse.

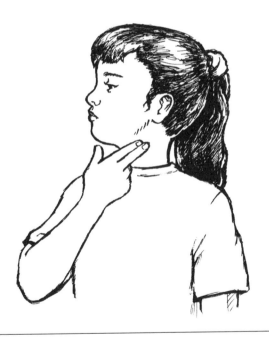

Figure 5.2 Carotid pulse.

Thus, THRZ is 147 to 168 beats per minute for a 10-year-old. Have each student capable of doing the math calculate their THRZ and monitor it during physical education class activities. But don't apply the information in the same manner recommended for adults, which asserts that to gain a cardiorespiratory effect you must exercise vigorously, four times

per week at THRZ for 20 to 30 minutes. Instead, build an awareness of this method of monitoring intensity, providing a significant learning experience. Two other ways to gauge intensity is for students to count the number of repetitions they perform during muscular endurance activity and to monitor the degree of tension of a particular stretching exercise.

Include a higher percentage of moderate to vigorous physical activity so that physical education better meets your students' exercise needs (Simons-Morton 1994). This is activity that requires repeated weight transfer using large muscle movements such as jogging, dancing, and rope jumping.

Time

This refers to the duration aspect of the exercise session, not including the warm-up or cool-down periods. In developmental levels I and II, limit the duration of activity to shorter bouts of 6 to 8 minutes with rest periods lasting at least 1 to 2 minutes between activity periods. In developmental level III, you can safely prolong physical activity for 10 to 20 minutes at a time. The amount of time in continuous or segmented physical activity, however, should total 30 minutes to 60 minutes per day for school-aged children for optimal health-related benefits (Corbin et al. 1994).

Type

This refers to the type, or mode, of exercise performed. Teach children a variety of exercises and activities that promote specific health-related fitness components. For example, provide students with choices to enhance cardiorespiratory endurance during a class period, e.g., jogging, roller skating, rope jumping, or step aerobics, encouraging them to select safe activities that they enjoy. Teach them that certain out-of-school activities, such as raking leaves, walking, washing the car, stair climbing, and house cleaning may contribute to the total physical activity time they accumulate throughout the day as well.

Appropriate Application of FITT

Keep in mind that the major purpose of a quality physical education program at the elementary school level is to emphasize the process and value of participating in physical activity. Don't lose sight of this by emphasizing product—fitness test scores and exercising to achieve awards.

Stages of a Physical Activity Session

Whether students are jogging, developing muscular endurance, playing basketball, or practicing kicking skills, you should teach them to follow the appropriate stages of a physical activity session: the warm-up, the main event, and the cool-down.

Warm-Up

The major objective of this stage is to prepare the heart, muscles, and joints for the main event. You may think stretching should come first, but it's important to warm the muscles before stretching as stretching cold muscles can increase the risk of injury. Therefore, the first step is to raise the body temperature and increase blood circulation to the muscles. For example, begin class with two minutes of moderate to brisk walking, marching steps with arm movements, slow galloping, or light aerobics performed to music. Once the muscles are warm, have your class perform a few static stretches for the major muscle groups. Keep in mind, however, that stretching for a warm-up is quite different from performing flexibility exercises. Concentrate on a few basic static stretches, such as the calf stretch, the sit-and-reach (hamstrings), the quadriceps stretch, and the leg hug (hip and lower back extensors). If necessary, add other stretches that fit the specific activity. But don't allow the muscles to cool off again before starting the main event; follow the warm-up period immediately with the main event.

Main Event

Have students spend the first two minutes of the main activity session in a moderate level of activity. This is what I call the "bridge" between the warm-up and the most vigorous stage of the class. For example, if students will be undertaking a jogging workout, have them move at a moderate pace for one to two minutes before they accelerate to their normal running paces. Students about to play soccer or full-court basketball should begin the main event with a lead-up game or with highly active skill activities. When possible, tailor the main event itself to each student's personal preference and physical needs. For the main event itself, concentrate on a specific health-related fitness component or simply include a high percentage of moderate to vigorous physical activity. Students in developmental level III working to improve cardiorespiratory endurance should monitor their target heart rate zones and use personal judgment whether to rest, drink water, or slow down. In developmental levels I and II, the main event should be active with intermittent rest periods spaced appropriately throughout the class period.

Cool-Down

Begin the cool-down immediately after the main event by gradually slowing down. Keep in mind that the large muscles of the body (legs, arm) return the blood back to the heart. If students stop suddenly after vigorous exercise, the blood will sit in their muscles, causing the blood to pool, possibly resulting in dizziness or nausea.

After vigorous activity, have students do approximately two minutes of brisk walking, slow jogging, or any other large muscle activity at a low-intensity level. Since the muscles are warm from the main event, this is a good time to have your class perform several static stretches as well. This may help prevent stiffness or muscle spasms after the physical activity. In fact, this might be the best time to develop flexibility since the body temperature and blood circulation are at optimum levels to maximize muscle stretching.

Components of Health-Related Physical Fitness

For your students to experience the optimal benefits of physical activity, you must balance the health-related physical fitness components. Each component is equally important: Cardiorespiratory endurance strengthens the heart and lungs. Muscular strength and muscular endurance maintain body support, helping students perform daily tasks and participate in recreational games and activities. Flexibility helps the muscles and joints move freely. Finally, proper nutrition and daily physical activity help maintain healthy body composition.

Keeping in mind that you should emphasize process over product, let's take a more in-depth look at the components of health-related physical fitness so you can plan a balanced physical activity program within—not instead of—your physical education curriculum.

Cardiorespiratory Endurance

Cardiorespiratory endurance is the capacity of your heart, blood vessels, and lungs to deliver nutrients and oxygen to your tissues and remove waste products (e.g., carbon dioxide), thereby providing the energy necessary for endurance exercises. Jogging, biking, swimming, and skating all build cardiorespiratory endurance. Regardless of the type of physical activity your students use to enhance cardiorespiratory endurance, however, the main goal is always the same: You're trying to increase the amount of oxygen the heart pumps to the working muscles. Without enough oxygen, the body will not be able to work for an extended period of time. Fortunately, continuous physical activity has significant positive effects on the heart. As the body begins to exercise, the muscles utilize the oxygen at a much higher rate, making the heart pump more oxygenated blood to meet this increased demand (Prentice 1996). As the blood continues to flow during exercise, it helps increase circulation because veins, arteries, and blood vessels, which transport blood, and oxygen and nutrients are kept elastic, free from any obstructions, and efficiently working in concert with the rest of the body. You can help your students improve their cardiorespiratory endurance through four different techniques:

1. Continuous activity
2. Interval activity
3. Fartlek training
4. Circuit course

Continuous Activity

Continuous activity may include both aerobic and anaerobic exercise. *Aerobic* means, "in the presence of oxygen." Activities that are continuous, longer in duration, and sustained are aerobic activities. *Anaerobic* means "in the absence of oxygen." During anaerobic activities, the body's demand for oxygen exceeds its ability to supply it. Anaerobic movements are explosive and short in duration, such as the 100-yard dash, playing basketball, running to first base in softball, and playing soccer. Anaerobic activity, if kept at a continuous pace, is highly appropriate for children since they are more able to handle short segments of activity. Good choices for continuous

activity include any activity that continuously uses large muscle and whole body movements, such as jogging, walking, roller skating, rope jumping, biking, swimming, hiking, aerobic dancing, step aerobics, and active games.

Interval Activity

Interval activity includes physical movements that alternate the intensity and active recovery time. In other words, periods of rest or lower-intensity training alternate with periods of higher intensity. Because of the lower-intensity periods, interval activity may actually allow for a higher total of intense activity over a longer period of time than the continuous activity approach, although research is not conclusive about this. Vary intervals by varying the distance, intensity, number of repetitions, number of sets, and recovery time. (See chapter 11 for a sample interval routine.)

Fartlek Training

Fartlek is Swedish for "speed play." The fartlek training course technique is similar to interval activity, however, the terrain controls the intensity and speed, not the clock. Most fartlek courses are designed to include uphill and downhill running. Some courses also include jumping or stepping obstacles, such as logs, rocks, or stumps. It's also beneficial to challenge and develop different muscle groups through the fartlek workout. Incorporate fartlek training into your physical education classes to add variety, thereby increasing motivation. (See chapter 11 for an example of a fartlek course.)

Circuit Course

This technique combines continuous activity with flexibility, strength, and muscular endurance exercise stations as students jog from station to station. Choose station activities that use large muscle movements continuously, arranging stations at least 30 yards apart. Task cards are helpful to instruct students at each station. (See chapter 11.)

Muscular Strength and Muscular Endurance

Muscular strength is the capacity of a muscle or muscle group to exert maximum force against a resistance. Muscular endurance is the capacity of a muscle or muscle group to exert force over a period of time against a resistance that is less than the maximum you can move. Muscular strength and endurance are related—to a point. For example, increasing muscular strength will enhance muscle endurance, but exercising for muscle endurance will not always produce significant gains in muscle strength (Powers and Dodd 1996).

We can classify muscle contractions in two major categories: *dynamic*, or isotonic, contraction, which is the force exerted by a muscle group as a body part moves (e.g., most sport skills, weight lifting, push-ups, pull-ups, and curl-ups); and static, or isometric, contraction, the force exerted against an immovable object in which movement does not take place (e.g., pushing against a wall, or placing your palms together and pushing as hard as you can for 8 to 10 seconds). An injured or disabled person may use isometric exercises to rehabilitate a body part when an adequate range of motion is not possible. In addition, isometric resistance exercises require little space, no equipment, and are easy to do. Encourage the classroom teacher to have students perform isometric exercises at their desks in five-minute fitness breaks several times during the week.

The general benefits of muscular strength and muscular endurance include the following:

1. Daily tasks: You're able to do the daily tasks of life more easily, such as opening a bottle, putting out the garbage, or cleaning out the garage.

2. Posture: Your neck and back get the support they need from strong, flexible muscles.

3. Joint support: Stronger muscles reduce the stress on major joints, especially the knees, shoulders, and hips.

4. Protection of internal organs: Strong abdominal muscles help keep the digestive organs intact. Well-developed shoulder, chest, and back muscles may help with general cardiorespiratory efficiency.

5. Sports and recreational activities: When muscles are strong and can work longer, sports that require leg and arm strength and endurance for running, jumping, striking, or demonstrating sudden bursts of speed are enhanced (e.g., basketball, softball, soccer).

Two common ways to develop muscle strength and endurance are resistance and calisthenics types of exercises. Resistance exercises usually include performing movement with added weight, such as dumbbells or resistance bands, to vary intensity. Calisthenics are a form of resistance exercise for which your own body weight and gravity provide the resistance, such as in a push-up or a pull-up.

To increase muscle strength, apply the overload principle, progressively increasing resistance. To gain muscle endurance, increase the number of repetitions within each set as well as the number of sets. At a fitness station, you can safely ask level III children to perform two sets of 8, 10, or 12 repetitions of the arm curl using two- or three-pound dumbbells, depending on each student's needs and fitness level. A one- to two-minute rest period between sets is usually sufficient. If a child is unable to complete the 8 repetitions, they may use alternative weighted objects such as a book or an elastic band.

Flexibility

As you know, flexibility is the ability to move the joints in an unrestricted fashion through a full range of motion. Generally, young children have flexible muscles, ligaments, and tendons, but still should be encouraged to stretch on a daily basis. To maintain flexibility, students should be physically active in a broad range of movement experiences (e.g., soccer, softball, swimming, biking, jogging). It is also important to include specific flexibility exercises in your program throughout the school year to

• prevent muscle-related injuries,

• reduce muscle soreness,

• maintain good posture,

• reduce stress on the joints, and

• improve movement performance.

As you can see, flexibility exercises bring many health-related fitness benefits that are well worth the time and effort they take!

Keep in mind, however, that the degree of flexibility is specific to each joint. For example, a student who scored in the 90th percentile on the back-saver sit-and-reach test, demonstrating flexible hamstrings and hip flexors, may not be flexible in other body parts, such as the shoulders or quadriceps. So include a wide variety of flexibility exercises for various muscle groups in your physical education program.

The two most common techniques used to improve flexibility in children are static and ballistic stretching. As always, have children warm up their muscles with a few minutes of brisk activity before stretching.

Static Stretching

Static stretching stretches a specific muscle group slowly and steadily to a maximum position. Teach children to find their own maximums by stretching until they feel slight tightness, *not pain*, then holding for a total of 10 to 30 seconds.

Ballistic Stretching

Ballistic stretching incorporates bouncing, jerking movements to stretch the muscles. Unfortunately, this force may cause a stretch reflex in which the muscle actually tightens instead of relaxes as a result of being stretched beyond its normal length. The bouncing may also place undue stress on the joints or cause muscle injury. For these reasons, I don't recommend that you add ballistic stretching to your flexibility program with one exception: When the student performs the movements around the joint slowly and with control, ballistic exercises may be helpful as a warm-up before a sport activity. But clearly, the controlled nature of static stretching places less stress on the joints and muscles than ballistic stretching and is therefore safer.

Body Composition

Body composition is the ratio of body fat to lean body tissue (e.g., muscle, bones, and internal organs). Pay special attention to this health-related physical fitness component since increased levels of body fat are not only closely associated with obesity but also to other health problems, such as elevated cholesterol levels, high blood pressure, diabetes, and a sedentary lifestyle. Many of these medical problems appear in childhood. The earlier the child has your help addressing high percentages of body fat, the better!

Increasing the levels of physical activity is a critical factor in controlling body fat; however, a quality fitness education program should also include nutrition instruction to assist children in maintaining a healthy body weight. In 1992, the federal government established new recommendations for healthy eating in the form of the Food Guide Pyramid (figure 5.3).

The Pyramid is broken into five major categories, each with a recommendation for the amount of servings per day. The breads, cereals, rice, and pasta

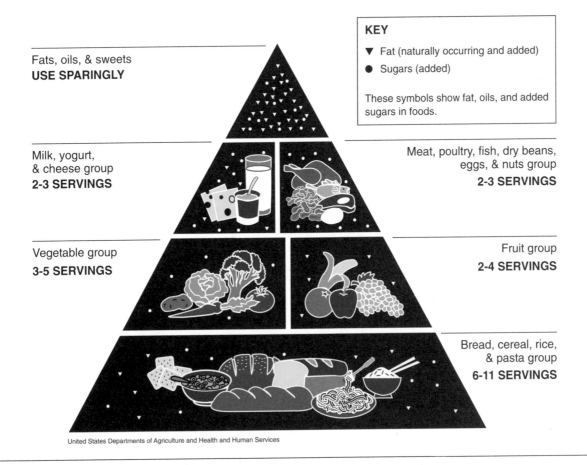

KEY

▼ Fat (naturally occurring and added)
● Sugars (added)

These symbols show fat, oils, and added sugars in foods.

Fats, oils, & sweets
USE SPARINGLY

Milk, yogurt,
& cheese group
2-3 SERVINGS

Meat, poultry, fish, dry beans,
eggs, & nuts group
2-3 SERVINGS

Vegetable group
3-5 SERVINGS

Fruit group
2-4 SERVINGS

Bread, cereal, rice,
& pasta group
6-11 SERVINGS

United States Departments of Agriculture and Health and Human Services

Figure 5.3 The Food Guide Pyramid.

group form the foundation of the Pyramid, and a healthy diet, with 6 to 11 servings daily. The vegetable (3 to 5 servings) and fruit (2 to 4 servings) groups share the next level. The milk, yogurt, and cheese group and the meat, poultry, fish, beans, eggs, and nuts group make up the next level, each with a recommendation of 2 to 3 servings. The fats, oils, and sweets group is at the top of the Pyramid. Foods from this group should be eaten sparingly as they are low in nutrients and high in calories.

Teach your students that the Food Guide Pyramid is a guide for the selection of a balanced diet high in carbohydrates, fruits, and vegetables, and lower in saturated fat and sugar and sodium. Use games and activities to teach and reinforce nutrition (see chapters 9, 10, and 12). Take this superb opportunity to collaborate with the classroom teacher to integrate the content of body composition and nutrition education with other subject areas (see chapter 10). A new product to help educate children is entitled "The Great Electronic Countdown Food Pyramid." It's a credit-card-size calculator that keeps track of daily food servings and counts down the number of portions that remain to be eaten in each food group. It sets the proper number of helpings based on the user's age, gender, weight, and level of activity (USA Nutritional Tracking, Inc. $22.95, 1-800-543-2144). This item may be shared with the classroom teachers and included in their budgets, thereby saving you the added expense and providing a way to collaborate with the classroom teacher.

Summary

Use the basic principles, guidelines, and components of health-related physical fitness as a foundation for planning a quality fitness education program. As you plan your specific program content, refer often to the SPORT-FITT acronym and the descriptions of its components as well as the guidelines for any activity session (warm-up, main event, and cool-down). Most importantly, however, remember that children need not adhere to a specific exercise prescription. In fact, a regimented approach to fitness will usually turn them off to physical activity. Simply encourage and facilitate physical activity 30 minutes to 60 minutes per day, most days of the week, while teaching students the value of an active lifestyle.

Fitness Education for Children With Physical Disabilities

CHAPTER 6

No one can make you feel inferior without your consent.

—Eleanor Roosevelt

Meeting the physical, mental, and social needs of each student is the most difficult challenge facing physical educators today. At the elementary school level, children's developmental levels vary widely in the areas of physical development, mental and social readiness, motor skill abilities, and fitness levels. This makes planning the typical physical education class lesson quite a challenge, often requiring instructional adjustments to ensure total participation.

Some children may not be able to meet the demands of traditional physical activity lessons because they have a developmental disability. In this chapter, we'll discuss how to plan activities for children with special needs. We'll cover specific disabilities and health limitations, including obesity, asthma, spinal cord impairments, and mental retardation. For more information, I highly recommend that you read *Adapted Physical Education and Sport* (second edition) (Winnick 1995) and *Adapted Physical Activity, Recreation and Sport* (fourth edition) (Sherrill 1996).

The Education for All Handicapped Children Act (Public Law 94-142), which Congress passed in 1975, requires that all disabled children of ages 5 to 21 receive an appropriate education in the least restrictive environment possible. "Least restrictive"

simply means that the child can participate successfully and safely in a setting as near to normal as possible. This law led to the educational practice of *mainstreaming*, which provides children with disabilities the opportunity to interact with and develop alongside nondisabled children in the same classes.

Individualized Education Plan

To comply with Public Law 94-142, each school district must locate, identify, and evaluate all students with disabilities. A team of specialists must work with the classroom teacher to develop an Individualized Education Plan (IEP) to carry out this mandate before placing the child. More recently, physical educators have been included in the IEP process to help develop, assess, and review each student's IEP. Formats vary from district to district; according to Winnick (1995), however, each IEP must contain these seven components:

1. **Present level of performance**—This section usually includes basic fitness and motor skill test results. The assessment may be a mixture of standardized and teacher-designed tests. Standardized tests should be included to

determine "special needs" and justify a stronger case for educational placement. See *Physical Best and Individuals With Disabilities* (Seaman 1995) for further information on assessment.

2. **Annual goals**—The annual goals are general statements that focus on the student's weaknesses as determined by the present level of performance (PLP) assessment. If, for example, the PLP reports that the student's level of flexibility is limited, it would be inappropriate to develop annual goals related to throwing skills.

3. **Short-term objectives (STO)**—The short-term objectives are specific statements that describe the intended outcome: for example, "Bobby will perform a total of three curl-ups, demonstrating good form and technique."

4. **Statement of services**—At this stage, the IEP team places the student in the least restrictive environment. It also recommends specialized instructional materials, equipment, and media at this point. Finally, it documents the need for special services, such as physical therapy, psychological services, and speech and hearing therapy.

5. **Schedule of services**—The IEP includes specific time frames for when related services will begin and end as well as a schedule for the special services with specified days, frequency, and time.

6. **Extent of mainstreaming**—The IEP team calculates the percentage of time the child with a disability will spend in regular classes. This section should state whether the IEP team recommends regular physical education classes.

7. **Criteria, procedures, and schedule for evaluation**—The IEP must specify how and when teachers will assess the student's progress. Monitoring should be ongoing, and the IEP team must review each child's IEP thoroughly annually.

Guidelines for Inclusion

For many years, opportunities for physical activity have not been accessible to children with disabilities. As a physical educator, you have a legal and moral responsibility to change this situation by providing the necessary health and fitness instruction to children with special needs. Adopt this simple philosophy of inclusion: All children have the right to good health through physical activity at school, at home, and in the community.

The following guidelines will help you develop physical activity programs that include students with disabilities.

Review Permanent or Cumulative Records

Check the student's school records carefully. Look for any medical problems or medication taken. Then study the student's IEP. If the IEP format does not include a fitness and skill component, meet with the IEP committee to establish an assessment standard.

Involve Parents

Parents will provide you with the history of their child's disability and helpful insights as to how to help their child. So establish lines of communication between school and home, informing the parents of your efforts in the area of health-related fitness development. If possible, schedule a conference with the parents at the beginning of the school year to discuss the IEP and how to help the student progress throughout the school year. (See also chapter 7.)

Employ Teamwork

Lobby to be on the IEP committee if you're not already. Discuss the student's progress with the classroom teacher, special education consultant, and special services professionals on a regular basis. Communication with others will help you plan and develop a quality experience for the student.

Put Safety First

Children with disabilities may need specific considerations to ensure their safety and well-being. Be certain that all students have specialized equipment as needed, such as helmets, gloves, knee pads, mats, and safety glasses. Make sure that your facilities allow for everyone to participate freely.

Modify Fitness Routines, Skills, and Games

In order to include everyone in your class activities, you may have to modify certain fitness routines, skills, and games. For example, enlarge a target or goal, make equipment lighter (e.g., plastic rackets, foam balls), reduce the distance the student must kick or throw a ball, or reduce the tempo of the game by allowing the student to walk instead of run. See Susan Kasser's *Inclusive Games* (1995) for specific ideas.

Modify Teaching Behaviors

Plan to include more visual and demonstration techniques to explain skills and give directions, especially when mentally retarded and hearing impaired students are enrolled in your classes. Physically "walk through" an activity or station rather than merely explaining the directions. Give step-by-step verbal cues that are direct and concise. Your special care in clearly communicating content will help all your students learn.

Be Sensitive

Provide the disabled student with plenty of positive reinforcement. Speak to the students about their friends, interests, hobbies, or favorite subjects in school. Children with disabilities will develop skills and increase physical activity levels when they feel a sense of belonging and warmth in your physical education classes.

Establish a Positive and Supportive Classroom Environment

Establish a class environment in which everyone helps and supports each other in the spirit of teamwork. Try not to pay special attention to or be overly cautious with the disabled child: This can be dehumanizing. Treat all students as equal members of your class. Concentrate on the physical needs, not the disability. Seek to plan activities the student can do; don't get hung up on what she can't do.

Use Class Tutors

Draw class tutors from many sources. Students within each class can tutor each other. These peer tutors can provide the disabled student with individual attention and one-on-one feedback. Big buddies are older students you have trained to work with younger students. Give special instructions as necessary to those students who will be working

with the disabled child. If the student needs more than a peer or a big buddy can provide, find the student an adult helper. The school district may hire a teaching assistant or you may be able to find a volunteer. Choose someone who possesses a caring, patient demeanor and make sure the assistant receives special training in special education. Can't find anyone suitable? Have parents help gather and program data, manage equipment, or supervise students, freeing you to focus on students with specific needs.

Obesity

Childhood obesity is one of the most serious health problems facing this nation. In fact, we'll look at obesity very closely since it is the most common disability in elementary schools. According to current statistics, over 20 percent of the children in this country can be classified as obese—and this estimate is on the rise! Children are classified as obese when they are 20 percent over the ideal body weight. It may not be necessary to assess an obese child with skinfold calipers or other body measurements. If a child looks obese, he is. Embarrassing tests and measurements may add more humiliation, creating a negative impression of physical education on the obese child.

Children who are obese may seem relatively healthy in their youth; however, they usually face serious medical complications later in life. For example, these children are at higher risk for coronary heart disease, respiratory impairments, diabetes, orthopedic problems, and certain types of cancer (Shear et al. 1988).

Serious psychological complications may develop through adolescence as well. Other children often taunt, tease, and humiliate the overweight child. This has a significant impact on a child's self-concept and feelings about the need for physical activity (Pangrazi and Dauer 1995).

Taking Action

Identifying obese students in your school is the easy part. But how can you help them? Follow these important steps as you begin to take action.

1. **Intervene early**. The earlier you begin intervening, the better. Once you have identified the obese students in your school, design a plan of

action. Intervening early can also help prevent serious psychological problems.

2. **Develop a team approach**. Organize a committee to help design a plan of action. This committee should consist of the school nurse, dietitian, psychologist, and you, the physical educator. Try to involve the family physician; it will give your committee credibility as well as an additional clinical perspective.

3. **Enlist the parents' support**. Ask the committee to meet with the parents of each student. This meeting is critical for the proper implementation of your program. State your concerns about the student's emotional and physical health. Ask the parents if they are willing to help; if they are, you're on your way! Provide the parents with a handout describing your program goals as well as a list emphasizing their responsibilities. Establish follow-up conferences at least every two to three months. If the parents are unable to come to the meetings, set up phone conferences and send home progress reports and literature through the mail. Organize a family health promotion night with the teachers and service professionals in the school cafeteria specifically for this group. Children may participate with their parents to learn how to eat and exercise together as a family. If the parents will not work with you, continue to work with the student at school and send literature home. Parents might need time to realize the severity of the problem.

4. **Design a plan**. The plan should address three major areas of intervention: eating behavior, physical activity patterns, and behavioral strategies. Each professional should be responsible for developing specific strategies and activities in his or her area of expertise.

5. **Develop a portfolio**. The portfolio will help organize the student's progress and make your efforts more credible. The portfolio may include a profile, contracts, log sheets to record eating and activity patterns, a plan with short- and long-term goals, schedules, and specific activities (see appendix A). Other committee members may add pertinent documents and instructional materials. This portfolio is the property of the student but keep it in the classroom unless the student uses it for home-based assignments.

6. **Schedule additional time**. You will need additional time to interact with the student to help increase physical activity levels. Request to meet with the individual student or arrange to meet with small groups of three or four students during the school week. Find time for a special physical activity class during recess, free periods, your planning time, early bird sessions before school, after-school activities, or during regular homeroom class time. Communicate closely with the principal and classroom teachers to help arrange special time for the obese student.

7. **Provide feedback**. Once the student has started working with the committee, be sure to provide feedback to maintain motivation and progress. Use charts and graphs to indicate improvement in such areas as weight, activity patterns, and eating habits. Give the student buttons, stickers, caps, or yogurt certificates as incentives for completing certain aspects of the program. As the school year continues, begin to phase out the incentives and accentuate the intrinsic value of weight loss, such as health, self-confidence, added energy, and greater success in games and sports.

Guidelines for Activity

The following techniques will help you design useful activities for obese students. Large muscle activities are the most beneficial because they expend the most calories. Activities such as walking, jogging, hiking, swimming, jumping rope, and tag games are just a few examples. Start with low-intensity activities, however, such as walking at a moderate, individually set pace. Do not demand or expect a certain level of performance during the initial stages. Instead, for example, design a mini-track around your outdoor facility and ask the students to walk and jog around the track until they feel uncomfortable. Have them record the number of laps they do and calculate any improvement.

Find out what types of physical activity they enjoy. Once you know their likes and dislikes, you'll be able to plan more exciting, interesting lessons. For example, try to individualize aerobic dancing by slowing the beats per minute to sustain moderate activity levels. Students seem to enjoy this activity as long as it is not too demanding, the music is up-to-date, and the activity environment is positive. When it comes to obese students, it's especially important to emphasize variety and fun in physical education. Introduce activities such as roller skating, games of low organization, dance and rhythms, lead-up sports, and recreational activities such as nature hikes to demonstrate a variety of ways to stay active. Never use performance expectations and competition to motivate obese (or any other) students.

Self-monitoring is a good way to reinforce increases in student activity levels. Have the students keep track of their physical activity times every day for a few weeks in their portfolios. Suggest a total of 20 to 30 minutes of continuous, large muscle activity, which students may break into different segments (e.g., three 7- to 10-minute segments completed any time during the day).

Include resistance exercises for strength and muscular endurance, using a low weight and high repetition format. Rubberized resistance equipment and light dumbbells (two to three pounds) are ideal. Students should perform five different exercises, one set of 10 repetitions each, creating a total body workout two or three times per week. After three weeks, gradually increase to two sets of 10 repetitions each. (See chapter 11 for specific exercises.)

Too many physical educators neglect to include flexibility exercises in obese students' physical activity programs because they are concerned about increasing large muscle types of exercise. But include flexibility exercises since the range of motion is usually restricted by excess fat around the joints. Encourage students to perform a series of stretching exercises each day for at least 7 to 10 minutes. (See also chapter 11.)

Assess each student's progress every four to six weeks. Arrange brief private meetings with the student and occasionally the parents to review the portfolio. Reinforce your interest in successes, talk about home-based activities, and encourage the student to evaluate and monitor his own progress.

Asthma

Over six million children have some form of asthma in the United States, and this figure is rising (U.S. Department of Health and Human Services 1989). Asthma constricts the airways, reducing the flow of air into and out of the lungs, causing panting, wheezing, or coughing.

Many years ago, educators did not encourage children suffering from asthma to exercise or engage in normal physical education activities. Research over the last 15 years has proven this approach wrong. Today, children with asthma who exercise on a regular basis can increase the duration of physical activity they can tolerate and reduce the severity of asthma attacks (Rimmer 1994).

Yet, you should be aware of a condition known as exercise-induced asthma (EIA). In this condition, exercise of high intensity or duration may make the bronchial tubes contract, causing an attack. If the EIA student follows certain guidelines, however, she may participate in physical activity.

Taking Action

To begin helping the student with asthma, consult with the school nurse and carefully review the student's medical records. Note special medications the student is currently taking and any physical activity limitations. Be aware of the student who uses an aerosol medication. He should use his medication 30 to 60 minutes before exercising and keep it with him throughout the physical education class.

Guidelines for Activity

It is extremely important to be certain the EIA student has warmed up before exercise. Sudden, high-intensity activity will place the student at high risk for an attack. Allow the EIA student more time to warm up than the rest of the class—at least 10 to 15 minutes of low-intensity activity, such as walking, calisthenics, moderate-intensity large muscle movements, followed by two to three minutes of stretching before beginning vigorous physical activity. The intensity of the activity should progress gradually to a level of no more than 50 percent of the target heart rate, progressing to 60 to 70 percent only when the student is physically ready. You may want the student to use a heart rate monitor to help determine a level suitable for physical activity.

The technique of interval activity we discussed in chapter 5 is ideal for the asthmatic student since the intensity level varies throughout the exercise session. Break the main event or bout into 5-minute intervals with 3- to 5-minute rest periods between sets. In more serious cases, decrease the amount of time in activity and increase the amount of rest. It is also important to end with a 10-minute cool-down period using exercises similar to those performed in the warm-up stage. This will enable the EIA student to gradually and comfortably bring the heart rate back to a normal range, preventing any sudden changes that could cause undue stress on the body. Experts recommend that these students engage in the typical length of a physical education class and that you should encourage them to be physically active for 30 minutes most days of the week—on the low end of normal frequency, intensity, and duration.

Certain types of strength-related activities can benefit the asthmatic child. For example, development of the abdominals, chest, back, and shoulder muscles may help the student breathe more efficiently. Other activities that should not give the asthmatic child major difficulties include activity circuits or stations, tumbling and gymnastics, resistance exercising, and softball and volleyball games.

Finally, as an extra precaution, you should establish an emergency procedure for dealing with an attack. You may ask the family to provide you with an extra inhaler, along with the instructions that come with it. Be prepared to call for an ambulance if the inhaler doesn't provide immediate relief.

Despite the potential problems, encourage asthmatic children to participate in a well-balanced physical education program. As they learn to pace themselves, they will become aware of the many benefits of enjoying physical activity. Your professional guidance and support is critical to developing a positive attitude about their physical capabilities.

Spinal Cord Impairments

Spinal cord impairments (SCI) are a result of a traumatic injury to or disease of the vertebrae or the nerves of the spinal column (Kelly 1995). For example, children suffering from serious injuries caused by car accidents, diving into shallow water, or falls may experience permanent nerve damage resulting in a form of paralysis. Diseases such as spina bifida may also cause similar paralysis. In this condition, one or more vertebrae fail to completely fuse during fetal development. The vertebrae become very unstable and cause severe nerve and tissue damage resulting in a loss of movement capabilities (Rimmer 1994). Whether due to a birth defect or an injury, the individual has limited upper body movement and usually uses a wheelchair.

Taking Action

The following guidelines will help you design appropriate physical activity programs for these children. Keep in mind that you should tailor your exercise recommendations to the individual's level of fitness, medical history, physical ability, and personality. You should also take into account certain safety precautions and equipment limitations.

Guidelines for Activity

First, children with spinal cord impairments may not have control of their bladders. If they do not have a catheter, you may suggest to the classroom teacher that the student use the restroom before each physical education class. To aid in kidney function and temperature regulation during exercise, the SCI student must have intermittent water breaks. As a precaution, the student should carry a sport bottle of chilled water on the wheelchair.

Normally, students with spinal cord impairments lack muscular endurance. So in the beginning stages of exercise, reduce the number of repetitions in resistance exercises as well as the number of arm movements in an aerobic dance routine in order to ensure success and continued physical activity. Through careful observation, assess what muscles the student can use, the strength and endurance of those muscles, and how they can be used in a physical education class. Often times, the SCI student develops muscle imbalances from the overuse of the same muscles needed to manipulate the wheelchair. Provide such a student with a number of flexibility exercises for the shoulder, back, and hip flexors. (*Caution:* Do not encourage extensive flexion of the back because overstretched, nonfunctional muscles may not keep the back well-supported, resulting in additional physical problems.)

Be especially aware of restrictions placed on a student who has a spinal rod or spinal fusion. Flexion and rotation may have an adverse effect on such a student's physical condition, creating a more dangerous situation during physical activity. It helps to closely monitor trunk balance and control during movement. If the student in the wheelchair needs additional support because of the physical activity, secure a two- to three-inch padded belt across the waist to keep the child stable in the wheelchair.

Students with SCI should follow the same basic principles of exercising and stages of physical activity (warm-up, main event, cool-down) as children without disabilities (see chapter 5). Some children with disabilities, however, must maintain a moderate overload to keep exercise safe and to prevent overexertion from causing a decline in normal functioning (Miller 1995). The following exercises may be appropriate for students with spinal cord impairments.

Flexibility Exercises

Flexibility is just as critical to a total physical activity program for the SCI student as anyone else. Unfortunately, this component of fitness is often overlooked. But for students who use wheelchairs, stretching may help to maintain muscle balance and certain functional abilities.

LATERAL TORSO STRETCHER

Slowly reach upward with one arm, fingers extended. Keep the opposite arm bent at the elbow. Bend the torso slightly to the side, reaching slightly across with the raised arm (see figure 6.1).

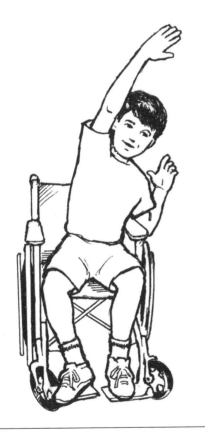

Figure 6.1   Lateral torso stretcher.

BACK STRETCHER

Keep the chin tucked to the upper chest and the back flat and stable. Bend forward from the hips. Support the upper body with the hands gripping the ankles (figure 6.2). Take care to ensure the student maintains balance to avoid a fall. (*Caution:* Postural changes may affect blood pressure and cause lightheadedness.)

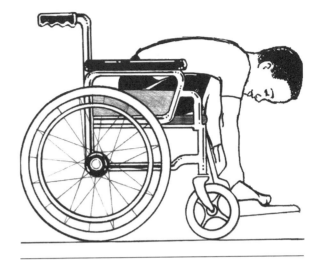

Figure 6.2   Back stretcher.

FOREARM AND SHOULDER STRETCHER

Clasp the hands in front of the body about shoulder height with the palms facing away. Extend the arms forward and slightly upward (figure 6.3).

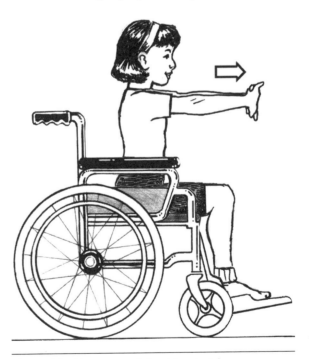

Figure 6.3   Forearm and shoulder stretcher.

SHOULDER AND CHEST STRETCHER

Reach back and extend both arms behind the mid-back area, palms facing upward. Gently lift the arms, stretching the shoulders and the chest (figure 6.4).

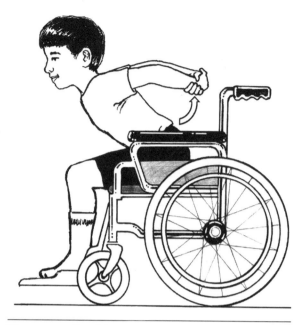

Figure 6.4   Shoulder and chest stretcher.

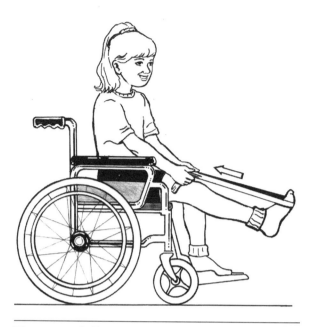

Figure 6.6   Calf stretcher.

HAMSTRING STRETCHER

Sit toward the edge of the chair, placing one leg straight out with toes up. Keep the knee slightly bent. Lean forward slightly, keeping the back stable (figure 6.5).

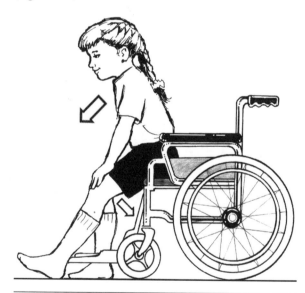

Figure 6.5   Hamstring stretcher.

CALF STRETCHER

Place a towel or strap around the ball of one foot and extend the leg, pulling the strap toward the chest (figure 6.6).

Strength and Muscular Endurance

The following set of exercises develops the major muscle groups of the body. I have not listed specific resistance levels, sets, or repetitions, however, because these depend on individual abilities. Remember, students should perform the exercise slowly and with control, and should never lock or hyperextend a joint. Keep the number of repetitions even on both sides of the body and remind students to maintain proper sitting alignment. The illustrations feature the rubberized resistance bands, the Toner from the Quik-Fit for Kids program (appendix B). You may substitute other resistance equipment.

BOW AND ARROW STRETCHER FOR SHOULDERS

Grasp the toner with one arm straight out to the side as if holding a bow. Draw the toner across the chest to the opposite shoulder (see figure 6.7). Hold for three seconds. Change sides and repeat.

FRONT BUTTERFLY FOR CHEST AND BACK

Grasp toner with both hands in front of the body with palms facing inward and elbows slightly bent. Pull the toner out to each side (figure 6.8). Hold for three seconds and return slowly.

Figure 6.7 Sequence for bow and arrow stretcher for shoulders.

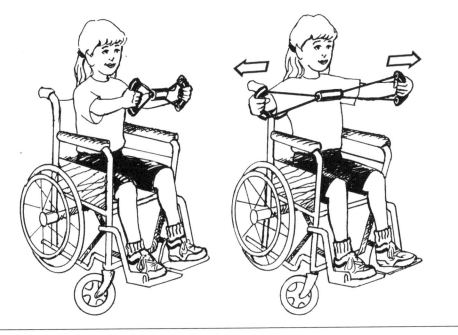

Figure 6.8 Sequence for front butterfly for chest and back.

OVERHEAD BUTTERFLY FOR BACK AND BACK OF ARMS

Grasp the handles overhead with palms facing outward. Extend the arms down to the side, making the toner go behind the back (figure 6.9). Hold for three seconds. Return slowly to the starting position.

CHEST PRESS FOR CHEST AND BACK OF ARMS

Place the toner directly behind the back with the center pad just below the shoulder blades. Grasp the handles with the palms facing inward. Extend both arms straight out, keeping elbows slightly bent (figure 6.10). Return slowly to starting position.

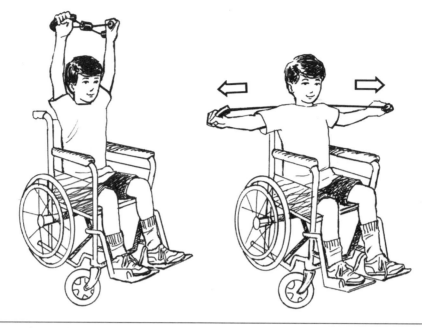

Figure 6.9   Sequence for overhead butterfly for back and back of arms.

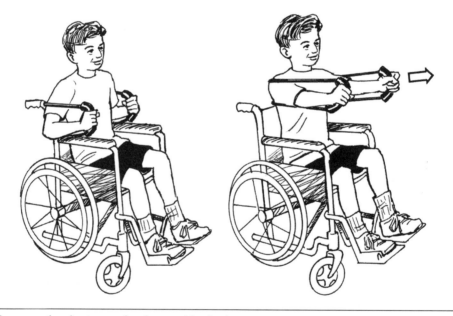

Figure 6.10   Sequence for chest press for chest and back of arms.

Cardiorespiratory Activities

Physical disabilities often limit large muscle movements in the lower body, making it difficult to develop cardiorespiratory endurance. The following activities utilize smaller movements to gain the benefits of cardiorespiratory endurance: wheelchair aerobic dance; wheelchair basketball; upper body ergometry, which is arm pedaling as illustrated in figure 6.11; and wheelchair ergometry, which is moving the wheelchair on stationary wheels.

Mental Retardation

According to the American Association on Mental Retardation, mental retardation refers to general intellectual functioning manifested during childhood that is significantly below average along with deficits in adaptive social behavior (Grossman 1983). Experts use several approaches to classify mental retardation (MR). But over the last 20 years, it has been judged primarily by intelligence quotient (IQ).

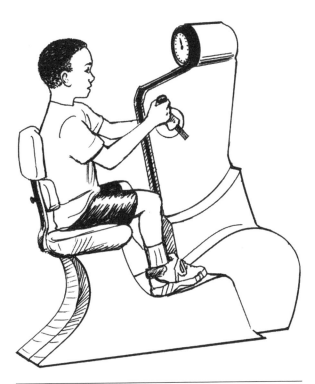

Figure 6.11 Upper body ergometry.

In schools, children categorized as mildly retarded or educable, with IQ scores between 50 to 75, are usually mainstreamed and scheduled for normal physical education classes. In terms of motor performance and physical fitness, mildly retarded children usually are 3.5 to 4 years behind their peers. Many children with mental retardation also have obesity, poor posture, gross motor coordination problems, and other physical disabilities.

Taking Action

The following guidelines will help you plan developmentally appropriate activities for children with mental retardation. These children might find exercise quite rewarding because they may exhibit a certain degree of success and accomplishment.

Guidelines for Activity

When teaching children with mental retardation, make sure they are aware of your verbal instructions and feedback cues. For example, most mentally retarded children will not understand such basic directions as "Pace yourself during the one-mile run" or "Do as many push-ups as you can."

Give slowly spoken, concise instructions. Repeat your directions if necessary.

Demonstrating instead of explaining a skill or concept may facilitate the child's understanding of the activity. Help the student walk through the game, skill drill, or fitness activity to get a feel for the movements before actually participating in the activity.

Give children with mental retardation praise and positive reinforcement at every reasonable opportunity for effort and participation as well as for accomplishments. Reward students with stickers, tokens, or similar incentives when they have successfully completed a task or a goal of their IEP. Use extrinsic rewards more liberally throughout the school year with these children to keep them on-task and motivated.

It is especially important for children with mental retardation to have consistent class procedures in a controlled learning environment. A certain amount of repetition may develop a sense of security and confidence. The following are a few examples of set procedures you may wish to try to help children with learning disabilities:

- Have the student walk on a line to enter the gym to take his place for the beginning of class.
- Always use the same attendance and warm-up procedures.
- Use the whistle for only one command, "*Stop, look,* and *listen.*"
- Always hold the closure segment of the lesson in the same place.
- Have children hold hands to form partners, small groups, or large circles.
- Use hula hoops for personal space or to indicate a set spot on the field or court.

Finally, establish small weekly goals in the area of health-related fitness. Monitor the progress each student makes, reinforcing it to help motivate participation in physical activity. Whenever you see a student improve, reward the positive behavior and design a plan to continue moving forward. Here's an example: week one, 10 minutes of physical activity, five times; week two, 15 minutes of physical activity, five times; weeks three and four, 30 minutes of physical activity, five times per week. If students have lower skill and fitness levels, give them short bouts of activity with longer rest periods. The rest periods are a great opportunity to provide immediate feedback.

In order to monitor progress, collaborate with the special education team to develop appropriate lesson plans and assure that students have physical education four or five days each week. For further information, see *Physical Activity for Individuals With Mental Retardation* (Eichstaedt and Lavay 1992).

Community-Based Opportunities

Mildly retarded children should have all the opportunities that other children have. Camps, playgrounds, YMCA and YWCA, CYO leagues, Jewish community centers, health spas, and other programs should have trained personnel able to serve the special needs of these youngsters.

For many years the Special Olympics program, sponsored by the Kennedy Foundation, has been a tremendous success story in this country. Each year, more than one million people, eight-year-olds to adults with IQs of less than 75, participate in this program. The Special Olympics, Inc., sponsors 14 events, including swimming, bowling, skiing, skating, hockey, and wheelchair events. Recently, the Special Olympics developed sport and fitness programs that occur throughout the year. Contact your local Special Olympics chapter for more information.

Summary

Increasing physical activity levels and enhancing the healthy lifestyles of all children remains a major goal of our nation's schools regardless of race, color, gender, or ability. Studies have indicated that children with disabilities are at higher risk for disease since they have lower levels of health-related physical fitness and are more likely to be obese. Therefore, give specific attention to children with disabilities by designing a physical activity plan to meet the individual needs of each student.

Use the specific guidelines, safety precautions, and activity recommendations I have listed for students with obesity, asthma, mental retardation, and spinal cord impairments to help you personalize and adapt your physical education program for students with special needs. Remember to always let this simple philosophy guide you in the instructional and moral decisions you make as a teacher throughout your career: All children have the right to good health through physical activity and should be afforded opportunities to be physically active at school, at home, and throughout the community.

Getting Parents and Your Community Involved

CHAPTER 7

> It takes a village to raise a child.
>
> —African proverb

For many years studies have shown that parent involvement is critical to success in school. Simply stated, when parents are involved in their child's education, the child has a greater chance of success, mentally, physically, and socially. Given the limited time you have with your students, it seems logical that school, parents, and community should work together to extend the time spent on physical activity and health to accomplish your comprehensive fitness education goals (Virgilio 1996).

The family has a powerful influence on a child's health and activity habits; however, few physical educators actually develop a specific plan to include parents and the community in their physical education programs. In this chapter, I'll provide you with practical information that you can begin using today, including communication techniques, conducting effective parent-teacher conferences, parent education, parent volunteers, home-based activities, and community involvement. The ready-to-use instructional materials such as letters to parents, a parent survey, a family fitness contract, and family activities will get you started right away!

Establishing a Plan of Action

First, it is important to recognize that parents may have negative attitudes toward physical education and may not value the benefits of fitness activity. Be sensitive to the following concerns as you plan to include parents in your program:

- Parents may have had negative experiences in physical education when they were in school.
- Parents may feel that physical education is a "frill" and should be eliminated from the school budget.
- Some parents may feel that physical activity is not really necessary for children, thinking, "They play enough at home."
- Parents may see physical education as an opportunity for athletic children to perform.
- Parents may recognize that exercise is important but do not have the time to get involved.

But don't be discouraged—move ahead with your plans! Your job is to initiate a plan to help parents recognize the importance of their involvement. Regardless of the parents' attitudes or lack of support, you must lead parents to more positive attitudes about physical activity. To get started, develop and follow a specific plan of action:

1. **Develop a written policy.** Written statements are more credible. Furthermore, they show the community that you are serious about enlisting their help. Finally, written policies allow school administrators to document your efforts, which may be important for yearly teacher reviews and tenure evaluations.

2. **Gain administrative support.** Support from the school principal is essential. Ask him or her to allocate a small budget for garnering parent and community support that will pay for guest speakers, meeting space, other facilities, audiovisual equipment, duplication costs, and mailing expenses. Brainstorm with the principal about other ideas that may help you find support.

Now that you have established a plan of action and have gained administrative support, you are ready to open the lines of communication to the community.

Communication

Strong lines of communication are necessary if parents are going to feel comfortable working with the school, sharing their ideas, and contributing to their children's education. First, write a letter to the parents introducing and explaining your new fitness education program and how it will fit in with your physical education program (see figure 7.1). Explain why it is important for children to develop healthy lifestyle habits at an early age. Attach a parent survey to the letter (one survey per parent or guardian). The survey will help you gain some perspective of the parents' exercise attitudes and habits. It will also tell you if they're willing to volunteer (see figure 7.2).

But don't stop with one letter. Keep the lines of communication open throughout the school year: Publish a newsletter three or four times a year and hold parent-teacher conferences.

Newsletters

Newsletters are an easy and efficient way to communicate with parents. Develop an eye-catching

format on your computer and choose an interesting title (see figure 7.3). Choose a different theme for each newsletter. Here is a list of headlines I have used successfully:

- Fitness Is Fun
- Let's Get Heart Smart
- Jump Rope for Heart
- Heart Healthy Month
- Family Fitness Fun
- Food and Fitness
- Active Summer Fun
- Winter Workouts
- Fit for a Lifetime
- Community Connections

What should you write about? Include fitness facts, which may dispel some common myths about exercise. For example, many parents may still believe that jogging one to two miles is too strenuous for their 12-year-old child. Include safety tips, such as the proper use of fluids during exercise. Add home-based family activities, such as the "Evening's End," for which the entire family meets in the family room to exercise for 15 minutes before everyone goes their separate ways. You could also cover a major health topic each month in a three- or four-paragraph article, such as, "Shake the Salt Habit" or "Low-Fat, No-Fat, Lite—What Does It All Mean?" Finally, include dates to remember such as an upcoming spring health fair or a fun run as well as reminders to parents about physical education days, sneakers, and medical notes, just to name a few.

Parent-Teacher Conferences

The general goal of a parent-teacher conference is to develop a partnership between home and school to benefit the child. A well-planned conference is an excellent chance for you to personally share your concern for the student while developing a positive relationship with the parents.

Setting Priorities

Elementary physical educators may serve up to 600 students during the school year. It may be difficult and time consuming to schedule a conference with even half of the parents at your school.

Save time by using less formal methods of conferring with parents. Use the phone or e-mail to have

(Date)

Dear Parents,

Heart disease remains the number-one killer and crippler of adults in the United States. On July 1, 1992 the American Heart Association announced that physical inactivity creates a major risk factor for heart disease along with high blood pressure, elevated blood cholesterol, and smoking. The good news is that premature heart disease is avoidable. We can all change our lifestyles and prevent this terrible disease from destroying our happy and productive lives.

Studies show that children develop healthy habits early in life. Generally, children who are inactive in elementary school will be inactive adults; children who are overweight will tend to be overweight adults; and children who grow up on a diet high in fat and sugar will continue eating unhealthily as adults. The elementary school is a great place to start teaching positive health habits!

This year I will be emphasizing health and fitness education within the physical education program through a program called _____, which I have specially designed for the children at _____ School. In every grade, children will be learning about the principles of exercise and nutrition and why plenty of physical activity and good nutrition are important to their health throughout their lives. Children will develop and maintain their own personalized fitness education portfolios in fourth through sixth grades, and all will participate in physically active, fun activities. The basic program of skills and sports taught over the last few years in physical education will remain; however, I will make fitness education a part of every unit throughout the school year. I have developed a team of professionals and parents to help accomplish this goal. Classroom teachers, school administrators, the school nurse, the school psychologist, school lunch personnel, and parent volunteers will be working together to ensure the present and future health of your child.

You are important to the success of this effort! Throughout the school year, your child and I will be asking for your help and support. Please take a few minutes from your busy schedule to invest in your child's health. If you wish to join the parent volunteer program or request any additional information about this new, exciting approach to physical education, do not hesitate to call me (phone number).

Let's get the ball rolling! Please fill out the enclosed survey and mail it back in the self-addressed, stamped envelope.

Sincerely,

(Name)

Physical Education Specialist

Figure 7.1 Letter to parents.

(Name of school)

Parent Physical Activity Survey

Instructions

Each parent or guardian should fill out the survey individually. Read each statement and circle the response that best describes your current health and physical activity habit or attitude. Be honest and fair—all individual surveys will be kept confidential. For the purpose of this survey, physical activity is any large muscle movement sustained for at least ten minutes, such as raking leaves, washing the car, jogging, playing tennis, walking, lifting weights, and aerobics (a total of 30 minutes per day).

Yes   No   Sometimes   1. I am physically active at least three days per week.

Yes   No   Sometimes   2. I am physically active with my child(ren) at least three days per week.

Yes   No   Sometimes   3. I encourage my family to be active rather than inactive.

Yes   No   Sometimes   4. On the average, I watch more than three hours of TV per day.

Yes   No   Sometimes   5. My child(ren) are physically active at least three days per week outside of school.

Yes   No   Sometimes   6. Teaching children about health and fitness in the school curriculum is very important.

Yes   No   Sometimes   7. Physical education is a positive time for my child(ren).

Yes   No   Sometimes   8. My child(ren) have too many outside interests that prevent them from active play after school.

9.   Parent Expertise

I have a strong background or expertise in the following activities (please check):

_____	Aerobic dance	_____	Jogging or walking
_____	Step aerobics	_____	Cycling
_____	Weight lifting	_____	Stretching
_____	Dance	_____	Swimming
_____	Team sport (specify)	_____	Hiking or jogging
_____	Skiing	_____	Individual sport (specify)
_____	Rollerblading	_____	Other (specify)

Figure 7.2   Parent physical activity survey.

10. I would be willing to share this background with the children of _____ School through the physical education program.

_____ Yes   _____ No   _____ Yes, if my schedule permits

11. I would be interested in attending parent health and fitness seminars sponsored by the school.   _____ Yes   _____ No

12. I would be interested in joining a parent-teacher advisory committee for physical education.   _____ Yes   _____ No

13. Comments, questions, or suggestions:

Circle your choices:

I could attend meetings or participate in school activities on

Monday   Tuesday   Wednesday   Thursday   Friday   Saturday   Sunday

I would like to participate:

Early bird (7:00-8:30 A.M.)   Morning   Afternoon   Evening

Parent's name _____

Address _____

Phone _____

Child(ren)'s name(s) _____

_____

_____

*** Please return in the enclosed self-addressed, stamped envelope. ***

Thank you for your cooperation,

_____

Physical Education Specialist

Figure 7.2   *(continued)*

FITNESS FACTS

Vol. 1, No. 2   May 1996

High Blood Pressure

What is high blood pressure?

Blood pressure is the force of the blood against the walls of the arteries as the heart pumps blood to all parts of the body. Normally, the blood flows easily through these vessels.

In some people, the arteries become narrow or closed off, making it difficult for blood to pass through. The heart must pump harder and the arteries must carry blood that is moving under greater pressure. Sometimes the heart starts working overtime, pushing too much blood through with each beat. This higher blood pressure adds to the workload of the heart and the arteries.

If the blood pressure remains higher than normal for a long time, the arteries and the heart may not function as well as they should and other body organs may be affected.

Who gets high blood pressure?

No one really knows for sure what causes high blood pressure, but regular blood pressure checks are critical if you

- are overweight;
- are black (African American people are twice as likely as Caucasians to have high blood pressure and are about four times as likely to die from it);
- have a parent, brother, sister, or child with high blood pressure;
- eat too much salt;
- are on birth control pills;
- are over 30 years of age (as people get older, their blood vessels become less elastic); or
- drink too much alcohol.

What are the symptoms?

Approximately half of those with high blood pressure are not aware of it, because they feel no sure symptoms. That's why it is often referred to as "The Silent Killer."

People with high blood pressure often associate sweaty hands, tense stomach, fast pulse, flushing, dizziness, fatigue, and tension with high blood pressure. But these symptoms are connected with other conditions as well. The only sure way to find out if you have high blood pressure is to have it checked regularly.

What can you do?

If you are at a higher risk than the average person for developing high blood pressure, you should do each of the following:

▶ **Get your blood pressure checked regularly,** especially if you are pregnant. High blood pressure can cause serious problems for both mother and baby.

▶ **Get rid of excess fat.** Ask your doctor for a sensible, balanced diet and begin to develop new eating habits. Diet may be the most important change you make. Losing weight and reducing your intake of high-fat foods and salty snacks usually help control high blood pressure—sometimes without medication.

Sugar Facts Quiz

1. Honey is better for you than sugar.
   True   False

2. Sugar is a carbohydrate.
   True   False

3. Sugar is a source of quick energy.
   True   False

4. How many teaspoons of sugar are in a 12-ounce cola drink?
   2   8   14

5. Which of these ingredients mean "sugar?"
   Dextrose   Sucrose   Corn syrup

6. Which of these contain added sugar?
   Ketchup   Orange juice   French dressing

Figure 7.3   Newsletter.
Adapted from *Heart Smart Gazette*.

▶ **Cut down on salt.** Salt contains sodium, which holds water and swells your body's tissues. Avoid foods high in salt, such as processed foods, condiments, smoked or cured meats, licorice, and baking soda. Choose low-salt foods, such as fresh and dried fruits, fresh vegetables, poultry, fish, lean meat, rice, and noodles.

▶ **If you smoke, decide to cut down or quit entirely.** Smoking not only increases your risk for respiratory damage, but also injures blood vessel walls and speeds hardening of the arteries. Heavy smoking increases the workload of the heart, increases pulse rate, and raises blood pressure. If you have high blood pressure, smoking more than doubles your risk of heart disease.

▶ **Exercise regularly.** Regular exercise chosen for cardiovascular conditioning, such as walking, bicycling, and swimming, can make your heart stronger, help relieve tension, and support your weight reduction efforts.

▶ **Reduce tension through activities such as reading and walking.** These can help temporarily lower your blood pressure, but don't depend on relaxation techniques to lower your blood pressure permanently.

▶ **Limit alcohol consumption.** Some research links heavy use of alcohol with elevations in blood pressure.

▶ If you have high blood pressure, **check with your doctor before taking birth control pills.** If you do take them, you should have your blood pressure checked regularly.

If lifestyle changes alone don't lower your blood pressure, your doctor may prescribe medication to help rid your body of excess water and sodium or to widen your blood vessels. Give the medication a chance to do what it is expected to do. If you stop taking it or if you take it now and then, it will not control your blood pressure.

Treatment only works when you are faithful in using it. Even if you feel fine, you usually have to stay with the treatment the rest of your life. In return, your life will probably be a much longer and healthier one.

ANSWERS

1. False.
Honey contains fructose, a sweeter sugar digested differently than table sugar. These differences, however, have little actual effect since fructose, just like table sugar, ends up as glucose—the food substance your body needs for energy. Unrefined sugars like honey, raw sugar, and turbinado ("washed" raw sugar) have no special benefits. Their mineral content is so low, you would have to consume all your day's calories in sugars to get a significant amount. These sugars provide only sweetness and calories, just like refined (table) sugar.

2. True.
Sugars are called simple carbohydrates, and starches are called complex carbohydrates. Compared to starches, sugars have a simpler chemical structure. Foods high in sugars and starches are our basic sources of carbohydrates.

3. True. . . .but . . .
Using sugar as a quick pickup—like eating a candy bar—will backfire. Your body uses the sugar very rapidly. You'll get a quick pickup and then a quick letdown. You can often end up feeling hungrier as well.

4. 8 teaspoons.
Remember that most of the sugar in our diets is from the sugar in processed foods like soft drinks or baked goods, rather than from naturally sweet foods like fruit.

5. All three.
Besides dextrose, sucrose, and corn syrup, common label terms include sugar, invert sugar, honey, molasses, sucrose, fructose, lactose, maltose, and galactose.

6. Ketchup, French dressing.
Look for "sugar" (and its many other names) on the ingredient label. Before you add table sugar to foods, remember that many foods like fruits, vegetables, dairy products, and grains already contain sugar naturally.

Figure 7.3 *(continued)*

brief but meaningful conferences with parents—more convenient for both you and the parents. Or have brief conversations with parents about their child's progress when you see them at school, after PTA meetings, or at an athletic event. Ensure, however, that you include positive comments and maintain the family's privacy. You may be surprised by what good public relations informal conferences are for your program.

Initially try to reach parents of students who are "high risk," for example, those who have low fitness scores, lead inactive lifestyles, are obese, have elevated cholesterol levels, have a family history of heart disease, or have disabilities. Develop a special program for these students, schedule additional class time, and arrange family health promotion nights to get parents motivated and involved in improving their children's health status. In this way, you can reach several families at the same time, thereby streamlining your efforts.

Sometimes, however, a situation calls for a more formal, yet nonthreatening, traditional conference. If, like most of us, your time is limited, concentrate on the parents of primary students (kindergarten through third grade). These parents are usually highly motivated and their enthusiasm may permeate the school. Perhaps most importantly, primary graders and their parents are usually more open to considering changes in exercise, nutrition, and lifestyle habits.

Before the Conference

Send home a "Fitness Flash" a few weeks before conference time to give parents some advanced idea of how their child is doing in physical education (see figure 7.4). The Fitness Flash is simply a progress report of the health-related physical fitness scores with comments attached. Place an asterisk next to each score that indicates that the student is in the healthy zone. Leave scores in need of improvement without an asterisk. Provide the student with specific exercises and recommendations when a score is not within the healthy zone. The Fitness Flash should be accompanied by a letter that explains that fitness tests are just one aspect of a physical education program. Emphasize that participation, effort, and physical activity levels are equally important, and that progress and improvement are your main goals.

When scheduling a conference, be sensitive to busy working parents by accommodating their schedules. If after school is not convenient, then an early bird or evening appointment may be neces-

sary. Being flexible will show you really care about the child.

Take advantage of regular conference days at your school as well. Make sure that the administration has included you when making room assignments and schedules and when signing up parents. Explain that you need a setting for the conference that will be more conducive for small group discussions than a cramped, noisy gym office and arrange to meet in an administrative office, conference room, or empty classroom. Once you have scheduled a conference, send a simple, yet professional, letter of confirmation stating where you'll be holding the conference and your willingness to work with the parents during the school year. Arrange to have a translator nearby if necessary.

Prepare for the conference by updating the student's personal fitness education portfolio for parents to review. Make notes as to the student's specific needs based on your assessments and observations of the student.

Don't plan to sit behind a desk or arrange chairs in a teacher-student lecture format. Arrange the chairs in a semicircle to project the message that you are all equal members of the same team and that information should be shared to help support the children.

During the Conference

Begin the conference by attempting to relax the parents with a calm, nonthreatening voice. Greet the parents by saying, "It's wonderful to get the chance to talk with you about [Joseph's] progress over the last few weeks."

Use direct, plain language, avoiding educational jargon. For example, parents may not understand the difference between static and ballistic stretching but may be too embarrassed to ask you to explain.

Lead, but don't dominate, the conversation. If a child is obese, ask a few leading questions rather than lecturing about the ills of overweight children. For example, "What does [Joseph] usually do after dinner each night?" Or, "What types of snacks are usually available in the house?" Put the parents at ease by acknowledging any poor habits as being common.

Use concrete examples from the student's fitness education portfolio. For example, discuss the student's activity log to show that the only exercise he is getting is in physical education class, twice per week. Then ask the parents how they think they can help increase the child's activity level after school and during the weekend. Next, review the Fitness

Fitness Flash

To the parent or guardian of _____ ,

Your child's fitness status was recently examined as a part of the physical education program. Listed below are your child's results and the date of the assessment.

An asterisk (*) next to the score denotes a healthy level of fitness in the particular component. Scores that appear without an asterisk are in need of improvement. I will provide specific exercises to help develop the specific fitness components that need improvement.

Fitness component	Date _____ Score	Date _____ Score	Comments
Flexibility (sit-and-reach)			
Cardiorespiratory endurance (one-mile run)			
Muscular strength (push-ups)			
Muscular endurance (curl-ups)			
Body composition (percent fat)			
Additional comments:			

Figure 7.4 Fitness flash.

Flash you sent home a few weeks before the conference. Ask the parents if they have any questions about the scores or your recommendations.

Asking leading questions and discussing the student's portfolio are nonthreatening ways to guide parents toward making their own conclusions about their child's health and fitness needs. At this point, they may be more interested in hearing your suggestions for improvement than before the conference.

Be honest, truthful, and concise when discussing the child and making suggestions. Parents may listen more closely to suggestions that begin with, "It may be helpful for [Joseph] to . . . ." than with, "You need to . . . ." However, try not to overwhelm the parents with too much information in one meeting.

To close the conference, summarize the discussion and ask if they have any further questions. Provide a few "action items" to help follow up and reaffirm what you have discussed. For example, ask the parents to review and sign the physical activity log each week for the next four weeks.

After the Conference

Documenting the conference is very important. Develop a conference file for each student and keep it in your office. Include the day, time, and which parent(s) attended. Add copies of any materials you reviewed. Note the main points of the conversation and any follow-up action you recommended. File a parent-teacher conference form in the school's main office if this is a requirement. Keeping an accurate account of what transpired can save you time and trouble later.

Finally, send a follow-up note or make a phone call to the parents when the student shows signs of improvement. This will indicate that the conference was worthwhile and that you still care.

Parent Education

Parent education is a natural extension of parent-teacher communication. Parents must understand what you are trying to accomplish and why it is so important. If you educate parents with up-to-date health and fitness information, they'll be more inclined to participate with you and their children during the school year. But what can you do beyond newsletters? Parent seminars, PTA demonstrations, a parent-teacher wellness room, and a health and fitness fair all educate parents in fun and practical ways.

Parent Seminars

Schedule a brief seminar as part of the monthly PTA meeting or schedule lengthier seminars before school, at lunchtime, directly after school, or in the evening. Schedule them at different time slots during the school year so different parents may be able to attend. You can even repeat the same seminar at more than one time slot. If possible, schedule guest speakers to lecture about a number of health and fitness topics. Contact the local university, American Heart Association, medical schools, and health clubs for possible speakers. Remember to advertise the parent seminars in the newsletter. Be specific and concise: topic, speaker, place, time, and date.

PTA Demonstration

Each year arrange to showcase your program through a PTA night. Select a theme, such as "North Side Elementary School Is Heart Smart." Here are a few suggestions to help you design your PTA night:

- Decorate the gym or cafeteria with the children's work, such as fitness posters, artwork, murals, exercise logs, the Food Guide Pyramid, and snapshots of children exercising.

- Introduce yourself. State the basic goals and philosophy of your new fitness education program.

- Have a guest speaker: a professor, medical doctor, or health educator. Ask the speaker to be brief (7 to 10 minutes is usually enough time) and very direct.

- Select about 25 children and give a physical activity demonstration. Music will help keep the activity upbeat (e.g., aerobics, jump rope workout, exercise bands and tubes, parachute play).

- Narrate a slide show. Slides should show your students exercising, having fun, doing family workouts, or eating healthy foods. Finish with an upbeat song such as "Reach" by Gloria Estefan as you continue to show slides of children exercising and cooperating with each other.

- Videotape several grade levels exercising and participating in the fitness education program. Set up three video monitors around the room so everyone can see the tape.

Parent-Teacher Wellness Room

Remember the staff wellness room we discussed in chapter 2? Expand it to include parents. Convert an empty classroom or turn the staff lounge into a combination wellness room and lounge. Include a reading area with a small reference space for books, magazines, brochures, and cookbooks. Use another section of the room for exercise. One mat and an exercise bike or a treadmill facing a television and a few dumbbells and exercise tubes on a shelf are all you need. And why not add a VCR and exercise tapes? Decorate the room with American Heart Association posters and place a small stereo on a shelf with soft rock playing throughout the day. No time to develop this idea? Delegate the responsibility to interested parents. The PTA could supply the funds and request the space from the principal. Ensure that the hours for using the wellness room are flexible for busy parents and teachers. A wellness room that includes parents creates excellent public relations.

Health-Fitness Fair

Schedule this event during a school day, on a weekend, or in the evening. Set up individual booths on the school grounds, for example, for posture analysis, body composition testing, healthy snack hints and samples, blood pressure and cholesterol screening, flexibility measures, and grip strength. Make each station a practical learning experience for the entire family. Plan this event with the local university, hospital, and business community. (See also chapter 14.)

Parent Participation During School Hours

Parents and grandparents (who may have more time) can help support your program during the school day. Your parent survey will give you a sense of the willingness of the parents to get involved during school hours. Then use the following approaches to help bring the parents into the school:

- Parent aides. Parents can help you with attendance, marking a field, recording fitness scores, and organizing large classes.

- Guest speaker. Schedule a parent who is knowledgeable in a specific subject to speak or demonstrate to your classes.

- Volunteers and monitors. Ask parents to supervise recess workouts, to videotape classes, to record fitness scores on the computer, or to act as a chauffeur or chaperone for special events.

- Facilities and equipment. Ask handy parents to help build or repair physical education equipment. Painting lines on your court or putting up equipment room shelves are activities that some parents would feel very comfortable doing. Organize a "Fitness Factory": Every three months parents meet on a Saturday morning to help you repair, build, and maintain your facilities and equipment.

- School governance. Establish a special committee of the PTA to help you with public relations, special events, fund-raising, and curriculum decisions. This committee also serves as an advocacy group, which may be the support you need in uncertain economic times.

- Guests and observers. Select certain days each month during which you open your classes to unscheduled parent visitors. Also, invite them to special event days as well as typical class periods. Parents will appreciate your openness and will be more likely to get involved. In addition, they'll see you in action and begin to develop an appreciation for the benefits of physical education.

Home-Based Activities

The home is the most influential environment in a child's life. Take advantage of this by suggesting creative family fitness activities. (*Caution*: Many parents are not accustomed to playing or exercising as a family. Begin slowly and don't expect too much progress at first. If you are persistent and follow some of the recommendations in this chapter, you will be quite successful.) Use your newsletter to communicate the following home-based activity possibilities.

Family Game: Fitness Fortune

Parents and children accumulate fitness dollars by engaging in moderate to vigorous physical activity.

Give each physical activity a specific dollar value. For example:

Jogging one mile = $1,000

Walking half mile = $500

Step aerobics 30 minutes = $1,500

Resistance training 30 minutes = $1,500

Raking leaves 15 minutes = $500

Vacuuming house 15 minutes = $500

Biking 30 minutes = $1,500

The family totals each member's dollars at the end of each week. Each family member describes how they would spend the hypothetical dollars. Dad may purchase a new Jaguar XJS! This activity may be logged in the fitness portfolio and shared with the rest of the class in a brief discussion.

Family Playacting

The family spends one evening writing and casting a miniplay based on a health and fitness theme. For example, the miniplay may at first depict how an unhealthy, tired, lazy family acts on a typical day. The second portion of the play depicts how, through exercise and nutritious foods, a healthy, active family responds to the day. Another evening, the family could perform their play for neighbors or videotape and show it later to grandparents, friends, or teachers.

Family Fitness Contract

A family fitness contract asks the family to make a commitment to exercise or engage in physical activity together. Use a contract to allow the family to decide what they would like to do and when they would like to exercise (see figure 7.5). If the family completes the contract, the physical education department gives them a reward, such as YMCA passes, frozen yogurt certificates, spa visits, or T-shirts.

Homework Helpers

Physical education homework assignments that involve parents can provide an exciting learning experience for the entire family. Select activities that support your module goals but that don't duplicate class activities. For example, send home the Heart Thump homework assignment (level II; see figure 7.6). Children and parents can graph their heart rates, using an X for parents and a dot for children. Have children explain to their parents how exercise makes the heart beat faster, making the heart stronger, and how after resting the heart rate is lower.

Neighborhood Fitness Trail

In this assignment, children and parents design fitness stations throughout the neighborhood. They draw a map and plan exercises at each station (see figure 7.7). Ask parents to calculate the total mileage of the course with their car's odometer. For safety's sake, emphasize that participants should jog and exercise on the sidewalk (level III).

Wake-Up Workout or Evening's End

Parents and children design a 10-minute exercise routine to perform before school or after dinner. Ask the family to keep track of their workouts on a large calendar placed on the refrigerator.

TV Time-Out

Ask the parents and children to watch a sporting event together. After the game, have the family answer questions such as the following:

1. What specific exercises would be important for this sport?

2. Did the players conduct themselves in a sportsmanlike manner?

3. Did physical conditioning play a role in the outcome of the game?

4. Name two players who used strength, endurance, or speed to gain an advantage in the game.

Fitness Minute

Each time a commercial is aired during a favorite prime-time show, the family does one to two minutes of exercise. Family members take turns leading and selecting the exercise for the group.

Family Fitness Contract

We, the _____ family, promise that today
_____ (date) we will adopt an active lifestyle and
become more physically active.

We acknowledge that general physical activity is very important
to the health of all family members. We promise to devote _____
minutes on Mon., Tues., Wed., Thurs., Fri., Sat., Sun. (circle at least
three days) toward making positive changes in our physical activity
levels. The best time of day for us to work on this change is
_____ A.M./P.M.

We will try our best to fulfill this one-month contract as we
develop our family fitness goals. We understand that by fulfilling
this contract, we will receive YMCA passes or frozen yogurt certificates from the school physical education program.

Family members: _____
(sign)

_____

_____

_____

This promise was witnessed by_____

Figure 7.5   Family fitness contract.

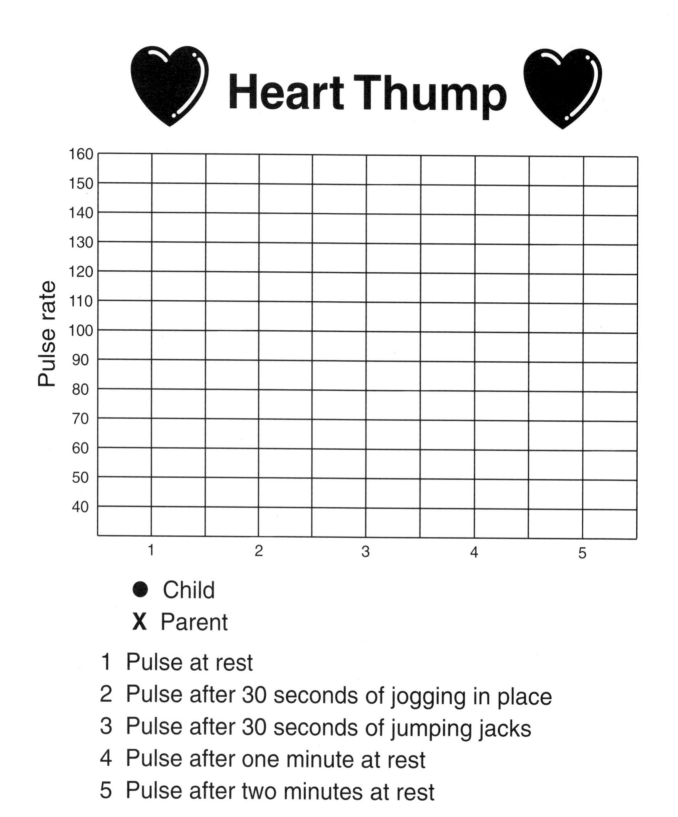

Figure 7.6　Heart Thump homework activity.

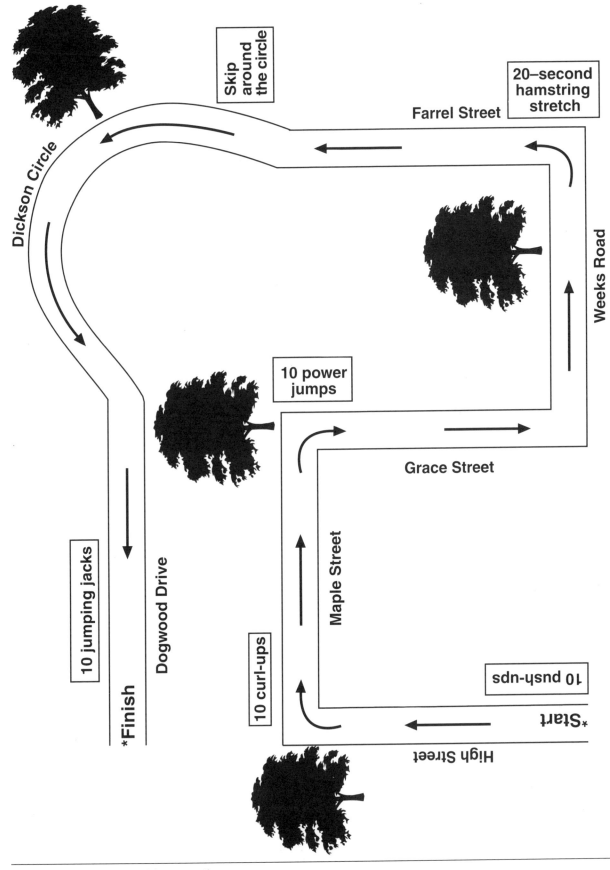

Figure 7.7   Neighborhood fitness trail.

Community Involvement

The community can be a gold mine for your physical education program. First, to establish a good relationship, organize a school-community wellness committee. (This can be a subcommittee of the school wellness committee discussed in chapter 2.) Invite local business leaders, parents, and senior citizens to join your program efforts; each will be a link to a different segment of the community. The following are guidelines for committee selection:

1. Select individuals from different social and cultural backgrounds, reflecting the ethnic and religious makeup of your community.

2. Encourage a gender balance.

3. Involve people from various age groups.

4. Choose volunteers who value health and fitness, for example, runners, fitness leaders, spa owners, and the like.

5. Invite proven community leaders to join.

The committee should meet once a month to discuss a variety of topics, including how to educate the community about healthy lifestyles and how they can help the school fitness education program plan special events such as a community health fair or fun run. It may also be helpful to identify your approach by giving it a name, such as the "East Williston Heart Healthy School-Community Program." One special event in the fall and in the spring will keep the committee active throughout the school year.

With the help of a strong committee you will be able to network throughout the community. The community support gained will strengthen your program and provide you with many advantages, such as the following:

- The city or another organization may let you use their swimming pool for classes or after-school programs.

- Sporting goods stores may donate athletic and fitness equipment.

- A local health club or YMCA may supply you with free passes to use as incentives for your students.

- Bowling facilities may give free or low-cost alley time for your classes or the opportunity to develop an intramural program after school.

- Restaurants may offer heart healthy choices and give your students special discounts.

- The local American Heart Association or American Cancer Society may provide workshops, brochures, videos, or educational kits for your school.

- Frozen yogurt stores may donate "buy-one-get-one-free" certificates for you to use as incentives.

- Local newspapers or radio stations may advertise your program and special events.

Give Back to the Community

School and community relations is a two-way street. It is very important to provide the community with a number of benefits and services in return for their support. Consider the following suggestions:

- Each year provide two or three community health seminars in the school cafeteria from 7:30-9:30 P.M. Possible topics: "Heart Disease—The Facts," "Exercise—For the Health of It," and "Eat to Your Heart's Content." Schedule medical doctors, university professors, or nutritionists to speak.

- Provide space for local clubs and organizations to meet during the evening.

- Help clean up and maintain the softball and little league fields at your school or in your town's public parks.

- Begin an exercise class for senior citizens in your community. Your compensation should come from the school district's budget since many seniors pay local school taxes.

- Have students keep the school grounds and surrounding streets clean. Plant flowers in the spring to show your community pride.

- Patronize the local businesses that support your school.

- Distribute flyers to your students about community programs like summer camps, little leagues, recreation centers, exercise classes, bowling leagues, swimming activities, and the like.

- Start a Saturday morning walking club. Meet at the school and walk through the neighborhood. Give your club a name, for example, "The Fitness Walkers."

- Provide your help and expertise to the local youth sports teams.

Fall Community Health Fair

Form a subcommittee to plan and carry out the details of this event. Plan to hold it on the school grounds on a Saturday or Sunday. First, it is vital to the success of the event to begin by establishing a budget. Ask local businesses such as banks and grocery stores to sponsor the event; in return, you place the businesses' names on the brochures that will be distributed throughout the day. To defray any unexpected costs, sell heart healthy refreshments during the event. Donate a portion of the profits gained from selling refreshments to the American Heart Association or a similar organization to give back to the community.

Make sure the committee remembers to advertise. They can approach your local or regional newspapers and TV and radio stations with public service announcements. Two other effective advertising tools are distributing flyers throughout the school and community and designing a poster advertising the fair and asking local merchants to display it in their windows. Students may also design and make posters for display at the public library and local businesses.

Establish a wellness booth as the focus of your fair, locating it in the middle of the fair. Let this booth serve as the general administrative area for questions, problems, or emergencies. You may also wish to include an array of information about a number of health topics, perhaps in the form of free brochures that clearly explain basic health principles. In addition, consider including a small bookstore at which community members may purchase more substantive books and materials related to healthy lifestyles. Locally owned bookstores may set this up and give the school a portion of the profits.

Finally, be certain you have planned for set-up, cleanup, security, and road supervision. Contact the local police several weeks before the event to inquire about traffic and security issues.

Possible health fair participants and ideas include the following:

Local restaurant	Heart healthy foods
Chiropractors	Posture screening
Health club owner	Equipment demonstration
Dance studio	Funky jazz dancing
Nurses	Blood pressure screening
Nutritionist	Healthy snacking
Medical school	Cholesterol screening
Body composition testing	University Health and Physical Education Department
Sports apparel store	Selecting the correct physical activity shoe
Exercise physiologist	Myths about exercise
Parents	Family fitness workouts
PTA	Personal hygiene

For ways to include children in developing a health fair, see chapter 14.

Spring Fun Run

As with the health fair, form a subcommittee to organize this event. If possible, route the run through the school's neighborhood. Contact local police to provide supervision and traffic control. (See figure 7.8.)

Sample fun run schedule (printed on flyer):

8:00 A.M.—Group warm-up with physical education teacher

8:30 A.M.—1.5 mile Community Fun Run (ages 7 and older) (Everyone receives a ribbon!)

9:30 A.M. —Little Tykes Run (ages 2 to 6) 200-yard run (Everyone is a winner! Each child receives a ribbon!)

11:00 A.M.—Awards for each age division

12:00 Noon—Community Picnic

1:30 P.M.—Parent-Child Softball Game

Grocery Store Tour

Arrange to visit the local grocery store just before they open in the morning. This is a great field trip for your fifth or sixth grade classes. Give each student 50 dollars in play money to spend on food they would purchase for the family if they were a parent. Meet as a group and introduce the store manager who may speak for a few minutes about the grocery business, how they order the food, and the basic store operations. Then have students get carts and go food shopping for 20 minutes. After checking out, students get computer readouts of exactly what

1996 - 17th Annual Memorial Day 5K Race

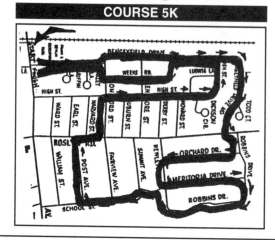

MONDAY - May 27, 1996
8:30 A.M. 5K Race

Lil' Tykes Fun Run • 6 years and under • Starts 9:30 A.M. • Rain or shine • Awards for all

Purpose This race is for local families and neighbors to walk, jog, or run together in a friendly, timed competition.

Registration Deadline for preregistration: May 23. Preregistration: $5.00. Late registration: $8.00.

Warm-up clinic A stretching and warm-up clinic from 8 A.M.-8:15 A.M. at starting line.

Awards Three best times for male and female runners in the following categories: 7-9, 10-12, 13-18, 19-29, 30-39, 40-49, 50-59, 60 and over; family team trophy.
Walkers 19 and over; three best times, male and female. L.T. Fun Run: Awards for all participants.

Figure 7.8 Community involvement fun run.
Adapted from Memorial Day 5K Race flyer.

they purchased. Later that day, have students analyze their purchases in comparison to the Food Guide Pyramid. Note major discrepancies in a child's selection; you might ask them to take the shopping list home and discuss the purchases with their parents.

Village Visits

Arrange to have a class review several businesses in your community. You may arrange to visit a frozen yogurt shop and study how yogurt is made and what it is made of. A health food store is another good place to visit. Ask students to analyze the fat, sugar, and sodium contents of the various foods on the shelf. Then arrange to view a local health spa. Perhaps the children could participate in a step aerobics class. Finally, visit a local restaurant that offers heart healthy items, and review how the chefs prepare the items and what makes them heart healthy. Then students could sample the food and discover how tasty healthy items can be.

Young at Heart

This effort enlists the help of the senior citizens in your community, matching them to first or second graders as exercise partners. Attend local seniors' meetings to explain your purpose and major objectives. During the first and third Friday of each month (or whatever works for your schedule), the seniors visit the school and walk and exercise with their partners. While exercising, they discuss how each is feeling and what is going on in their lives. This program may be especially meaningful for those children who have lost their grandparents or have grandparents who live out of town. This is also another way to give back to your community.

Can It

Collect canned foods from the community to help the homeless or natural disaster victims. Taking civic responsibility to help a charity is good public relations. Announce that you are interested in healthy foods that are low in fat, sugar, and sodium, reinforcing your support of healthy foods. Students may also use healthy canned foods for resistance exercises such as arm curls, or study and analyze the labels.

Fund-Raising

When the community at large is aware of your physical education program, they will be more inclined to help you financially. Individuals and businesses who have participated in the community-based activities will gladly sponsor children for such fund-raising events as "Jump Rope for Heart,"

"Step for Heart," and raffles to buy equipment. The American Cancer Association and the American Heart Association have various fund-raising events during the year. The school may join these events and share a percentage of the donations.

Once you have developed a comprehensive community involvement program, it's much easier to apply for local, state, or national grants for your school. Speak to the Department of Health and Physical Education at the local university. Professors may be interested in using your school as a health and fitness intervention model for their research. Funds may be available for graduate assistants, equipment, and instructional materials through the university. As we have already touched on, local businesses may be interested in sponsoring community-based programs. They may volunteer to adopt a grade level at your school to support the cost of curriculum materials, fitness equipment, cholesterol screening, and special events.

Summary

Work with your students' parents and community organizations to expand your opportunities to develop physical activity and healthy lifestyles in children. Keep in mind that family and community influences have a significant impact on the health behaviors of children. Channel these influences by including parents and the community in your fitness education plans. Indeed, never underestimate the power of parent and community involvement. The time you invest in communication and building bridges to parents and your community will ultimately bring tremendous dividends for your physical education program. Remember, "It takes a village to raise a child."

PLANNING AND TEACHING FITNESS EDUCATION

Planning for Fitness

*Our plans miscarry because they have no aim.
When a man does not know what harbor he is
making for, no wind is the right wind.*

—Seneca

Curriculum planning is one of the most difficult responsibilities facing physical educators today. In the past, physical educators usually assumed that movement skills, games, dance, gymnastics, and sports developed health-related physical fitness levels and maintained physical activity patterns in children. A more contemporary approach supported throughout this book is that health-related physical fitness and motor skills should be taught in concert throughout the school year.

In this chapter, I will provide you with model curricula, including an example of a yearly plan for developmental level III in which I have integrated health-related physical fitness concepts with the various skill themes. We'll also take a look at sample fitness education and fitness integration lesson plans for developmental levels I, II, and III.

My fitness education lesson plans focus solely on providing instruction in health-related physical fitness. My fitness integration lessons illustrate how to integrate health-related physical fitness and increase physical activity levels in a skill or sport theme lesson. I'll demonstrate how fitness, values, physical activity concepts, and skill themes can work together to develop a quality program of physical education.

Sample Yearly Plan for Developmental Level III

Block out segments of time for the major components of your curriculum on your school calendar. Consider overall body development and strive for a well-balanced curriculum. Look for opportunities to combine a skill activity with a fitness activity if the skill-related lesson includes a high percentage of vigorous physical activity. For example, a rhythmics and dance unit may include an aerobic dance routine.

Figure 8.1 shows a yearly plan for developmental level III, designed for classes meeting twice a week for 30 minutes. See chapter 9 for lesson plans that address health-related physical fitness concepts in detail (levels I, II, and III).

Later in this chapter, I'll give you detailed fitness education lesson plans for weeks 7 and 8 in figure 8.1 (level III). Then I'll give you a model fitness integration lesson plan that corresponds with weeks 12 through 14 of the same yearly plan. Use this structured approach to curriculum planning, such as the examples illustrated in this chapter, to ensure that your physical education program has appropriate fitness education content and continuity.

Weeks	Curriculum focus	Fitness activities	Fitness concepts
1	Introductory activities, cooperative games	Flexibility stretches	Wellness concepts
2-3	Health-related physical fitness pretest	Sit-and-reach, push-ups, curl-ups, one-mile run, body composition	Physical activity and wellness exercise techniques
4-6	Health-related physical fitness activities and concepts	Fitness circuits, muscular strength and endurance	Heart smart concepts
7-8	Health-related physical fitness activities and concepts, using the fitness education portfolio	Cardiorespiratory endurance (CRE)	Fitness principles (components, FITT, heart rate, interval activity)
9-11	Soccer skills	Active soccer skills and lead-up games	Fitness principles (training HR, HR recovery, preventing injuries)
12-14	Basketball skills	Upper body exercises, lower body exercises	Exercise science: upper body anatomy and lower body anatomy
15-17	Volleyball skills	Medicine ball exercises, fitness games	Exercise science: specificity, progression overload, reversibility, train and maintain (SPORT), and bone anatomy
18-20	Tumbling and gymnastics	Push-up routine, flexibility, fitness games	Foods for fitness
21-22	New games	Fitness circuits	Making healthy food choices
23-27	Rhythms and dance	Aerobic dance, step aerobics	Family fitness: parent and community involvement
28-31	Softball skills	Free choice fitness activities	Maintaining a personal fitness education portfolio
32-34	Physical activity for healthy lifestyles	Individual contracts for physical activity choices	Fitness forever: making choices, decision making
35-36	Health-related physical fitness posttest	(See pretest, weeks 2-3)	Review major fitness principles, summer fitness, summer safety, recreational opportunities
36	Field day activities	Total body development	Activity review

Figure 8.1   Sample yearly curriculum plan for developmental level III.

Sample Lesson Plans

The following lesson plans are examples of fitness education and fitness integration. Each example will illustrate a lesson from developmental levels I, II, and III. Keep in mind that these lessons are single class period lessons that I have extracted from a unit plan.

Since the amount of class time varies, the following format has been suggested as percentages of time:

Lesson segments --------------- Class time

Set induction	15 percent
Fitness education	30 percent
Developmental movement	45 percent
Closure	10 percent

Each teacher has his or her own approach to lesson plan formats, and content may be integrated within lesson segments. Certain guidelines, however, should remain consistent regardless of the level or content of the class.

- **Lesson focus**: This is the specific content in which you should direct class instruction.
- **Objectives**: The lesson plans illustrated in this chapter will use student-centered objectives. These objectives describe what students will do as a result of the lesson activities in the cognitive (knowing), psychomotor (moving and physical development), and affective (valuing) areas.
- **Equipment and facilities**: This category lists all equipment, instructional materials, and fa-cilities you need to present the lesson. I have described specific equipment in an equipment-to-student ratio.
- **Safety considerations**: Proper safety planning will help prevent accidents and keep your classes running smoothly.
- **Set induction**: Also called the anticipatory set, the purpose of the set induction is to motivate children, orienting them to what they will learn, why it is important, and how they will accomplish the learning objective.
- **Procedures**: Here I'll give a detailed account of each activity, the instructional strategy I have planned, the time allotment breakdown, and class management tips.
- **Closure**: This may be difficult to include due to time limitations, however, it's necessary for a number of reasons. First, use it to review the lesson content. Second, use it to help you evaluate whether students grasped the concept of the lesson. Third, use closure as a culminating activity, showing how the lesson is relevant to the students' daily lives. Finally, this is an opportune time to prepare students for the next class activity by giving a brief preview of the exciting lessons to come.

As you read through the lessons, think about how you can update your own lesson plans to include each essential component. Remember, incorporate fitness into your lessons throughout the school year.

Fitness Education Lessons

Superpump (Level I)

Lesson Focus -------------------- Increasing physical activity levels through creative expressive movement, heart rate, and exercise

Objectives ----------------------- **Cognitive:** The student knows that physical activity increases the heart rate, which in turn exercises the heart.

Psychomotor: The student participates in a wide variety of activities to enhance physical activity levels.

Affective: The student values physical activity as both a means to strengthen the heart and a form of creative expression.

Equipment and Facilities ---- Music, tape player, and open playing surface with line markings.

Safety Considerations -------- Check playing surface for any hazards. Make sure students are dressed properly for active movement.

Set Induction (3 minutes) --- Say "All muscles are important and should be exercised, but the heart is the most important muscle in the body." With the class sitting in a circle, ask them to feel their hearts beating on the left side of the chest. Ask them to notice the rhythm of the beats. Reinforce that as the heart beats stronger, it sends fuel to the muscles. Say "Have you ever felt your legs get real tired? It may be that you need to exercise to strengthen your heart muscle. Today we will actively move to strengthen the heart, and we'll make it fun by adding music."

Procedures ---------------------- **Warm-Up   (6 minutes)**

Students stand in a circle. Direct them to do the following:

Walk in circle.	30 seconds
Walk briskly in circle.	30 seconds
Skip in circle.	30 seconds
Sidestep in circle.	30 seconds
Gallop in circle.	30 seconds
Do arm-cross stretch (L-R).	1 minute
Do hamstrings stretch.	1 minute
Do quadriceps stretch.	1 minute

Activity 1:   Creative Movement to Music   (7 minutes)
Have students move throughout the playing area, staying in their personal spaces. When the music stops, students perform a seal crawl walk.

Do	**Instruct**
Begin music.	Walk.
	Walk with stiff legs.
	Walk with spaghetti legs.
	Walk on your heels.
	Walk on your toes.
	Walk in a straight line.
Stop music.	Seal crawl.
Begin music.	Jog lightly.
	Jog lightly and give a friend a "high five."
	Jog and pretend you are a bird.
	Jog and pretend you are a car.
Stop music.	Seal crawl.
Begin music.	Hop like a kangaroo.
	Hop like a rabbit.

	Leap like a frog.
	Can you name another animal to imitate?
Stop music.	Seal crawl.
Begin music.	Walk as if you are very happy.
	Walk as if you are very sad.
	Walk as if you are very angry.
	Walk as if it is a sunny, warm day.
	Walk as if it is a cloudy, rainy day.

Activity 2:   Heart to Heart   (7 minutes)

Divide students into pairs and have them scatter throughout the playing area. Give students a series of movement problems. Say "When I give the command 'Heart to heart,' find a new partner and stand left shoulder to left shoulder and place your right hand over your own heart to feel it beat." Try the following commands:

- Take three giant steps forward.
- Take two giant steps backward.
- Balance on one foot.
- Heart to heart!
- Skip around the gym.
- Gallop like a horse.
- Heart to heart!
- Take five steps forward.
- Take five steps backward.
- Take five steps sideways.
- Heart to heart!
- Take two hops, then one leap.
- Walk on a line painted on the floor.
- Walk backward on the line.
- Find anyone in class and shake their hand.
- Heart to heart!

Cool-Down   (2 minutes)

Say "Everyone walk quietly and feel your heart beating. This faster beating means you are exercising your heart."

Closure (3 minutes) ----------- Have students stand in a circle. Conduct the following discussion:

"What movements made your heart beat faster? What other types of activities make your heart beat faster? Everyone feel their heartbeat again (place your right hand on your chest). Feel how it has slowed. That is because we are resting. The heart needs rest, but we should all exercise our hearts every day! Next week we are going to use the parachute to exercise and play a fun fitness game."

Back to the Basics (Level II)

Lesson Focus -------------------- Building general body development and performing exercises correctly for neck and back care

Objectives ----------------------- **Cognitive:** The student knows how to perform certain exercises to prevent stress on the neck and back.

Psychomotor: The student participates in cardiorespiratory endurance, muscular strength and endurance, and general physical activity specific to each station.

Affective: The student makes a personal choice of activities based on individual physical fitness level.

Equipment and Facilities ---- Large playing area, 1 horizontal ladder, 4 task cards, music, tape player, 4 to 6 tumbling mats.

For every 4 students: 1 hula hoop, 1 jump rope, 1 streamer, 1 soccer ball, 1 basketball.

For each student: 1 8.5-inch playball, 1 foam soccer ball.

Safety Considerations -------- Ensure that mats are clean. Check playing area, all equipment, and horizontal ladder.

Set Induction (3 minutes) --- Explain to the class that this lesson will help develop the following components of fitness: cardiorespiratory endurance and strength and muscular endurance. Each station will have a different fitness objective. Say "Does anyone know someone who got hurt from exercising? Sometimes exercise can hurt our bodies if it is not done properly." Demonstrate the curl-up with bent knees, not straight legs, and the neck exercises—drop head, look over, tilt neck (not the head straight back). Remind students to perform these exercises correctly to avoid placing stress on the back or neck. (See chapter 11 for additional unsafe exercises.)

Procedures ---------------------- **Warm-Up   (5 minutes)**

Have students form a single line around the basketball court. Direct students to

- walk around the outside of the basketball court area,
- dribble a playball around the basketball court area, and
- kick a foam soccer ball around the basketball court area.

Activity: Circuits (16 minutes)

Divide students into groups of four. In this small group activity, color-code the choices at each station. Play music during activity. Tell students "When the music stops, move to the next station." Move around class, providing individual feedback to students. The selections should be posted at each station with a reminder to do their physical best.

Station 1: Upper body strength and endurance

Yellow	Walk across the horizontal ladder, two turns.
Red	Bent-knee push-ups—perform two sets of maximum repetitions.
Green	Seal crawl, two times up and down tumbling mat.

Station 2: Cardiorespiratory endurance

Yellow   Jog around the court area three times.

Red   Jump rope, three sets of 15 jumps with rest.

Green   Soccer or basketball dribble—dribble a soccer ball or basketball at a jogging pace until it is time to change to next station.

Station 3: Abdominal strength and endurance

Yellow   Curl-up—5, 10, or 15 repetitions.

Red   Curl-up twists—5, 10, or 15 repetitions.

Green   Diagonal crunch—5, 10, or 15 repetitions.

Station 4: Free play for physical activity (Students select desired movements and create a physical activity.)

Yellow   Hula hoops

Red   Playballs

Green   Streamers

Cool-Down   (1 minute)
Have students walk around the play area in any direction.

Closure -------------------------- Ask "Why is it important to perform exercises correctly? What were the two dangerous exercises we reviewed at the beginning of class? Why are they so dangerous? Remember, perform the exercises correctly so you won't put any additional stress on your neck or back. Next week we will be playing an active game to increase fitness."

Smart Heart (Level III)

Lesson Focus -------------------- Increasing cardiorespiratory endurance through interval activity

Objectives ------------------------ **Cognitive:** The student knows the technique of interval activity to enhance cardiorespiratory endurance.

Psychomotor: The student participates in interval routines at individual ability level.

Affective: The student values intervals as a means to enhance his or her personal best.

Equipment and Facilities ---- Stopwatch, music ("Twenty-Five Miles to Go" by Edwin Starr), tape player, 10 cones, whistle, outdoor playing area, outdoor playing field.

Safety Considerations -------- Check playing surface for glass, debris, potholes, and other hazards. Check facility availability.

Set Induction -------------------- Say "Has anyone thought about how certain sports such as basketball, soccer, and floor hockey require a great deal of running with short rest periods? Basketball, for example, is active until the game flow changes or there is a violation. Then all the running stops for a short while. Well, this is a form of interval training. Today we will perform interval activities that will enhance your heart and lungs, maybe enabling you to play certain sports without tiring so quickly."

Procedures ---------------------- **Warm-Up**   (5 minutes)

Have students form a single line around playing area. Have students walk around playing area to the song "Twenty-Five Miles to Go" by Edwin Starr.

Activity 1:   Leader Change   (3 minutes)

Divide students into groups of five and have groups stand in single file. The line leader begins jogging in any direction at a moderate pace. Say "When I say 'Change,' the last student in line becomes the leader and the previous leader becomes the second person in line." Change leaders every 30 seconds. If you wish, have leaders vary the movements, for example, allow them to skip, hop, sidestep, seal crawl, crab walk, or the like.

Activity 2:   Walk-Jog Intervals   (8 minutes)

Use cones to mark the perimeter of a large running track on your outdoor facility. Spread students around the track to avoid a "bunch up." Say "We'll start by walking briskly around the track. When I whistle, start jogging at a pace that is comfortable for you. When I whistle again, you walk briskly again and so on." Alternate walking and jogging in 45-second intervals. Continue for seven to eight minutes total.

Activity 3:   Destination Choice   (7 minutes)

Stand in the middle of the field and ask the students to walk briskly to you. Explain to students that in this next activity they have a choice of destination. Provide them with a number of possibilities from which to select their jogging destination. Be certain that all destinations are within your view so you can properly supervise. Examples:

- Large oak tree
- Basketball standard on court
- North edge of the school building
- Pull-up bars
- Soccer goal
- Softball field backstop

Say "Jog to your destination at a moderate pace then run back to this spot at a faster pace. But this is not a race!" Then allow students to select their own destinations.

Cool-Down   (3 minutes)

Ask the class to walk back to the court area from the field. Discuss how they felt performing the interval activities.

Closure -------------------------- Ask students if they enjoyed the interval activity: "What other activities do we participate in that are considered interval activities? What types of intervals do you do at home?" (Possible responses: Biking, roller skating.) "Next week we will learn another exercise principle: heart rate recovery. We will be taking our heart rate before, during, and after exercise and calculating what we'll call the 'recovery index.'"

Fitness Integration Lessons

Heart Jump (Level I)

Lesson Focus ----------------------- Jumping, leaping, doing support movements, moving at various levels, identifying shapes and letters to develop the heart muscle through jump rope activities

Objectives ----------------------- **Cognitive:** The student knows the heart is a muscle that needs to be exercised and becomes aware of various movement forms, levels, and support.

Psychomotor: The student participates in various movement skills using the jump rope as well as a highly active game to increase physical activity levels.

Affective: The student values using the jump rope and game-related activities as a way to exercise the heart and stay active.

Equipment and Facilities ---- Music, tape player, 1 jump rope per student, flat playing surface.

Safety Considerations -------- Check jump ropes and playing surface for hazards; make sure that no one is wearing jewelry.

Set Induction (3 minutes) --- Introduce the use of the jump ropes as a way to develop movement skills and stay physically active. Review the muscles used for jumping. Ask students to tighten the thigh muscles and place a hand on the muscle as it tightens. Ask students to make a fist and place it on the left side of the chest. Say "This is where your heart is and your fist is the size of your heart. The heart is also a muscle and is exercised when you jump and leap."

Procedures ---------------------- **Warm-Up   (3 minutes)**

Arrange students in one large circle. Use music and direct cues. Have students walk around the circle, then walk briskly, shake their arms and walk, skip, bunny hop, and jog at a moderate pace.

Activity 1:   Rope Shapes   (15 minutes)
Have students scatter throughout the playing area, staying in personal spaces. Use guided discovery with these individual jump rope activities:

- Shape your rope into a circle.
- Can you place one body part inside the circle? Two? Three? Four?
- Can you get inside your circle?
- How small can you get?
- How big can you get?
- Can you jog around your circle?
- Discover ways you can move around the outside of the circle.
- Shape your rope into a square.

- Can you take one giant leap over your square?
- Show me how you can hop in and out of the square.
- Lay your rope in a straight line.
- Can you walk on your rope as if you were a tightrope walker in the circus?
- Can you walk backward?
- Can you move down the rope at a low level?
- Can you move down the rope at a high level?
- Can you travel down your rope from side to side?
- Shape your rope into the letter "V."
- Can you leap over the letter "V" at the widest part?

Divide students into groups of three:

- Can you place three letters together?
- Step through your letters without touching the rope.
- Can you jog around your letters?
- Can you walk in and out of your letters?

Activity 2: Lifeline   (7 minutes)
Divide students into small groups of four or five with one standard jump rope. Explain the game: "One student in each group holds the end of a jump rope, which is the 'lifeline.' At the signal 'Go!' he or she runs throughout the play area dragging the rope along the ground and shaking it. The other students in the group try to pick up the end of the jump rope. The student who picks up the lifeline then gets to run with the rope." Make sure each student in the group has a turn running with the lifeline. Remind the class "The reason the rope is called a 'lifeline' is that jumping rope is a good exercise for the heart, and exercise will improve your life and keep you healthy." Remind the students to keep the rope at floor level.

Cool-Down   (1 minute)
Have students find a line on the court area and walk as if it were a tightrope; walk sideways, walk backward, walk on toes, walk and dip, walk on heels.

Closure (2 minutes) ---------- Reinforce the value of the jump ropes for fitness development. Ask "What muscle besides the legs are exercised when you jump rope or run?" (Heart.) "Next week in class, we will try long rope jumping. This is when two students turn the rope and another student jumps through."

Chute the Works! (Level II)

Lesson Focus ------------------- Ball handling, tossing and catching skills, and increasing muscular strength and endurance

Objectives ---------------------- **Cognitive:** The student knows that muscle strength and endurance are important to accomplishing a variety of activities in life.

Psychomotor: The student participates in a variety of ball handling skills and develops upper body strength and endurance through parachute activities.

Affective: The student gains confidence in ball handling skills and values the need for arm and shoulder strength and endurance.

Equipment and Facilities ---- 1 large parachute, 2 medium parachutes, 1 8.5-inch playball for each student, large playing surface or grassy field.

Safety Considerations -------- Parachutes should be checked for small rips or holes. Children should be instructed to hold the handles with an overhand grip.

Set Induction (5 minutes) --- Say "Today we're going to develop our ball handling skills and our upper body strength and endurance, using the playballs and the parachutes. To enjoy this lesson, it's important that we cooperate as a group."

Ask "What kinds of chores around the house require you to use your arms and shoulders?" (Washing the car, vacuuming, cleaning windows.) "What sport activities require strong arms and shoulders?" (Throwing a softball, hitting a softball, bumping a volleyball, shooting a basketball.) "What other types of things do you do that require strong arms and shoulders?" (Climbing trees, hanging on the playground equipment, digging, swimming.) "In order to do all those things without getting tired, you need to exercise your arms and shoulders. Today we will be using the parachute in class to help strengthen our upper bodies."

Procedures ---------------------- **Warm-Up**   (3 to 5 minutes)

Arrange students around the large parachute. Ask students to walk, skip, or jog around the parachute. Then, have all students grasp the parachute with both hands, raise it overhead, and lower it back to the waist two times. Next, have all students grasp with their left hands and jog counterclockwise in a circle while holding the chute—skipping, hopping, galloping.

Activity 1:   Have a Ball   (12 minutes)

Have students scatter throughout the playing area, staying in personal spaces, each with an 8.5-inch playball. Present the following problem-solving situations:

1. Holding the ball in two hands, waist high, walk in general space without dropping the ball.
2. Repeat 1, jogging with ball.
3. Place the ball on the floor in front of you. Find a way to go over the ball without touching it.
4. Hold the ball and roll it on different body parts.
5. Toss the ball in the air, let it bounce once, then catch it.
6. Toss the ball in the air and catch it on the fly.
7. Throw the ball in the air and count how many times you can clap your hands before catching it.
8. Can you toss the ball in the air and catch it while you are running?
9. Throw the ball in the air and catch it at a high level, medium level, and a low level.
10. Throw the ball up while sitting, then stand and catch it.
11. Find ways of keeping the ball in the air without using your hands.

Activity 2:   Group Chute Catch   (5 to 7 minutes)
Divide the class into two equal groups. Have each group grasp a medium-sized parachute. Have the two groups stand about 10 feet apart. Place a playball in one chute to begin the game.

The objective is for the group with the ball to pop the ball over to the other group's parachute. Emphasize teamwork and cooperation. Say "See how many times our two groups can catch without dropping the ball. See if you can beat your own record!"

Activity 3:   Popcorn   (5 to 7 minutes)
Arrange students around the large parachute. Place several types of balls in the parachute. Have the students grasp the parachute with overhand grips. Explain "When I say 'Simmer,' you shake the chute, creating small ripples. When I say 'Cook,' make the balls move more rapidly by adding a slight chop in the ripples. When I say 'Popcorn,' make large, fast ripples by waving your arms and jumping up and down to pop the balls straight up, trying to keep the popcorn in the pan. When I say 'Pop Out,' pop the balls outside the chute."

Cool-Down
Have students place the chute down and walk around it performing arm-cross and overhead arm stretches.

Closure -------------------------- Ask "Do your arms feel a little tired and sore? Good, that means you were exercising the arm and shoulder muscles. But you also need rest. Whenever you are feeling bad or experience pain, you should stop and tell an adult. Who can name different games and sports that use round balls and require arm and shoulder strength and endurance?" (Basketball, volleyball, baseball, softball, four square, tetherball, parachute play, etc.)

Basketball Cats (Level III)

Lesson Focus -------------------- Practicing basketball skills—layup, dribbling, upper body strength and endurance; developing physical activity levels through basketball play

Objectives ----------------------- **Cognitive:** The student knows the proper techniques for a right- and left-sided layup and can identify the biceps and triceps as well as the exercises that strengthen each.

Psychomotor: The student practices the layup and dribbling skills, using proper form and technique.

Affective: The student cooperates with classmates in small group activities.

Equipment and Facilities ---- 18 cones, 6 hula hoops, 15 plastic pins, 4 task cards, 1 roll gym tape, whistle.

For every 4 students: 1 yellow tube, 1 green tube, 1 red tube.

For every 2 students: 1 2-pound medicine ball, 1 3-pound medicine ball, 1 5-pound medicine ball.

For each student: 1 junior-size basketball, 1 3-by-5 index card, 1 jump rope, 2 2-pound and 2 3-pound dumbbells.

Safety Considerations -------- Check all equipment and facility surfaces for hazards. Allow a sufficient buffer zone between the station activity and the gym wall. Ensure that students maintain proper spacing as they move through the obstacle course.

Set Induction ------------------- Say "Does anyone have a basketball goal at home or nearby at a local playground? This is a great way to stay active and practice the basketball skills you learn in physical education. The purpose of today's class is to practice skills that will help you play the game better so you may enjoy basketball in school as well as at home with friends and family."

Procedures ----------------------- **Warm-Up**   (3 minutes)

Have students line up around the gym, each with a basketball. Have students jog around the gym floor, dribbling a junior-size basketball two times. When students complete their second trip around the gym, have them enter the basketball dribble obstacle course (figure 8.2). Have students jog and dribble to each activity within the obstacle course. Remind them to move slowly and not to race.

Activity 1:   Basketball Dribble Obstacle Course   (7 minutes)

Area 1   Weave through cones: Have students dribble around cones.

Area 2   Hoop dribble: Place hoops at least three feet apart. Have students dribble the ball once in each hoop, alternate dribbling hands as they change sides.

Area 3   Half-moon left then right; half-circle left, half-circle right. Have students dribble around the cones placed in a left

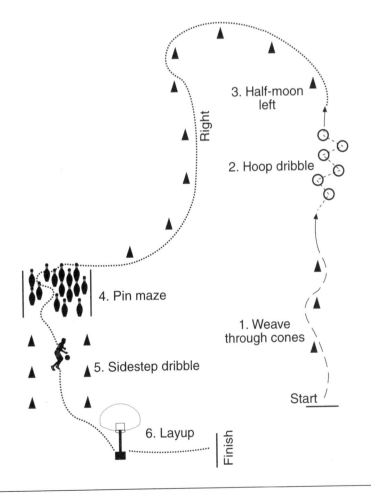

Figure 8.2   Dribbling obstacle course.

curve then around the right curve, using hand farthest away from the cone.

Area 4   Pin maze: Set up 15 plastic bowling pins in a maze configuration. Make lines with tape on both sides to set the boundaries. Have students try to dribble through without knocking the pins over.

Area 5   Sidestep dribble: Set up large cones in a narrow pathway, approximately 15 yards long and 2 yards wide. Students must attempt to sidestep through the area while dribbling with dominant hand.

Area 6   Layup: Have students attempt one right-handed layup.

Activity 2:   Stations   (16 minutes)

Divide students into four equal groups. Create task cards for each station, giving directions and skill and fitness instruction. Ask students to perform the exercise with proper form for a maximum of 10 repetitions. Ask them to record the number of sets, repetitions, weight, and type of exercise performed at each strength and endurance station on a 3-by-5 index card.

Station 1   Layups—right side and left side: Have students form two even lines, 20 feet from goal. One is a layup line and one is a rebounding line. Have students practice dribbling while waiting for their turns.

Station 2   Quick-shot layup challenge: Give each student 30 seconds to make as many layups as possible. Have two students shooting at once. Allow them to position themselves on any side at any angle. Have students waiting for a turn participate in individual rope jumping activity.

Station 3   Center layups with students in two lines: Have one line perform center layups from the line at the top of the key. Have the other line form a rebound line on the left side, angled to the basket. Remind students that they should shoot center layups just over the front of the rim. Using the backboard is optional.

Station 4   Muscle up: Have students select a cat group and the number of repetitions and sets they wish to perform. Give each cat group a task card that illustrates the biceps and triceps. Label and shade the two muscles to highlight them.

Jaguars: Use resistance tubes with color codes to denote various resistance levels (yellow, easy; green, medium; red, hard). Have students do arm curls (biceps) and arm extensions (triceps).

Cougars: Use the medicine ball. Have students select from three different weighted balls (2, 3, or 5 pounds) and choose a friend to toss ball. (See chapter 9 for specific activities.)

Mountain lions: Have students do push-ups, either bent-knee or straight-leg.

Bobcats: Have students do dumbbell arm curls (biceps) and arm extensions (triceps), using 2- or 3-pound weights.

Cool-Down   (2 minutes)

Have students jog around court two times and perform hamstrings stretch, quadriceps stretch, calf stretch, and arm-cross stretch.

Closure --------------------------- Emphasize the importance of basic skills to the game of basketball. Say "Basketball is a game you can play for many years ahead, especially if you have a goal at home or at a nearby playground. If you would like to join a local basketball league (park district or community center team) I have the phone numbers and sign-up sheets. This would be a nice way to develop your basketball skills. Who can tell me what muscle the arm curls exercise? (Biceps.) How about the arm extensions? (Triceps.) It may not appear to be important, but arm strength *is* an important factor in the game of basketball. Who knows Shaquille O'Neal from the LA Lakers? Next time you see him play, look at the strength in his biceps and triceps! Next week we'll learn the muscles of the legs."

Summary

Reform your physical education program by changing your approach to physical education curriculum planning. Use the level III sample yearly plan in this chapter as a model as you plan how you'll include health-related physical fitness in harmony with skill and sport activities throughout the year. Next, use the traditional fitness education lesson plan models as you plan fitness units. Remember, a fitness unit is a great way to kick off the school year, making it easier to integrate fitness throughout the year. Then you'll be all set to follow the fitness integration lesson plan models as you strive to integrate fitness activities and concepts throughout your skill- and sport-related units. Adopt this new perspective on including physical activity and fitness concepts in your physical education curriculum, and your overall program is sure to reap great benefits. Keep in mind, if change is going to take place in our physical education programs, careful planning must remain as a major priority.

Teaching Health-Related Physical Fitness Concepts

CHAPTER 9

Only the educated are free.

—Epictetus

Now let's discuss a plan for teaching health-related fitness concepts within your physical education classes. To help get you started, I'll give you models of practical learning activities for each developmental level. Then, we'll extend our discussion of teaching health-related fitness concepts in chapter 10 with a discussion of ways to collaborate with your partner, the classroom teacher.

As we discussed in chapter 3, knowledge is the foundation for teaching children the necessary skills and behaviors for an active lifestyle. Each major learning domain (cognitive, affective, and psychomotor) is important to a well-balanced quality program of physical education. Try not to fall into the trap of neglecting the cognitive component of your curriculum to ensure ample physical activity. Instead, take the time to help children get the most out of new activities by teaching them the relevance of the exercises. Indeed, students need a strong background in health-related fitness concepts to better understand the value and importance of physical activity. This understanding, in turn, will help them pursue active lifestyles long after they leave your program.

Just as you plan the physical activity components of your curriculum so that they occur in an appropriate sequence, plan the knowledge components. Use the Rainbow to Youth Fitness and Active Life-styles (chapter 3, pages 19-20) to guide your selection of developmentally appropriate health-related fitness concepts. Begin with simple learning experiences that are associated with active fun and creativity found in developmental level I. Progress to level II, the level of concrete facts with relevant examples and activities that apply to a concept. Finally, move your students to independence by giving them the opportunity to problem solve and make decisions, as characterized by developmental level III. Remember, teach health-related physical fitness concepts throughout the school year, incorporating them into each unit of your curriculum.

Strategies for Teaching Fitness Concepts

You can incorporate concepts into a physical education class through five basic strategies:

- Set induction
- Teachable moments
- Class activities
- Closure
- Classroom sessions

Set Induction

Tailor this vital component of a carefully planned lesson to introduce a health-related fitness concept, giving a concrete example to create interest in the lesson's objective. In other words, don't just tell students what they'll be learning, tell them why, relating the concept to the unit you are presently teaching. Let's look at a set induction for level II. Have students find their heart rates at rest. Conduct one soccer activity two to three minutes in length, then have students take their heart rates once again. Explain why they are elevated. Say "Soccer requires a lot of running." Then make the concept connection for the students. Say "Soccer is a great exercise for your heart. To play any sport well, you must keep active and exercise on a regular basis. Today in class we will be practicing several skill drills that will call for a great deal of running. This will prepare you for soccer games and also keep you healthy."

You can also use set induction as a lecture to introduce a concept. Visual aids and props will help make your point and add interest to the lesson. Be brief and succinct, limiting your minilecture to no more than three minutes with level I, four minutes with level II, and five minutes with level III.

Teachable Moments

A great way to incorporate fitness concepts is through teachable moments. With experience, you can pinpoint class opportunities when students are ready to truly learn. This can be an exciting way to teach fitness concepts since most children find it difficult to sit and listen for more than a few minutes in physical education class!

For example, at level I, you may find a quiet, shy child laughing and having fun during a game activity. Reinforce this behavior by letting the student know how great it is to see him enjoying your physical education class. Then, ask him how he feels when he plays and moves with his friends. This type of interaction will begin to create a positive feeling within the student about physical activity. At level III during a basketball activity, you may notice a student who is constantly losing possession of the ball by having it taken from her hands. Through private instruction, show the student specific skill techniques to protect the ball. Then, help the student increase wrist and forearm strength (see chapter 11 for specific exercises). Explain how she needs muscular strength and endurance to control the ball, rebound, and even shoot baskets. The student will appreciate your concern and feel supported.

Class Activities

Incorporate fitness concepts into the class activity itself. Task cards can help introduce or reinforce a concept, such as muscle identification at a fitness station (see chapter 4). A game-related activity such as Jogging Through the Circulatory System will help children understand the cardiovascular benefits of exercise (see description later in this chapter). Games can reinforce fitness concepts, such as learning food groups through active participation.

Closure

Don't simply summarize the activity: Use this vital lesson component to teach or reinforce a fitness concept. You can briefly review the concept that you introduced during the set induction portion of the class. Or you can integrate a health-related fitness concept example with the specific sport or game activity the class just completed. At level III, you might remark "OK class, it seems everyone is making progress developing their dribbling skills. Just remember to keep your head up so you can see the entire court. Also, remember to keep exercising since basketball does require a great deal of cardiorespiratory endurance. What types of cardiorespiratory endurance exercises would be helpful for the sport of basketball? Who can identify other types of exercises that may help basketball players?" In this example, you refer to the class objective—dribbling skills—as well as a fitness concept, cardiorespiratory endurance. Another technique is to have a varsity basketball player visit your classes to discuss her exercise routine, preseason and in-season workouts, and how they helped her become an effective player.

Classroom Sessions

Sometimes, a few minutes during regular lessons in the gym are not enough for teaching fitness concepts. So occasionally hold a classroom session to prepare and motivate students for upcoming class activities. Take the opportunity to present a concept with added depth through a variety of classroom techniques and visual aids. Videotapes, slides, overhead transparencies, books, handouts, guest speakers, and cooperative learning groups can all help you expand upon a concept. But avoid scheduling classroom sessions only when there is inclement weather or a facility problem. If you use fitness concept education as a replacement lesson, it will give students the message that concepts are only a filler when something goes wrong—rather than valuable instruction. Instead, schedule and plan these class periods at least one day per month—another way to routinely incorporate fitness concepts into each unit of your physical education curriculum. (See also chapters 7 and 10 for ways to gain parent and classroom teacher collaboration to integrate concepts into other subjects and daily life.)

Scope and Sequence

Tables 9.1, 9.2, and 9.3 represent scope and sequence models for developmental levels I, II, and III. Each month focuses on a different health-related fitness concept. When you have a fitness concept theme planned, you can easily organize several relevant learning activities throughout the month to facilitate the primary concept. As children move through the developmental levels, you can repeat the primary concepts adding appropriate information to advance student understanding of the concepts.

Study the following learning activity examples to get more ideas as to how you might incorporate fitness concepts into your physical education classes throughout the year. Think about how you can best include these concepts in your program.

Table 9.1 Developmental Level I Fitness Concepts: Fitness Is Fun		
Title	**Concepts**	**Month**
Fit Is Fun	Promotion of an active lifestyle. Send the message: Fitness is fun with friends and family.	September
I'm Important—Inside and Out	Children learn to feel good about themselves and their bodies.	October
Body Part Identification	Body part identification. Body awareness. Exercise is important to growth and development.	November
Fitness Is for Everybody	All children must be included in physical activity. Developing sensitivity to others.	December & January
Superpump	How the heart works, listen to the beat, value of exercise, types of exercise.	February
Safety First	Rest, exercise, safety precautions (e.g., heat, water breaks, sneakers, traffic safety).	March
Fuel for Fitness	Eating healthy snacks, making good food choices, weight control.	April
Summer Fitness Fun	Swimming, summer fitness ideas, biking, swimming, hiking. Review of major concepts.	May & June

Table 9.2   Developmental Level II Fitness Concepts: The Best I Can Be

Title	Concepts	Month
Superstretch	Warming up: static stretching techniques, flexibility exercises.	September
Muscle Mania	Muscle identification and accompanying exercises.	October
The Heart Facts	Basic anatomy of the heart, circulation, effects of exercise, safety (e.g., exercising in heat).	November
Back to the Basics	Neck and back care, anatomy, posture, lifting techniques, dangerous exercises.	December & January
Heart Healthy Habits	Eating and exercising for heart health.	February
Exercise Techniques	Critical components of exercise movements, proper body alignment, and positioning.	March
Body Systems	How exercise impacts different body systems: skeletal, muscular, nervous, circulatory, digestive, respiratory.	April
My Choice	Promoting student choice, decision making, and responsibility for physical activity.	May
Recreational Time	Selecting recreational activities to promote an active lifestyle (e.g., hiking, swimming, biking, individual and team sports, skating, and the like).	June

Table 9.3   Developmental Level III Fitness Concepts: Let's Get Heart Smart

Title	Concepts	Month
Wellness	Wellness concepts: physical, mental, social, emotional, spiritual. Exercise techniques. Establishing a personal fitness education portfolio.	September
Heart Smart	Risk factors of heart disease, anatomy, good and bad cholesterol, heart healthy foods, snacks. Effects of exercise on the heart.	October
Health-Related Physical Fitness Principles	Why fitness? Components of health-related fitness: FITT (frequency, intensity, time, type of exercise). Interval techniques, heart rate, training heart rate, recovery stages of a workout. Identifying, preventing, and treating injuries.	November & December
Exercise Science	Basic anatomy and physiology. Exercise foundations, specificity, progression, overload, reversibility, train and maintain.	January & February
Food for Fitness	Heart healthy nutrition for an active lifestyle. Food Guide Pyramid, snacking ideas, food for fuel.	March
Family Fitness and Community Involvement	Parent and student homework assignments, family activities, parent and child learning experiences.	April
Personal Fitness Education Portfolio Review	Review of goal setting, designing an individualized program, logging eating and exercise patterns. Monitoring fitness levels. Review main exercise concepts.	May
Fitness Forever	Understanding fitness levels, techniques to improve scores, designing independent workouts, making responsible lifestyle choices. Planning for summer fitness.	June

Developmental Level I Fitness Concepts: Fitness Is Fun

Fit Is Fun

Concept ----------------------------- Students express why they like the physical activity in physical education class.

Equipment ----------------------------- Large colored banner paper, instant camera with film, tape, markers, magazines, and one pair of scissors per student.

Activities ----------------------------- Select one grade level for this project. Take individual pictures of each student moving. Attach the pictures to a large piece of colored banner paper for each class. Label the banner "Fit Is Fun." Ask your students to cut out pictures from magazines of active people to add to the collage. Then have students write a word or draw a picture under their photos about physical activity. Finally, have students write what they enjoy most about physical education. (Teachers may have to write what younger students dictate or have older "buddies" do so.)

    This is a great activity just before an open house at the beginning of the school year. Place the banners for each grade you select around the gym or in the hallway.

Body Part Identification

Concept ----------------------------- Students practice body part identification and develop body awareness.

Equipment ----------------------------- Chalk, outdoor playground surface, large roll of colored banner paper, and markers.

Activities ----------------------------- Before class, draw a large figure of a child about 15 feet long on the outdoor playground surface with colored chalk. Divide the class in half, making one group the "hearts," and the second group, the "smarts." Call out specific directions, such as, "Hearts walk to the knee, smarts skip to the ears. Hearts gallop to the elbow, smarts hop to the ankle." Remind students to stay in their own personal spaces.

    Divide students into pairs. Give each pair a section of banner paper and a marker. Have each student trace the other lying on the paper. When they are finished, have them draw in the body parts they have learned. Then ask them to verbally identify different body parts.

I'm Important—Inside and Out

Concept ----------------------------- Students learn that as they become older, they grow, becoming stronger, enabling them to do advanced physical activities.

Equipment ----------------------------- 5 to 6 feet of cord, 5 clothespins, 5 socks of different sizes (infant to adult), 5 clothespins, 5 index cards, markers.

Activities ----------------------------- Attach the cord along a wall or fasten it between two standards to resemble a clothesline. Hang five different socks on the cord of various sizes from infant to adult. Attach an index card to each sock identifying the appropriate age. Have students identify the differences between the socks. They will notice the socks get bigger as the wearer gets older. Ask them to describe the changes people go through as they get older: physically, mentally, and socially. Ask "What kind of physical activities can an infant, 6-year-old, 10-year-old, 16-year-old, adult do? Why can't a 6-year-old run as fast or climb as well as a 10-year-old?" They will probably remark "Because the 10-year-old is bigger." Reinforce that physical activity promotes growth and makes bones and muscles stronger. Ask "What other body parts change in size as a person gets older?"

Fitness Is for Everybody

Concept --------------------------- Students learn about the physical differences among people.

Equipment ----------------------- Mats, playground equipment, playballs.

Activities ------------------------- Ask students to think about the people in their neighborhood. Ask them to describe them; short, tall, dark, light, blonde hair, black hair, thin, heavy. Remind the class that people are different and that is a wonderful, natural part of life. "Just as people are different looking—they also have different physical abilities. Just think about our class; some are strong, fast, or quick, and some are graceful and very coordinated. Over the next few minutes think about what you do best and practice that activity or exercise." After a few minutes ask each student to demonstrate and explain what they do best.

Each student should be guided to a certain physical ability. For example, a student with a weight problem may be able to exercise with the "heavy" resistance bands or may be powerful enough to pick up a tumbling mat. The student who may be unskilled may be very flexible. A student confined to a wheelchair may perform arm exercises. At the end of the activity, emphasize that exercise, games, and sports are for everybody. It's just that some students have certain abilities, but everyone has their own personal strengths.

Safety First

Concept --------------------------- Students learn about exercise breaks, use of water during exercise, and traffic safety.

Equipment ----------------------- 15 to 20 cones, 1 medium-sized hoop for each student, paper stop signs.

Activities ------------------------- Plot a simple roadway course on your gym floor or outdoor facility. Use cones to create driving lanes and place stop signs at some intersections. Provide each driver with a medium-sized hoop to use as a steering wheel. Have students tell you what type of car they are driving (give them hints: Jaguar, Bronco, van, and so on).

Send students through the course four at a time. Students may only jog, not sprint, to pass other students or to go in reverse. When they come to a stop sign, they must make a full stop, then look left-right-left.

Set up a water station to allow the automobiles to cool off and rest. Remind students "Everyone needs water and rest periods when they exercise to be safe, especially in hot weather." Teach and reinforce personal safety: Allow several students to be pedestrians crossing at an intersection. Students must look left-right-left for oncoming automobiles.

Developmental Level II Fitness Concepts: The Best I Can Be

Superstretch

Concept ---------------------------- Students recognize that flexibility is the range of motion of a joint. Stretching prevents muscle and connective tissue injuries, improves the range of motion in order to fully benefit from the activity, and prevents muscle soreness that overtraining can cause.

Equipment ---------------------- 1 pound of uncooked spaghetti, 1 pound of cooked spaghetti, 1 tennis ball (kept warm), 1 tennis ball (from freezer).

Activities ------------------------ Explain the need for warming up before physical activity. Say "We need to raise the temperature of our muscles before stretching through a couple of minutes of large muscle activity like jogging or brisk walking. A warmed muscle is less likely to become injured because it takes more force and stretching to tear the muscle. Experts now feel that to improve flexibility we may be better off stretching directly after an exercise or activity session since the muscles are warm and circulation is increased." Give examples of typical activities such as little league games, physical education class, housework, and gardening. Then, demonstrate the difference between warm and cold muscles. Hold up one pound of uncooked spaghetti, which represents a group of cold muscle fibers. Remark that the muscle fibers are cool, stiff, and brittle, limiting any movement. Now hold up a pound of cooked spaghetti. Show the class how warm and flexible muscles can move and bend more freely.

Demonstrate the same concept with two tennis balls. First, bounce the warm ball. Ask the class to notice how high it bounces. Next, bounce the frozen ball. Reinforce the difference in performance between the two tennis balls.

Have students practice a typical warm-up:

- Walking in large circle (30 seconds)
- Walking with long strides (30 seconds)
- Walking briskly (30 seconds)
- Jogging slowly (30 seconds)
- Static stretching (2 minutes)

Muscle Mania

Concepts -------------------------- Students practice muscle identification, learn the difference between muscle contraction and relaxation, and learn specific exercises for arm muscles.

Equipment ---------------------- 1 long balloon, posterboard for task card, markers, several exercise toners (rubberized resistance equipment).

Activities ------------------------ Ask students to extend their arms with palms facing the ceiling. Show the class where the bicep is located. Have students place the opposite hand across the muscle. Remark that the muscle appears flat. Now ask them to "make a muscle," keeping the hand on the bicep muscle. As the muscle pops up, explain that the muscle is contracting.

Blow up the long balloon. Grab both ends and stretch it (see figure 9.1). Show the class that the balloon becomes *elongated* (stretched out) just like a muscle when it is relaxed. Then explain the concept that a muscle in a *contracted* state will shorten and become wider. Tell students that the balloon is now going to contract. Push gently from both ends to make the balloon come back slightly. Have students describe why the balloon becomes wider. (Because it shortens; Meeks and Heit 1992).

Design a fitness station with arm strength and endurance as its primary focus. Develop a task card with the picture of the entire arm illustrating the bicep. Color the bicep red and label it. Describe the arm curl movement using the exercise toner (see chapter 11) and illustrate it on the task card. Ask students to perform the arm curl five repetitions with the resistance toner of their choice.

Figure 9.1   Muscle contraction using long balloon.

The Heart Facts I

Concept ----------------------------- Students learn the benefits of good circulation: Exercise will increase blood flow throughout the body and help keep the veins and arteries from clogging.

Equipment ---------------------- 2 rubber tubes about 2 feet long, small pieces of Play-Doh, 2 cups of water, cranberry juice, gym tape, hula hoops, posters, markers, cones, 2 boxes, tennis balls, paper balls.

Activities ----------------------- Hold up two separate pieces of rubber tubing approximately two feet in length. Tell students "The tubes represent arteries, which carry blood from the heart." Fill one tube with a few pieces of Play-Doh and keep the other clear. Pour a cup of cranberry juice through the clear tube. Ask "See how easily and free-flowing the juice passes through?" Now, pour a cup of juice through the tube with Play-Doh. The juice will trickle. Explain "Exercise may help keep your arteries clear so blood may get to various parts of your body. Eating fatty foods (e.g., cheeseburgers, ice cream) and not getting enough exercise can clog your arteries. What other fatty foods might clog your arteries?"

Jogging Through the Circulatory System: Have students act as the blood traveling through the heart, arteries, and veins (see figure 9.2). Explain "The arteries and veins are the one-way highways that the blood travels through." Remind students of the following concepts: "Arteries carry blood away from the heart, veins carry blood to the heart. The blood carries oxygen to the working parts of the body. As you jog through the lungs, pick up oxygen (tennis ball) and deposit (leave) carbon dioxide (a ball made of paper). As you enter the working parts of the body, deposit the oxygen and pick up the carbon dioxide. Jog throughout the system following red arrows on the gym floor. Read the signs that tell you the different areas of the circulatory system. Bright red signs mark the parts of the system with oxygen. Light brown signs mark the parts without oxygen" (Kern 1987; Ratliffe and Ratliffe 1994). Refer to figure 9.3 to see the anatomy of the heart.

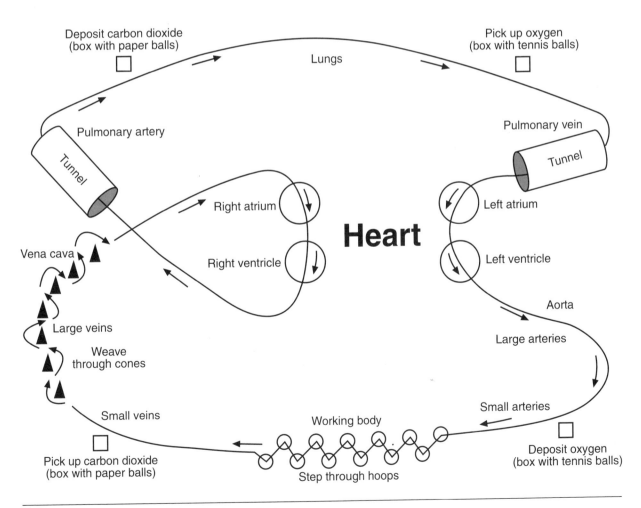

Figure 9.2   Jogging Through the Circulatory System.

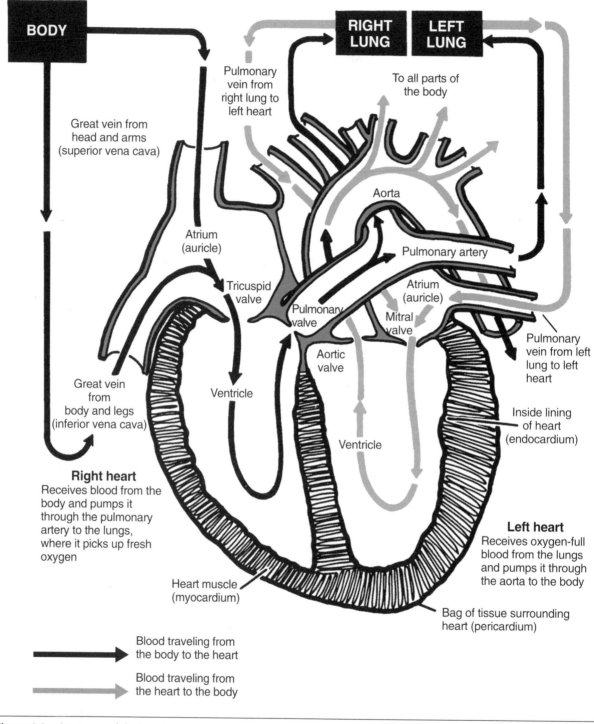

Figure 9.3 Anatomy of the heart.
Source: American Heart Association.

The Heart Facts II

Concept -------------------------- Students explore safety at home, especially the warning signs of a heart attack, and learn that exercise may prevent heart disease.

Equipment ---------------------- 6 cones.

Activities ------------------------- Discuss with students that when there is an emergency at home, they should call 911, stay on the phone, and give the operator specific information, such as their name, address, and the situation.

Review the warning signs that tell us someone is having a heart attack:

- Shortness of breath
- Clutching left side of chest
- Pain down the left arm

Heart Alert! Reinforce your discussions with this active game. Mark boundaries in the gym with cones. Select two "its" who will be taggers. Explain "At the signal 'Go!' the its try to tag the rest of you. The first time a student gets tagged, he grabs his chest. The second time, he grabs his left arm. The third time, he grabs his throat and yells 'Heart alert! Heart alert!' Then another student runs over to him, and they both perform 10 power jumps (jumping straight up as high as possible). After doing the power jumps, the student who had the heart alert is symptom-free. But the other student keeps any symptoms he already had from being tagged earlier. While the two students are exercising, they are safe from the 'its' tagging them again." Rotate the "its" every two minutes using a random selection process such as picking names from a hat.

Back to the Basics

Concept ------------------------- Students learn about back anatomy and proper posture, specifically: The vertebral bones and disks are the supportive columns and cushions for the entire upper body, and correct posture is important for a healthy back.

Equipment ----------------------- 4 hockey pucks, table, 3 jelly donuts, 5.5-foot piece of white string per small group, 1 small 3- to 5-pound dumbbell.

Activities ------------------------- Ask the students in class to reach back and feel the bones in their backs. Then, show them a stack of four hockey pucks on a table. Explain "When you run or jump, the pucks (bones) come together. To prevent the bones from compressing (pushing) into each other, a soft jelly-like substance called a disk is located between each pair of bones." Now place the medium-sized jelly donuts between the hockey pucks. Say "The jelly donuts represent disks. One way to prevent injury to the disks (so they don't get stressed by the bones) is to have good posture.

Poor posture can lead to backaches. Flexibility and strong neck and back muscles are very important to good posture." (See chapter 11 for specific exercises.) Tie a weight to a piece of white string that is as long as the students are tall. In pairs or small groups of three or four, have one student hold the string just above the head of another student who is standing sideways. Or, you may want to assess each student individually. Either way, with the string hanging straight along the side of the student, check the following posture points:

- Is the head straight up or does it lean forward or backward?
- Are the upper back and shoulders even like the string or curved forward or backward?
- Are the hips even with the string or are they tilting forward or backward?

Report any significant imbalances to the school nurse and parents. You may want to assess each student to avoid any embarrassment.

Body Systems

Concept --------------------------- Students explore the effects of exercise on the digestive system.

Equipment --------------------- 1 22-foot piece of white yarn.

Activities ------------------------ Crumble the yarn against your body where the intestines are located. Explain "The yarn represents the intestines. A section of the intestines called the 'small intestines' is the part through which food is absorbed into the bloodstream. The other section is called the 'large intestines' where food is released from the body." Have two children hold the yarn in a straight line. Ask students to guess the length of the small and large intestines.

Explain that active play and vigorous exercise help you digest your food properly by allowing the blood to flow evenly so the intestines can work better. Remind students that after a complete meal, they should wait at least one to two hours before participating in vigorous physical activity. The digestive system needs the blood flow for a period of time to help process the food; exercise would interrupt this and may cause nausea. Ask "What exercises would help improve digestion?" (Walking, jogging, biking, swimming, hiking, active games, any continuous large muscle activity.) Explain to students that one of the reasons why you ask them to do curl-ups is to strengthen the abdominal muscles, the supportive area of the intestines. Strong abdominal muscles protect the digestive system and help keep the intestines in the right place so they can digest properly. Say "If the abdominal muscles are flabby and weak, the intestines will move lower and not work as well. This is why some adults have stomachaches."

Developmental Level III Fitness Concepts: Let's Get Heart Smart

Wellness

Concept --------------------------- Students consider accepting friends for what they are as people, not what they look like, and recognize that games and sports are a good way to enjoy old friends and an opportunity to make new friends.

Equipment --------------------- 1 roll of yarn, 1 book with a plain cover, 1 book with a colorful cover but that has blank pages, 1 large parachute.

Activities ------------------------ Show the class two books, the plain book and the colorful, fancy book. Ask "Which book do you like the best? Why?" (Most students will prefer the colorful book.) Now show them what is inside the fancy book: nothing but blank sheets of paper. Now explain to them that the plain book is an important work of a famous author. Explain "Just because someone is a little heavy or they wear glasses, it does not make them less of a person. That's just the outside. What really counts is what's on the inside." Ask "Have you heard the expressions 'Beauty is only skin deep' or 'You can't judge a book by its cover?' These old expressions hold true even more so today!"

Friendship Knots: Have students sit in a large circle. Take a roll of yarn, tie it around your index finger and state a human characteristic that you like in friends, for example, "Honesty." Now pass the yarn around the circle and have each student tie a knot around his or her index finger and state a positive human characteristic he or she values. When everyone has had a chance, ask the class what the yarn has done. (It connected us together.) Explain to the group that classes in school should work together as a team, help each other, and develop close friendships.

Parachute Jog: Have each student grasp the parachute with the inside hand. Explain that they will be going on a class jog up to the large oak tree and back. Say "Some in class are faster runners, but in this activity, everyone has to stay together as a class." Jog with the class the first time you introduce this activity, reinforcing working as a team and some of the positive characteristics mentioned earlier in the class.

Hold up a poster with the word TEAM written on it. On the back of the poster show the class what team stands for: Together Everyone Achieves More. Ask students to describe the benefits of teamwork when they play a game or team sport. Ask them to name a popular professional team that plays well together and is a good example of sportsmanship.

Components of Health-Related Physical Fitness Principles

Concept ----------------------------Students learn that the components of health-related physical fitness are cardiorespiratory endurance, muscular strength, muscular endurance, flexibility, and body composition and that they can develop each component by incorporating certain exercises into a balanced physical activity plan.

Equipment ----------------------5 boxes, each labeled as a different fitness component and colorfully decorated; 20 3-by-5 index cards, each labeled with various activities or foods (e.g., 10 push-ups, 10 curl-ups, jog in place, frozen yogurt, sit-and-reach, and so on).

Activities ------------------------Organize a learning station for a small group of students. Set up the five fitness component boxes. Offer task cards face down to students so they can each select one. Have them turn their cards over, perform the activities on the cards, then place them in the appropriate fitness component boxes. Have at least 2 cards for each member of the group so the students can repeat the process. When the students are finished, go over to the boxes and check the cards. If you find mistakes, don't ask who placed them incorrectly. Simply reinforce the correct answers.

Health-Related Physical Fitness Principles: Intensity of Exercise

Concept ----------------------------Students learn that intensity of exercise refers to how vigorous an activity must be to help develop the specific area of fitness; that they might, at times, exercise at a level that is too high for their individual needs; and that higher levels can become dangerous and often result in muscle injury.

Equipment ----------------------Paper and pencil for each student.

Activities ------------------------Say "To have a safe, productive physical activity session, you should monitor your intensity level. Knowing how your body responds to activity can also help you plan your individual fitness program. One way to monitor cardiorespiratory endurance is by calculating your target heart rate zone (THRZ). To figure out what your THRZ is, follow the three-step formula." Display this example of a 12-year-old child's calculations:

1. Subtract 220 minus age to get the maximum rate (MHR). 220 – 12 = 208.

2. 208 (MHR) × 0.70 = 146 beats per minute.

3. 208 (MHR) × 0.80 = 166 beats per minute.

THRZ = 146 to 166 beats per minute.

Have students calculate their own THRZs. Have them work in pairs in case the math is too difficult for some students.

Several heart rate monitors are on the market. The monitors are a fun and easy way to show students their intensity levels during physical activity. Encourage students to adjust their intensity levels according to the digital readouts of their heart rate.

Many heart rate monitors (figure 9.4) consist of a wristwatch and chestband device. Students may program their THRZ into this device. An alarm will sound if the student falls out of the zone. Some monitors also allow you to store heart rates into a memory bank so you can play them back and record them at a later time. Computer programs are now available to record and analyze scores using interface software for the IBM PC and Macintosh. (See Polar Electro, Inc., in appendix B for more information.)

Figure 9.4   Heart rate monitor.

Health-Related Physical Fitness Principles: Heart Rate Recovery

Concept ---------------------------Students learn that their heart rates will increase less during exercise and will return to a normal level faster after exercise if they lead active lives than if they lead sedentary lives.

Equipment ---------------------Stopwatch, 1 bench (or box) 8 inches from ground level for each student, 1 chair (or bench) for each student. Optional: Metronome.

Activities ------------------------- (*Caution:* Students who have experienced knee problems in the past should not participate in this assessment.) This is a baseline assessment to teach students the concept of HR recovery. Begin with three to five minutes of warm-up. Then say "At the signal 'Begin!' start with your right foot and step up on the box (or bench), then step down again (four count: left-right-up, left-right-down). Continue stepping up and down, alternating feet for three consecutive minutes at a rate of 24 steps per minute (two steps every five seconds)." A metronome can help maintain the rhythm, or students can count in unison. Stop at the three-minute mark and have the students sit on their chairs (or on benches). At exactly one minute after completing the test, have the students take their pulses for 30 seconds, then multiply by two to obtain a one-minute pulse recovery score.

Average HR recovery scores for boys ages 10 to 19 should be 72 to 88 beats per minute. Girls the same age should range from 82 to 96 beats per minute. Heart rate above these levels could mean a student needs to increase physical activity to enhance cardiorespiratory endurance. Scores closer to the lower end may indicate higher levels of cardiorespiratory endurance and heart rate recovery.

If you decide to retest periodically, remember to assess under the same conditions, equipment, time of day, exact warm-up routine, and test procedures.

Exercise Science: Overload Principle

Concept -------------------------- Use the overload principle to improve cardiorespiratory and muscular fitness by exercising at higher than normal levels. This involves working against increased resistance to progressively make advances in physical development.

Equipment --------------------- 1 pound of regular spaghetti, 1 pound of angel hair pasta, 1 pound of thick spaghetti, 1 exercise tube with handles for every 2 students (rubberized tubing), 1 resistance band for each student.

Activities ----------------------- Divide the students into pairs and have one partner stand behind the other. Have the front partner place an exercise tube around his waist and the back partner hold the rubber tubing by the handles, applying light resistance (see figure 9.5) Tell both partners to walk briskly in the same direction. Point out that the front partner should experience how much more difficult it is to have the band resist movement. Reverse roles and repeat. The resistance provides an overload to the normal walking movement.

Hold up one pound of regular spaghetti. Explain "Each piece of spaghetti represents a muscle fiber and many fibers make up the muscle. When you increase the resistance on a muscle, the muscle fibers grow thicker." Hold up the pound of angel hair spaghetti. Remark "This is how the muscle fibers look before you begin an resistance program for muscular strength and endurance." Now hold up the thick spaghetti. "The fibers (just like the spaghetti) become larger when you progressively increase the resistance in your muscular strength exercises."

Explain to the class that lifting weights or using the exercise machines may be dangerous without the supervision of a trained instructor. Give examples of how students may safely practice this principle by slightly increasing their jogging distance, doing two more push-ups with open

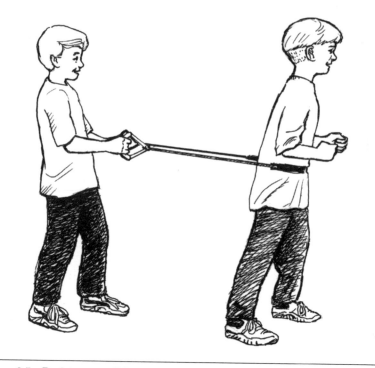

Figure 9.5 Resistance walking.

hands or using the next color level of the rubberized resistance exercise toners or bands.

Have students do several leg kicks from a standing position in front, back, side, marching step, and cross-kicking. Now have them use a resistance band suited for their levels. Do the same leg movement exercises. (See chapter 11 for instructions.) Ask "How does the added resistance feel on your leg muscles?" (Harder, heavier.) Explain "This resistance will build strength in the particular muscle group you exercise."

Food for Fitness

Concept ----------------------------- Students learn that eating according to the Food Guide Pyramid can help limit the fat in their diet and increase the complex carbohydrates and fiber. Eating properly will aid in physical performance and energy levels.

Equipment ---------------------- 1 Food Guide Pyramid for each student (U.S. Department of Agriculture, U.S. Department of Health and Human Services), 4 cones, 4 paper grocery bags, pictures of various food groups on a different color paper for each bag, chalk or gym tape, 1 large Food Guide Pyramid drawn on gym floor or outdoor surface as shown in figure 9.6.

Activities ----------------------- Hand out copies of the Food Guide Pyramid to each student. Explain to the class the importance of the number of recommended servings per day. Discuss how you can increase energy levels by eating more calories from

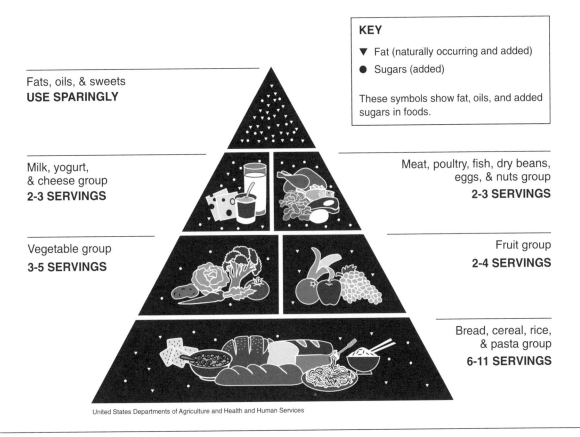

Fats, oils, & sweets
USE SPARINGLY

KEY

▼ Fat (naturally occurring and added)
● Sugars (added)

These symbols show fat, oils, and added sugars in foods.

Milk, yogurt,
& cheese group
2-3 SERVINGS

Meat, poultry, fish, dry beans,
eggs, & nuts group
2-3 SERVINGS

Vegetable group
3-5 SERVINGS

Fruit group
2-4 SERVINGS

Bread, cereal, rice,
& pasta group
6-11 SERVINGS

United States Departments of Agriculture and Health and Human Services

Figure 9.6   The Food Guide Pyramid.

bread, pasta, fruits, and vegetables than foods with empty calories and high sugar content, such as chocolate cake, ice cream, or candy bars. Remind them to use their nutrition log (in their personal fitness education portfolio) to keep track of their daily eating (see appendix A).

Pyramid Power: (Before class: Paste pictures of various foods on colored paper. Have the students help cut out pictures from magazines in previous classes, reinforcing a nutritional concept while saving you time. Use four different colors of paper so that each team will have its own color. Fill a paper grocery bag with pictures of food for each team. Position the large Food Guide Pyramid on the gym floor and label the sections.) Divide the class into four groups. Give each team one grocery bag. Place the four teams in lines 25 yards from the Pyramid. Use a cone to mark where each team should line up. "At the signal 'Go!' the first student from each team reaches down and grabs a food picture, then runs to the place on the Pyramid where it belongs. Then the student runs back, gives a high five to the next student, who goes next." The first team to finish is not the winner. (Remind students of this before they do the activity.) Go over to the Pyramid and check the food pictures placed in the Pyramid sections by matching the color to the team. The winning group is the one with the most correct responses. Say "And you thought this was another typical relay race!"

Summary

We must teach more health-related physical fitness content in our physical education programs so that our students will have the knowledge they need to lead healthy, active lives. But how do you find the time without reducing physical activity time? A well-designed curriculum plan is the answer, one that includes important fitness concepts planned in sequence each year throughout the elementary school experience. Use the examples of a yearly plan for each developmental level and the sample learning activities as models of how to incorporate fitness education into your program without sacrificing precious physical activity time.

Encouraging children to achieve their personal fitness goals and increase their physical activity levels remain as very important objectives in a fitness education program. I cannot stress enough, however, that knowing "why" they are doing certain activities is just as valuable as doing the activities themselves. Most importantly, however, knowledge builds a foundation for understanding and valuing health-related fitness. This, in turn, increases the probability that your students will develop healthy and active long-term behaviors. So integrate fitness education into your program as you hope your students will integrate fitness and physical activity into their lives.

Collaborating With the Classroom Teacher

> *Reading furnishes our minds only with materials of knowledge; it is thinking that makes what we read ours.*
>
> —John Locke

Most of us simply do not have enough time to accomplish the cognitive, affective, and psychomotor objectives of a yearly physical education curriculum. Classroom teachers at the elementary school level can be an important ally in helping you reach your program goals. Certainly, if you intend to develop positive long-term attitudes toward the benefits of physical activity in your students, then the classroom teacher should become a member of your team (Virgilio 1996).

In this chapter, I'll provide you with practical strategies for developing a cooperative relationship with the classroom teacher and a sample of a cardiovascular health thematic unit with instructional activities for developmental level II to help you begin your collaborative relationship. This interdisciplinary unit incorporates content around a major theme into several subject areas. Then, I'll illustrate how you can integrate health-related physical fitness concepts into the subject matter content areas of the classroom at other levels as well.

Collaborating With the Classroom Teacher

Classroom teachers serve as excellent role models for young children and have extraordinary potential as change agents. With the exception of family members, few people have more influence on the health of children than the elementary teacher (Downey et al. 1987). As a former elementary physical educator, I have worked with hundreds of elementary classroom teachers at three different public schools, and as a teacher educator, I have interacted with thousands more through professional seminars and workshops. In general, I have found elementary classroom teachers to be caring individuals, sensitive to the needs of their students, and receptive to new ideas. Classroom teachers become especially interested in physical education objectives when they can clearly see the educational as well as the health benefits for students in their own classrooms.

The responsibility for establishing a close relationship with the classroom teacher is yours; you must initiate the interaction. Classroom teachers are not very comfortable with the subject of health-related physical fitness. As the authority, they expect you to provide the leadership in this area, educating both the students and the faculty about the benefits of an active, healthy lifestyle.

Administrative Support

To ensure success gain the administrative support of the principal and school steering committee. Arrange a private meeting with the principal to discuss your plans to include classroom teachers in your endeavors to meet your curriculum goals. Reinforce the belief that the health and well-being of the students should be a school-wide goal shared by the entire school and community. Once you have gained the principal's support, request to meet with the school's steering committee.

Identifying Your Role

Physical education specialists are often isolated from the school curriculum and classroom teachers simply because they are considered a "special" subject. Physical educators also perceive their roles in the school as separate or different because the medium for student learning is through the physical, not through the intellect. This traditional stereotype will inhibit collaboration. Thus, as a physical educator, you must look at yourself as a true professional and a valuable member of the school community. When you perceive yourself in this manner, others will too!

Communication Strategies

As with parents and the community, communication is the key to establishing a good relationship with classroom teachers. Follow these strategies to help open the channels of communication.

School-Wide Health Committee

Establish a school-wide wellness committee consisting of several representatives from the school and community. The ideal committee consists of two classroom teachers (one each from the primary and intermediate grade levels), the lunch director, the guidance counselor or school psychologist, a parent, and a member of the community (perhaps a senior citizen). Have the committee meet every two weeks to discuss any health issues, assessment plans, or special projects, such as a health fair. Good communication through committee meetings helps promote a multidisciplinary team approach.

Newsletter

The school-wide wellness newsletter we discussed in chapter 7 shouldn't only be for parents and students. Classroom teachers can also benefit from the health and fitness information. In addition, they'll enjoy your reports of special fitness events as much as everyone else. Insert an extra page directed solely at them that describes specific activities to help integrate health-related concepts into the classroom and announces different activities that various grade levels are participating in during physical education (Virgilio and Berenson 1988).

Meeting With Level Leaders

Ask to attend a level leader meeting. At this meeting, discuss your desire to work closely with the faculty. Provide each grade level with a copy of the scope and sequence of health-related fitness concepts that you intend to cover during the year (see tables 9.1 through 9.3 for examples). Then simply ask for their help. Allow teachers to brainstorm: They will feel more enthusiastic about your plans when they know you value their input.

Faculty Meetings

Establish a physical education report as a segment for each general faculty meeting. Report upcoming events, special projects, and announce updates of the curriculum integration approach using specific examples. This is a surefire technique to keep everyone informed as you take advantage of this opportunity to motivate teachers who have yet to participate in your new curriculum strategy.

Memos and E-Mail

Send updates, announcements, and any other pertinent news in the form of a memo to the faculty on a regular basis. Create your own stationery by developing a letterhead with graphics on your computer. Or send messages via e-mail if your school has the capacity.

Education

Focus your efforts to educate the faculty on two specific areas: health-related fitness content and school curriculum materials (Downey et al. 1988). In order for you to be successful, teachers need to understand what health-related physical fitness is all about. Remember the wellness room we discussed in chapters 2 and 7? Use this as a fun way to reach and educate your colleagues. In addition, plan to provide the instructional materials and learning activities you want them to use in the classroom curriculum.

Health-Related Fitness Content

In this stage, your primary purpose is to educate the faculty and staff relative to the benefits of exercise, basic fitness principles, cardiovascular health, wellness concepts, and the like. It's also helpful if the school physical educator establishes an exercise class for the teachers and staff in addition to increasing their knowledge of physical fitness. The following are strategies to help educate the elementary classroom teachers, staff, and administrators.

- **Fitness class for teachers**: Teach a fitness class after school. Include step aerobics, resistance training, and flexibility. For each class include a health concept, such as "lowering your cholesterol" or "how to have a healthy back," as well as at least 20 minutes of physical activity. This is a great opportunity to show teachers how they can learn through the physical—as their students do. It is also a superb way to get to know your faculty better and establish deeper professional relationships.

- **Inservice workshops**: Give inservice workshops to the faculty and staff. The county or school district may sponsor this workshop and award inservice credit as an incentive for all teachers to attend and become better informed. Enlist the help of local physical education professors at a nearby university.

- **Guest speakers**: Schedule guest speakers in the area of health and fitness to speak at a faculty meeting. Speakers may also be scheduled during early bird sessions before school, lunchtime seminars, or at PTA meetings in the evening (see chapter 7).

- **Health fair**: Teachers can benefit from the information and activities at the school-wide health fair alongside parents and students (see chapter 7). Consider asking each grade level to design a health station (see also chapter 14). Request assistance from a local university, AHA, or hospital.

- **Health-fitness reading area**: If you're not able to do so in a teacher-parent wellness room, designate an area within the school library, faculty lounge, lunchroom, or curriculum lab in which teachers have an opportunity to read various articles, brochures, and books related to general health.

Curriculum Materials

A hands-on inservice workshop is the ideal setting to introduce curriculum materials to teachers. You may elect to design your own classroom activities, use published material, or pull together a combination of materials that will best match your curriculum goals. The contents of this book make an ideal resource for the classroom teacher.

Remember, however, to always keep the classroom learning activities simple, concise, and easy to follow. If the content is too technical, teachers will not feel comfortable using this new curriculum approach. Moreover, in order to match the content and concepts being taught in physical education with classroom instruction, you will need to become aware of the curriculum guidelines on each grade level for other subject areas.

Once classroom teachers recognize the value of health in their own lives and the important role it plays in the overall development of children, they will become important allies in your efforts. So let's get down to business and study sample thematic units, health-related physical fitness classroom activities, and practical strategies you can use to help, support, and guide the classroom teacher. Remember: You are the key!

Thematic Units: An Approach to Integrated Learning

Over the last several years, the thematic unit has been recognized as an exciting and challenging approach to learning at the elementary school level. The basic notion of thematic units is that learning should be integrated, multidimensional, and multidisciplinary. Simply put, a thematic approach provides students with a series of lessons on a particular topic that students find interesting and meaningful (e.g., dinosaurs, Native Americans, environmental issues, cardiovascular health), integrating a variety of subject areas, such as language arts, science, math, and art. When designing thematic units, teachers take into consideration the needs, interests, and developmental levels of their students. Furthermore, they try to incorporate a selection of children's literature and a number of instructional resources to help establish connections across the curriculum. Thematic units are planned to include a number of hands-on activities with many opportunities for decision making and critical thinking.

Thematic units enable the classroom teacher to combine students whose attitudes and skill and knowledge levels vary greatly with a wide variety of resources both in and out of the classroom. According to Meinbach, Rothlein, and Fredericks (1995), using thematic units offers numerous advantages. They refer to these advantages as the seven Cs:

1. **Contact**: Thematic units break the boundaries of the clock and schedules. This approach creates an "open" feeling to learning. The blocked time periods of traditional education, which separate one subject from another, may limit learning opportunities and motivation.

2. **Coherence**: Thematic units send children the message that learning is not an isolated activity: It takes place continuously and throughout one's life.

3. **Context**: Learning must have a purpose. Many times children study or read merely because they were told to or because the content will be on a test. Thematic units help children identify the meaning and context of the content as they apply the experiences to the real world.

4. **Connections**: Thematic units help children understand the relationships among subject areas, such as between math and language arts or between science and physical education. This approach offers the learner opportunities to make connections among the facts in different subject areas, thereby enhancing comprehension and opening the door for more meaningful learning in all subject areas.

5. **Choices**: Thematic units give students a sense of ownership of their educational time. Instead of telling students what they should learn, ask them what they would enjoy learning and how they would like to learn it. When students feel they have made important choices, they will be more active and enthusiastic learners.

6. **Cognitive expansion**: Children will inherently learn at the level they are taught. If you ask a majority of low-level or rote memory types of questions, students will approach learning in the same manner. The purpose of thematic units is to have children investigate, discover, and explore with very few predetermined answers. In fact, you can even ask children to develop their own questions, then solve the problem or research the answers on their own.

7. **Cooperation**: Learning can be enhanced by interacting with peers. Children need experiences working as a team rather than as competitors for grades. Thematic units create a purpose for cooperative learning groups when they emphasize group, rather than individual, achievement.

Cardiovascular Health: A Thematic Unit

The following is an example of a thematic unit for developmental level II. Enlist classroom teacher support by discussing with them how vital the study of cardiovascular health is to your program and how important it is to have students learn about health as a school-wide goal. Explain to them that this thematic unit will help them integrate curriculum areas, providing the students with a wide range of activities and opportunities to enhance their learning across the curriculum.

When introducing the unit on cardiovascular health, suggest that the teacher begin by assessing what the students *know* about the topic and what they *want* to learn about the topic. While the classroom teacher may have a clear direction of what content to plan for the unit, as illustrated in the cardiovascular health curriculum web (see figure 10.1), it is important to be flexible and willing to use student ideas and interests to enhance the learning experience.

Brainstorming, making lists of what students know and what questions they want to investigate, is a good method to use. At the end of the unit, ask the classroom teacher to have the students list what they have *learned* about the topic. Making and displaying these lists in the classroom is an effective technique for reinforcing the learning objectives, empowering children by allowing them to make decisions within the context of the theme.

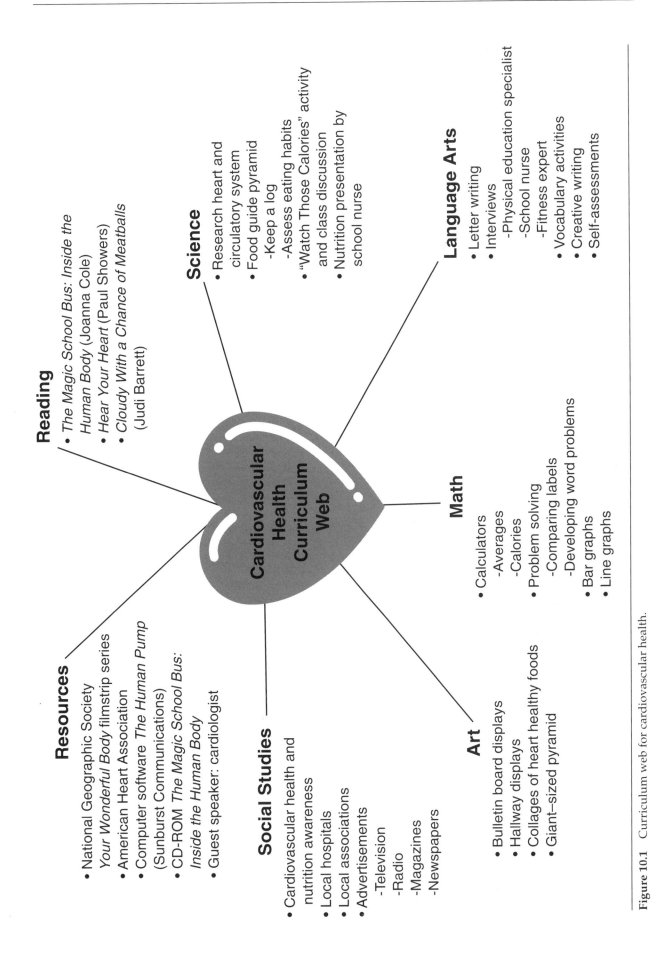

Reading
- *The Magic School Bus: Inside the Human Body* (Joanna Cole)
- *Hear Your Heart* (Paul Showers)
- *Cloudy With a Chance of Meatballs* (Judi Barrett)

Science
- Research heart and circulatory system
- Food guide pyramid
  -Keep a log
  -Assess eating habits
- "Watch Those Calories" activity and class discussion
- Nutrition presentation by school nurse

Language Arts
- Letter writing
- Interviews
  -Physical education specialist
  -School nurse
  -Fitness expert
- Vocabulary activities
- Creative writing
- Self-assessments

Resources
- National Geographic Society *Your Wonderful Body* filmstrip series
- American Heart Association
- Computer software *The Human Pump* (Sunburst Communications)
- CD-ROM *The Magic School Bus: Inside the Human Body*
- Guest speaker: cardiologist

Cardiovascular Health Curriculum Web

Math
- Calculators
  -Averages
  -Calories
- Problem solving
  -Comparing labels
  -Developing word problems
- Bar graphs
- Line graphs

Social Studies
- Cardiovascular health and nutrition awareness
- Local hospitals
- Local associations
- Advertisements
  -Television
  -Radio
  -Magazines
  -Newspapers

Art
- Bulletin board displays
- Hallway displays
- Collages of heart healthy foods
- Giant–sized pyramid

Figure 10.1   Curriculum web for cardiovascular health.

The classroom teacher can plan learning activities for specific content areas or can integrate them throughout the day in the blocks of time set aside for the unit. Although I list the following activities under the broad categories of language arts, math and science, and art, they can be easily integrated into several subject areas. The classroom teacher may use the activities as is, modify them to meet the needs of the students, or use them to supplement his or her own creative ideas on this topic.

Overall Introduction

Collaborate with the classroom teacher to collect a library of books to display and use in the classroom for this unit. When introducing a unit, the display can create excitement in the classroom about the approaching topic. Ask students to bring in other books or resources that will help in their study of cardiovascular health. Check with the local chapter of the American Heart Association for more titles and materials. Suggest that the classroom teacher introduce the idea of the importance of the heart to the body by reading *The Magic School Bus: Inside the Human Body* by Joanna Cole.

Language Arts

Suggest to the classroom teacher that the class integrate language arts skills with the content of cardiovascular health by writing and producing a "Heart Healthy Newsletter." The process of writing a newsletter automatically includes a variety of skills that are essential to children at this developmental level. Reading, writing, communication, computer applications, and math are all integrated in such a way that it brings a certain confluence to the learning experiences.

Let the students brainstorm many of the components of this newsletter and then divide the class into appropriately sized groups to handle each task. Allow students to work on more than one area in order to make the newsletter as comprehensive as possible.

Sections may include the following:

- Crossword puzzles: Use exercise and fitness terms and healthy foods.
- Wordsearches: Include important terms relating to the heart, exercise, and nutrition (see figure 10.2).

- Unscrambling activities: Scramble key words relating to the heart, exercise, and nutrition.
- Teacher highlights: Have students interview a teacher in the school who exhibits healthy eating habits or who is often seen exercising to stay healthy (e.g., walking or jogging during lunch time).
- Family involvement: Encourage students to brainstorm several family-oriented activities that would be fun to do on a weeknight or during the weekend (e.g., biking, a hiking trip at the local state park, and the like).
- Heart healthy recipes: Have students find two or three heart healthy recipes (perhaps one each for breakfast, lunch, and dinner). A list of healthy snacks for school would be also be helpful as a reminder to parents to avoid packing too many sweets!
- The Lunch Bunch: Have students interview the principal, cafeteria manager, teachers, and other students to gather information on ways to improve the school lunch program.
- Cereal Alert: Have students survey the students in the school for their favorite cereal and graph the results on a poster displayed in the hallway. Next to the graph, have students compare the labels on the five most popular cereals. Show them how to analyze the calories, fat from calories, and sodium content using the new nutrition facts label (see figure 10.3). Include these results in the newsletter as well.
- Fitness tips: Have students interview a fitness expert or you and list tips for staying healthy through physical activity.
- Nutrition tips: Have students interview the school nurse or district dietitian to help make a list of nutrition tips to share in the newsletter (e.g., list of low-fat substitutes such as skim milk, frozen yogurt, and fat-free cookies.)
- School highlights: Help students list special events that are scheduled at school such as the dates for the Jump Rope for Heart or the updated results of the Geography Run (see chapter 14).
- Family survey: Have students develop a survey to ask families about their favorite physical activities. Compile the results and list the top 10 family activities.
- A message from the school nurse: Have students interview the school nurse for a special

section of the newsletter. The message may include general health and hygiene information.

- A message from a special guest: Encourage students to interview a university faculty member or an exercise physiologist for information about the latest trends in exercise science research or the latest equipment.

Encourage the classroom teacher to work closely with the students as the editor of the newsletter. Ask that the classroom teacher provide time each day for students to use the computer, discuss progress on the various sections, and problem solve any concerns that arise. As the physical educator, you should come in once or twice during the week to consult with students, distribute materials, and offer support.

Wordsearch

H	E	A	R	T	O	B	C	Z	L
C	Y	O	G	J	O	G	E	R	W
A	O	S	Y	O	G	U	X	H	A
L	G	U	B	F	A	T	E	E	L
O	U	G	I	O	S	G	R	A	K
R	R	A	C	E	O	N	C	L	I
I	T	R	M	A	D	I	I	T	N
E	X	I	C	I	I	K	S	H	G
S	W	O	L	D	U	I	E	Y	C
S	A	T	E	O	M	B	E	A	X

Find these words:

HEART	SWIM	SUGAR
BIKING	YOGURT	CALORIES
FAT	SODIUM	WALKING
JOG	EXERCISE	HEALTHY

Figure 10.2 Wordsearch.

The new food label carries an easier to use nutrition information guide. It is to be required on almost all packaged foods (compared to about 60 percent of products until now). The label below is only an example.

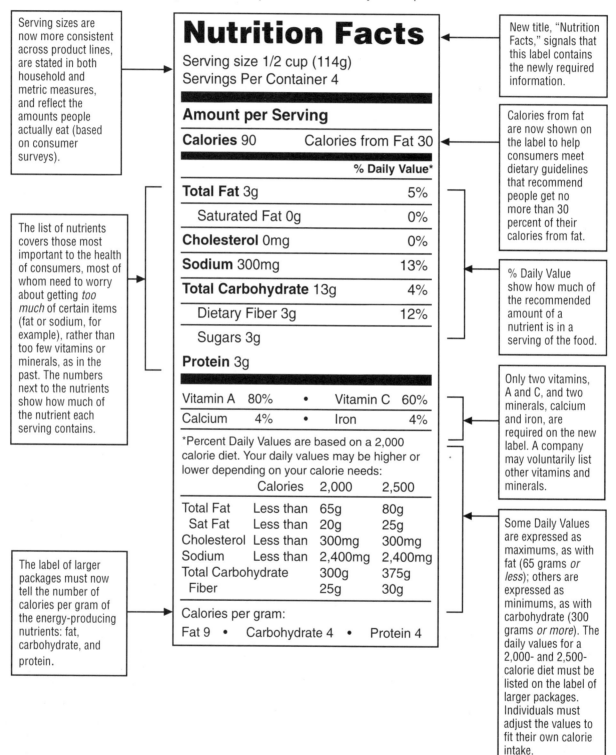

Serving sizes are now more consistent across product lines, are stated in both household and metric measures, and reflect the amounts people actually eat (based on consumer surveys).

New title, "Nutrition Facts," signals that this label contains the newly required information.

Calories from fat are now shown on the label to help consumers meet dietary guidelines that recommend people get no more than 30 percent of their calories from fat.

The list of nutrients covers those most important to the health of consumers, most of whom need to worry about getting *too much* of certain items (fat or sodium, for example), rather than too few vitamins or minerals, as in the past. The numbers next to the nutrients show how much of the nutrient each serving contains.

% Daily Value show how much of the recommended amount of a nutrient is in a serving of the food.

Only two vitamins, A and C, and two minerals, calcium and iron, are required on the new label. A company may voluntarily list other vitamins and minerals.

The label of larger packages must now tell the number of calories per gram of the energy-producing nutrients: fat, carbohydrate, and protein.

Some Daily Values are expressed as maximums, as with fat (65 grams *or less*); others are expressed as minimums, as with carbohydrate (300 grams *or more*). The daily values for a 2,000- and 2,500-calorie diet must be listed on the label of larger packages. Individuals must adjust the values to fit their own calorie intake.

Nutrition Facts
Serving size 1/2 cup (114g)
Servings Per Container 4

Amount per Serving

Calories 90   Calories from Fat 30

% Daily Value*

Total Fat 3g	5%
Saturated Fat 0g	0%
Cholesterol 0mg	0%
Sodium 300mg	13%
Total Carbohydrate 13g	4%
Dietary Fiber 3g	12%
Sugars 3g	
Protein 3g	

Vitamin A	80%	Vitamin C	60%
Calcium	4%	Iron	4%

*Percent Daily Values are based on a 2,000 calorie diet. Your daily values may be higher or lower depending on your calorie needs:

	Calories	2,000	2,500
Total Fat	Less than	65g	80g
Sat Fat	Less than	20g	25g
Cholesterol	Less than	300mg	300mg
Sodium	Less than	2,400mg	2,400mg
Total Carbohydrate		300g	375g
Fiber		25g	30g

Calories per gram:
Fat 9 • Carbohydrate 4 • Protein 4

Figure 10.3   The new food label.
Source: Food and Drug Administration, 1993.

As a culminating activity, help the classroom teacher plan a publishing party. Invite parents, administrators, school nurse, and other teachers to a special gathering in the classroom. Give each guest a copy of the published newsletter. Serve healthy snacks and refreshments to the guests. You might even consider using this classroom-generated newsletter as a school-wide project during the school year. Be sure to acknowledge the hard work done by the classroom teacher and all of the students throughout the process of planning and publishing the newsletter. Remember to emphasize the collaboration between the classroom teacher and yourself.

Math and Science

Math and science have their places in health-related physical fitness, too. In fact, integrating math and science into your curriculum can make these subjects more meaningful and interesting to children. Try these fun and relevant activities but work with the classroom teacher to ensure that the students are capable of doing the activities you choose.

• Watch Those Calories! Divide students into cooperative groups. Provide each student with a handout or make a large poster entitled "Watch Those Calories!" that describes several meal choices (see figure 10.4). Ask the students to predict which meal will prove to have the fewest calories. Then have them use a calorie chart to find the total number of calories for each meal (see figure 10.5). (Have them do calculations by hand or use calculators, depending on which specific skill the classroom teacher wishes them to practice.) Compare their predictions to the meal that was actually the lowest in calories. Discuss why the two meals are different.

• Places in the Pyramid: Ask students to keep track of their food intake for three days, recording the foods they eat on a blank handout of the food pyramid each day (see figure 10.6). Use the data to determine if students are eating nutritious meals.

Prepare a small booklet together in class, including a cover, title page, a Food Guide Pyramid record sheet for each of the three days, and a self-assessment form (see figure 10.7). At the end of the week, plan an assessment activity. Discuss what types of foods the students eat more often, whether they're eating foods from all the food groups, whether they're eating the recommended number of servings from each of the food groups, and how to improve their eating habits. Then ask the groups to make six large charts listing the foods they ate in each of the food groups. Display these charts in the classroom or hallway.

• I Can Take My Pulse! Distribute the handout "I Can Take My Pulse!" (figure 10.8). Have students record their heart rates after each of the four activities under the column labeled "Me." Make sure that students rest for a moment before they begin another activity. After completing and recording all four readings, have the students figure the class average for each one and record it under the column "class." Give a minilesson in finding averages, then let students use calculators.

Not enough room for the pulse-taking activities in the classroom? Use the hallway, too. Modify or change activities you use to meet individual needs.

• Graphing: Take the results of the I Can Take My Pulse! activity and ask the students to develop a bar graph. Make a giant-sized graph for the class to put on display. Ask students to compare their personal results and the class-wide results by creating a line graph. Students may do this activity at home with at least one family member, recording results on a line graph using different colors to denote each family member. You can also incorporate graphing activities using the food group information that the students have gathered throughout the week. For example, cooperative groups could use their charts to make bar graphs or line graphs of favorite snacks or drinks and display them in the hallway.

• Cereal searching: Have students bring in empty boxes of their favorite cereals. Begin the activity as soon as there are enough boxes for each cooperative group to do comparisons. Give a minilesson on the importance of reading labels for fat and sodium content. Discuss other items found on the labels and the importance of reading the ingredients on labels. Make transparencies of sample labels to use on the overhead so that they can easily be seen by all students. Then ask students to choose three different cereal labels and compare them for calories, fat from calories, and sodium content. Have students discuss their findings with group members and present one healthy cereal to the rest of the class, discussing why their group selected it. Prepare and share a healthy breakfast at the end of the week. Include the cereals that were found to be the healthiest. (You may wish to do this activity in conjunction with the Cereal Alert and newsletter activity already discussed.)

Watch Those Calories!

Meal choices	Total calories
1. Hamburger patty, french fries, cola	_____
2. Pizza, cola	_____
3. Three pancakes, bacon, orange juice	_____
4. Turkey, whole wheat bread, salad, water	_____
5. Cornflakes, banana, low-fat milk	_____
6. Spaghetti and meatballs, salad, water	_____
7. Tuna salad, potato chips, apple juice	_____
8. Steak, broccoli, mashed potatoes, water	_____
9. Fried shrimp, green beans, rice, cola	_____
10 Macaroni and cheese, salad, skim milk	_____
11. Chicken cutlet, baked potato, spinach	_____
12. Hot dog, french fries, cola	_____

Figure 10.4   Watch Those Calories!

Art

You can develop and enhance a child's awareness of shape, form, texture, and color by connecting art in a classroom unit of study to the child's life. Curriculum specialists have historically suggested integrating art with other subject areas in order to meet intellectual (problem-solving), emotional (self-expression), and perceptual (experiencing the environment through the senses) needs of students. It's important to include several artistic opportunities in a thematic unit to reinforce the idea of healthy lifestyles.

• Draw a giant-sized heart on the bulletin board. Ask students to make it look like a giant puzzle by

Calorie Chart

Food Item	Calories
Apple	125
Apple juice (1 cup)	120
Bacon, two strips	97
Banana	100
Broccoli (1 cup)	55
Carrots, cooked (1 cup)	44
Chicken cutlet, fried (3 ounces)	160
Cola (8 ounces)	107
Cornflakes (1 cup)	88
Egg, one scrambled	106
French fries (8)	157
Fried shrimp (3 ounces)	190
Green beans (1 cup)	30
Hamburger patty (6 ounces)	632
Hot dog	124
Macaroni and cheese (1 cup)	430
Mashed potatoes (1/2 cup)	120
Milk, low-fat 2 percent (1 cup)	120
Milk, skim (1 cup)	85
Milk, whole (1 cup)	210
Orange juice (1 cup)	120
Pancakes (3)	177
Pizza (cheese, 2 slices)	360
Potato, baked	97
Potato chips (10 chips)	115
Rice (1/2 cup)	100
Salad (1 cup)	96
Spaghetti (1 cup with 1 ounce cheese)	331
Spaghetti and meatballs (1 cup)	260
Spinach (1 cup)	92
Steak (3 ounces)	330
Tuna salad (1 cup)	350
Turkey (2 slices)	150
Water	0
Whole wheat bread (2 slices)	130

Figure 10.5   Calorie chart.

drawing small heart healthy pictures (e.g., biking, swimming, exercising, nutritious foods or meals, and so on) and adding them to the inside of the giant heart.

• After a visit from a guest speaker such as the school nurse, pediatrician, heart specialist, or the like, ask the students to create "flow charts" of the heart showing how the blood circulates throughout the heart and body.

• Have students construct a giant-sized three-dimensional Food Guide Pyramid using a variety of art materials. Display the pyramid in the hallway for other students to view.

• Invite the art teacher into your classroom to work with your students on a special project. This teamwork will benefit everyone and create a positive environment in your class and throughout the school.

Health-Related Physical Fitness Classroom Activities

The classroom learning activities for health-related physical fitness for each developmental level described here extend the concepts discussed in chapter 9. Remember to stay in close touch with the teachers in your school so they are aware of the units you will be covering throughout the year. By working closely with the classroom teachers, the fitness education concepts integrated in their classrooms can reinforce and compliment the content you are teaching in physical education.

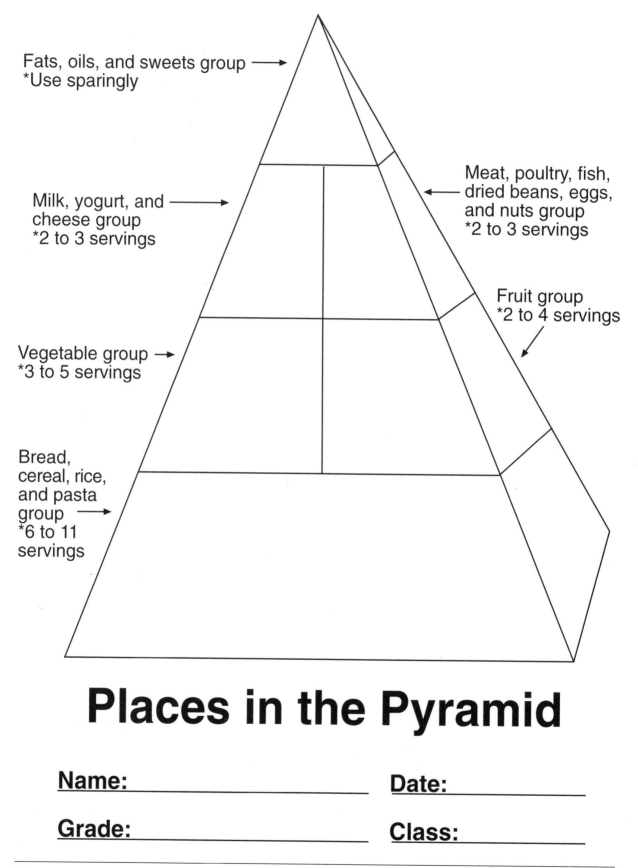

Fats, oils, and sweets group →
*Use sparingly

Meat, poultry, fish,
dried beans, eggs,
and nuts group
*2 to 3 servings

Milk, yogurt, and →
cheese group
*2 to 3 servings

Fruit group
*2 to 4 servings

Vegetable group →
*3 to 5 servings

Bread,
cereal, rice,
and pasta
group →
*6 to 11
servings

Places in the Pyramid

Name: _____   **Date:** _____

Grade: _____   **Class:** _____

Figure 10.6 Places in the Pyramid.

Places in the Pyramid Assessment

Name _____   Date _____

Grade _____   Class _____

Use this assessment sheet to tally and record the total number of foods you ate in each food group over the three-day period.

Food groups	Day 1	Day 2	Day 3	Total
Fats, oils, and sweets group				
Milk, yogurt, and cheese group				
Meat, poultry, fish, dry beans, eggs, and nuts group				
Vegetable group				
Fruit group				
Bread, cereal, rice, and pasta group				

Figure 10.7   Places in the Pyramid Assessment.

I Can Take My Pulse!

	Me	Class average
Resting (30 seconds)	____	____
Walking (30 seconds)	____	____
Jogging (30 seconds)	____	____
Jumping jacks (30 seconds)	____	____

Figure 10.8   I Can Take My Pulse!

Developmental Level I Classroom Activities

I'm Important—Inside and Out

Lesson Focus ---------------------- Children learn to value their self-worth and care about others as they become more aware of their personal health.

Equipment ----------------------- 1 pencil, 1 copy of "Me Tree" handout, and 1 colored marker for each student; cassette recorders; blank cassette tapes; construction paper; pictures of body parts; paste.

Activities ------------------------ **Language Arts**

Incorporate language arts by having students fill in the "Me Tree" illustrated in figure 10.9. Have them write the names of family members on the branches and personal strengths on the roots (e.g., athletic, funny, good student). The first name goes on the trunk. This will enhance a student's personal feelings of self-worth.

Incorporate oral language by asking students to select their favorite physical education activity. Have each student make an audiotape, stating why they enjoy that particular activity. Ask them to also include the physical activity they enjoy most at home. If you wish, ask students to interview each other, asking set questions about activity preferences. (See Sample Personal Fitness Education Portfolio, "My Favorites," in appendix A.)

Science

Have students make a list of their favorite body parts (knees, hands, toes, and so on). Ask them to explain what they like about these particular body parts.

Math

Ask students to solve the "Body Part Addition" worksheet illustrated in figure 10.10. This makes a good cooperative learning activity.

Art

Ask students to give some color to the Me Tree and also create a scene of children playing around the tree. When the class has completed this activity, display the artwork in the classroom. After two to three weeks, send the Me Tree home with each student and have them share the activity with their families. Remind students not to color over the words on the "Me Tree."

Divide students into groups of four. Provide each group with a number of body part pictures you've cut out from magazines. Ask students to select different body parts to develop an entire body by pasting the parts on a large piece of colored construction paper. (Older students or parent volunteers may help you with this activity.)

Safety First: Rest and Exercise

Lesson Focus -------------------- Children learn that they need to rest periodically during vigorous physical activity. They should be aware of the basic signals of their body telling them to slow down or take a short break.

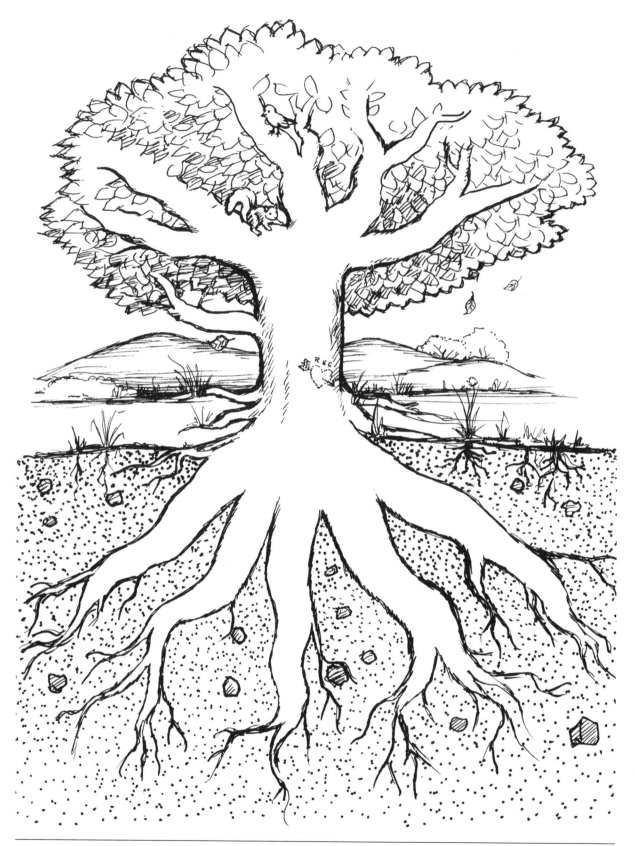

Figure 10.9   Me Tree.

Body Part Addition

Count the number of body parts and write the number on the blank to the right. Now add and find the total number of body parts.

Body part		**How many**
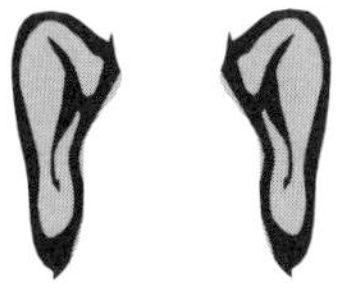	Ears	_____
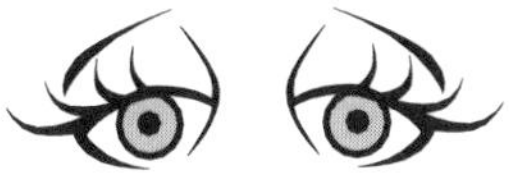	Eyes	_____
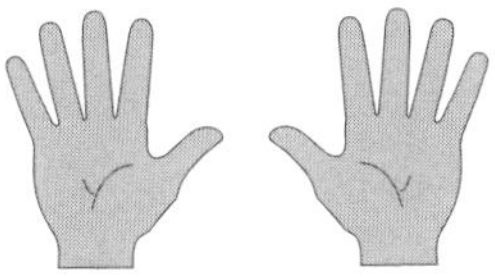	Fingers	_____
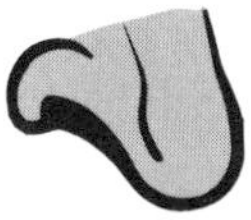	Nose	_____
	Shoulders	_____

Total number of body parts _____

Figure 10.10   Body Part Addition.

Equipment ----------------------1 ruler or 1 large pencil, 1 twist tie, and 1 pair of scissors for each student; several magazines.

Activities ------------------------**Language Arts**
Review the recommended responses to fatigue or overexertion:

- Slow down.
- Rest.
- Take sips of water.
- On hot days, rest under a shady tree.
- If experiencing sharp pains, immediately stop and tell an adult.

Have the students describe an incident when they were playing vigorously and began to feel uncomfortable (tired, sick to stomach, pain in side, breathing very hard). Ask them to describe how they felt and what they did to recover.

Science

Give each student a twist tie and a pencil or a ruler. Ask them to fold the twist tie in half and place it over the pencil or ruler. Have the students hold the pencil or ruler out with the arm slightly bent (but not supported) over their desks about an inch high. In about 10 seconds, the twist tie will begin to move in time with the muscular jitters. This is an example of muscle fatigue (Anderson and Cumbaa 1993).

Ask students to place one hand on their desks with palm facing up. Ask students to open and shut that hand as many times as possible in a one-minute period. Ask students to describe the feeling in the hand, wrist, and forearm. They will answer "pain, tightness, tired" and so on. Say "This is also called muscle fatigue." Remind them "When your body is giving certain signals such as pain or the feeling of exhaustion, it's time to rest."

Math

Ask students to count in seconds (one-one-thousand, two-one-thousand) before the twist tie starts to dance. Ask students to count how many times they make a fist in the one-minute period. Record the numbers from the two experiments for each student and find the class average for each activity.

Art

Ask students to help you make a large poster or bulletin board entitled "Rest and Exercise." Include in the display the responses to fatigue. Have students cut out pictures from magazines of people exercising and people resting, drinking healthy liquids, exercising, and walking. Display the poster in the classroom, hallway, or gymnasium.

Developmental Level II Classroom Activities

Back to the Basics

Lesson Focus -------------------- Students learn that posture is the way your body is supported when you are standing, sitting, walking, or lying down. Good posture prevents or relieves strain on the neck and back. Posture is important to the way you look and feel about yourself. When body posture is correct, internal organs will get enough blood supply to function properly.

Equipment ---------------------- Chalkboard and chalk, poster paper, 4 balloons, 1 marker, instant camera. For each student: paper and pencil, 1 chair, 1 copy of figure 10.11, 1 8.5-inch playball, 1 copy of figure 10.13, 1 chalkboard eraser.

Activities ------------------------- **Language Arts**

Have the class sit in their chairs. Ask the students to demonstrate poor sitting posture. Ask "Why is it harmful to sit incorrectly?" Discuss the benefits of good posture, making a list on the chalkboard:

- Keeps the neck and back supported and healthy
- Enables you to sit for longer time periods without strain

- Keeps internal organs in place and functioning normally
- Keeps you alert and attentive
- Makes you feel good about yourself

Ask the class to write a description about what a person's posture tells you about the way he feels about himself.

Science
Explain to the class, whether sitting or standing, good posture depends on the strength and flexibility of key muscle groups.

- Stomach muscles: Weak stomach muscles allow the pelvic region to tilt forward, creating strain on the lower back. Remark "This is why people who are overweight have frequent back strain. Strong stomach muscles will keep the back straight." (The recommended exercise is curl-ups.)
- Back muscles: Back muscles support the neck and shoulders. These muscles should be strong and flexible to keep the back in proper alignment. (The recommended exercise is pull-ups.)
- Leg muscles: Leg muscles that are inflexible—especially the hamstrings (back of thigh)—can pull the pelvic region out of alignment. Strength in the leg muscles will help support the body while standing, getting up from a seated position, and lifting. Strong legs will relieve the stress on the lower back. (The recommended exercises are the back-saver sit-and-reach stretch, resistance exercising, and jogging.)

Have one student lie down on her back on a large roll of poster paper. Trace the student's body with a marker. Now place the body outline on a chair. Attach small balloons to the front of the body to represent the stomach and the heart. Attach balloons to the back of the outlined body to represent the neck and lower back. Move the body into different positions. Ask "What happens when the body is bent over?" (The stomach and heart are crunched.) "What happens to the blood supply?" (The blood cannot move freely.) (Optional: To further illustrate the point, you may use a small pin to burst the balloons when the outlined body places pressure on the organs.)

Move the outline down the chair in a backward slump. Ask "What is stressed now?" (The neck and back.) Give the outline a name such as "Slumping Steve" (but do not use the name of a child in the class). Place it in the corner of the room to remind students of their sitting habits.

Duplicate the illustration shown in figure 10.11 for each student in class. Review the major points for good sitting posture:

- Ears, shoulders, and hips aligned
- Shoulders relaxed
- Weight evenly distributed on both hips
- Chair close to desk
- Feet flat on the floor

Have each student take the picture (figure 10.11) home and ask their parents to post the picture near the computer or on the refrigerator in the kitchen. Ask the students to help mom, dad, sister, or brother sit correctly while eating dinner, doing homework, or watching TV.

To reinforce proper posture, have students sit up straight with feet flat on the floor. Ask them to place their hands, palms down, directly aligned with the hips on the chair. Have them push down on the chair but not lift their bottoms and count to five. Repeat three times.

To develop the pelvic muscles and reinforce good posture, ask students to sit toward the front of a chair with the hips and knees aligned. Give each student an 8.5-inch playball. Have them place the ball between the knees as shown in figure 10.12. Ask the students to squeeze the ball between the knees, hold for five seconds, and release—all while maintaining good posture. Have them do 10 repetitions.

Give each student a chalkboard eraser to balance on the head. Take a walk down the hallway or outside. When you return to class, discuss how having correct posture with the head remaining over the center of gravity (trunk) helped keep the eraser balanced.

Figure 10.11   Good posture while sitting at computer.

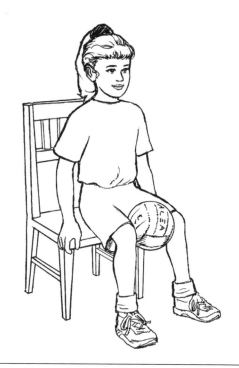

Figure 10.12   Seated ball squeeze for developing good posture.

Math

Give each student the "Measuring Madness" activity sheet (figure 10.13). See how many they can guess. Review the answers.

Art

Ask students to help develop and decorate a bulletin board entitled "Positive Posture." Take a photograph of each child sitting in class participating in various learning activities, such as at a computer, in a cooperative group, reading independently, or the like. Mount the pictures on construction paper to make them look framed and display them on the bulletin board.

Measuring Madness

Name _____   Grade _____

Date _____   Class _____

Try to match the amounts on the left with the items on the right.

A. 75 times

B. 2 to 3 million

C. 650

D. 1.2 to 1.6 gallons

E. 2.5 pints

F. 16 percent

G. 60 percent

H. 208

I. 15 to 30 feet

J. 4 million

_____ 1. Number of new red blood cells made per second

_____ 2. Percentage of body weight that is bone

_____ 3. Number of hairs on your body

_____ 4. Amount of water sweated per day

_____ 5. Amount of blood in body

_____ 6. Bones in the body

_____ 7. Percentage of body weight that is water

_____ 8. Approximate number of times your heart beats in one minute

_____ 9. Length of the small intestine

_____ 10. Number of muscles in the body

Answers: 1. B 2. F 3. J 4. E 5. D 6. H 7. G 8. A 9. I 10. C

Figure 10.13   Measuring Madness.

Body Systems: Skeletal

Lesson Focus ------------------- Students learn that proper eating and daily exercise will produce strong bones. A newborn's bones are comprised of soft cartilage and become harder as the child develops into the late teens. Food choices rich in calcium and phosphorus, as well as vigorous physical activity, will ensure proper bone growth and development.

Equipment --------------------- 1 poster of the skeletal system; 2 chicken bones; 1 jar of vinegar; 1 jar of water; 1 tape measure; 1 calculator, pencil, and piece of paper for each student; crayons, 5 pieces of colored poster paper; graphics of different bones for each group.

Activities ----------------------- **Language Arts**

Display a large poster of the skeletal system. Only label several of the major bones of the body (at this developmental level it is not necessary to review every bone). Review one bone each week. Have students feel the bone that you are discussing on their bodies. After they have studied the skeletal system, ask students to match the body part with the medical name of each bone (see figure 10.14). If you like, you can give the students a word bank from which to choose the medical terms. The answers are skull (head), clavicle (collarbone), ribs (chest), vertebrae or spinal column (back), iliac crest (hip), tibia (shin), femur (thigh), radius and ulna (lower arm), and humerus (upper arm).

Science

Strip two chicken leg bones clean and allow them to dry out for two days. Place one bone in a jar of vinegar and the other in a jar of water. Allow the bones to soak for three or four days. Remove the bones from the jars. The bone from the water jar will still be stiff, but the bone from the vinegar jar will be soft because its minerals have been dissolved by the acid in the vinegar. Reinforce to the class that when bones do not get a good supply of minerals, they become soft and underdeveloped.

Ask "What are good food sources of calcium?" (Low-fat milk, low-fat cheese, yogurt.)

"What exercises or sports build strong bones?" (Jogging, basketball, soccer, hiking—any large muscle continuous activity.)

Math

Explain to the class that in the next few years they will begin to grow quite rapidly. Between the ages of 10 and 14 years, they may grow about six inches taller. Their hands and feet will grow first and they may feel awkward or uncoordinated for a short time.

Here is a method that uses bone measurements to calculate height. Using a tape measure, measure each student's arm from the shoulder joint to the bony point on the outside of the elbow. This is the length of the humerus, or upper arm bone. Follow the formula to calculate the students' height in inches (Anderson and Cumbaa 1993).

Girls:

Length of humerus = _____ inches.

Multiply by 3.14.

Add 25.58 = _____ height in inches.

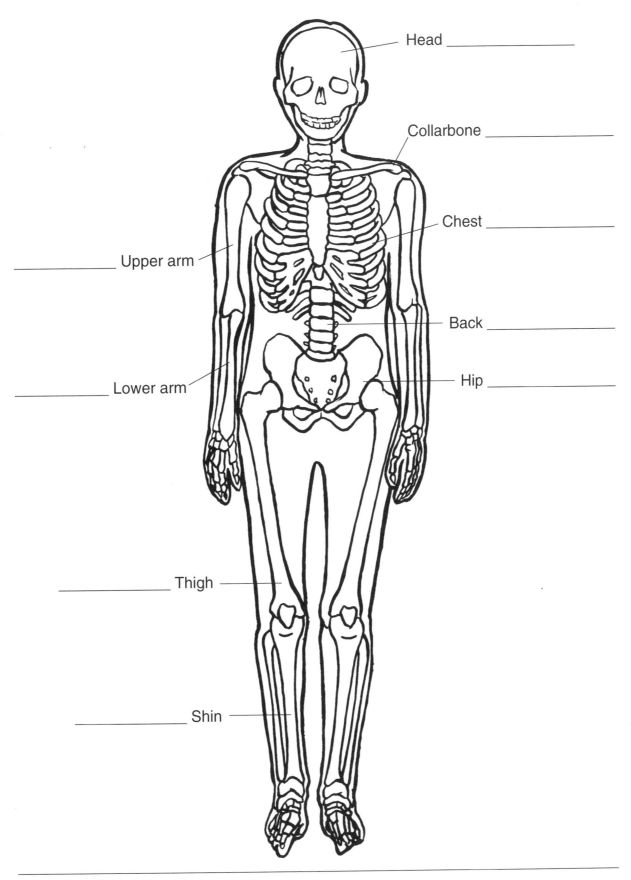

Head _____

Collarbone _____

Chest _____

Upper arm _____

Back _____

Lower arm _____

Hip _____

_____ Thigh

_____ Shin

Figure 10.14   The skeletal system.

Boys:

Length of humerus = _____ inches.

Multiply by 2.97.

Add 28.96 = _____ height in inches.

Help students at this level with the calculations. Compare the final calculations with each student's actual height in inches.

Art

Divide the class into five groups. Have each group select a portion of the body, such as legs, feet, back, shoulders, arms, hands. Ask each student to trace the bones of the body part from the sketches you provide. Instruct them to label and color the bones. Give each group a large piece of poster paper. Have the groups create a large drawing of the body part they selected. Display the students' work around the room.

Developmental Level III Classroom Activities

Fitness Principles: Components of Health-Related Physical Fitness

Lesson Focus --------------------Students review the five components of health-related physical fitness: strength, muscular endurance, flexibility, cardiorespiratory endurance, and body composition.

Equipment ----------------------1 graph worksheet, colored markers, paper, pencil, glue, and scissors for each student; 5 dictionaries, 10 fitness books, several fitness magazines, 1 large piece of poster paper; 20 fitness index cards for every 2 students.

Activities ------------------------**Language Arts**

Divide the class into five cooperative learning groups. Write the words "strength," "muscular endurance," "cardiorespiratory endurance," "flexibility," and "body composition" on large chart paper or on a piece of posterboard. Give each group two fitness books, one dictionary, and several fitness magazines. Ask each student to write the definition of the components of fitness on an individual learning activity sheet, using the resources to define the words. Now ask each student to look through the fitness magazines and cut out pictures of people exercising, depicting the components of physical fitness they have selected. Have them paste these on the lower portion of a learning activity sheet. Ask students to also look for a healthy food item and a picture of a person with low body fat to represent body composition.

Divide the students into pairs. Give each pair a set of 20 fitness index cards (10 cards with the fitness component and definition and 10 with the corresponding pictures). Shuffle the decks of cards for each pair of students, spread the cards out, and place them face up. Have students take turns trying to match the components with the pictures. If a student successfully makes a match, he keeps both cards. If the match is unsuccessful, he returns the cards to the table and the other student takes a turn. The student with the most cards is the winner. To avoid confusion and arguments, place a corresponding number on the back of each picture to denote the correct answer.

Science

Discuss with students the medical benefits of each fitness component, such as how cardiorespiratory endurance prevents heart disease. Then have students make a list of at least five physical activities for each fitness component. Under body composition have them list five healthy snacks.

Math

Ask students to record their fitness scores for each component, using an individual bar graph labeled "Pretest, Interim Test, Posttest." Help students calculate the percentage of improvement made throughout the school year (see figure 10.15).

Art

Divide students into pairs. Ask one student to strike an active pose (jogging, curl-up, shooting a basketball, kicking a soccer ball) while lying on a large section of colored poster paper. Have the other student trace the activity onto the paper. Have the students color the drawing and decorate. Ask them to give the picture a name or title with the appropriate component it represents, for example, "Jo Jo the Jogger," representing cardiorespiratory endurance.

Foods for Fitness

Lesson Focus -------------------- Students learn that foods that are high in carbohydrates provide the body with energy to meet the daily needs of physical activity.

Equipment ---------------------- Pictures of assorted foods; 5 sheets of newspaper; samples of different foods (cheese, crackers, white bread, bologna); iodine solution; 5 eyedroppers; food magazines; 10 boxes (5 marked "GO" and 5 marked "STOP"); 5 pieces of posterboard; several food labels; scissors, paper, graph paper, and pencil for each student.

Activities ----------------------- **Language Arts**

Divide the class into five groups. Provide each group with a number of food pictures, such as candy, steak, pasta, cheese, carrots, and bread. Have each group decide which food pictures are high or low in carbohydrates by placing the pictures of foods high in carbohydrates in the "GO" box and pictures of foods low in carbohydrates in the "STOP" box.

Science

Divide the class into five groups by pulling the desks together. Provide each group with a sheet of newspaper to place on their desks. Give each group samples of food (cheese, crackers, white bread, bologna) and an iodine solution. Ask students to place a drop of iodine on each food sample with an eyedropper. Record what happens to the food. (The foods high in carbohydrates will turn blue.)

Math

Ask students to review food labels from cereal boxes, candy bars, crackers, canned soups, and so on. Have the students design a bar graph of each label, listing the fat, protein, sodium, and carbohydrate content. Ask students to attach the label to each bar graph. Use this analysis to teach the different percentages of ingredients in various food choices.

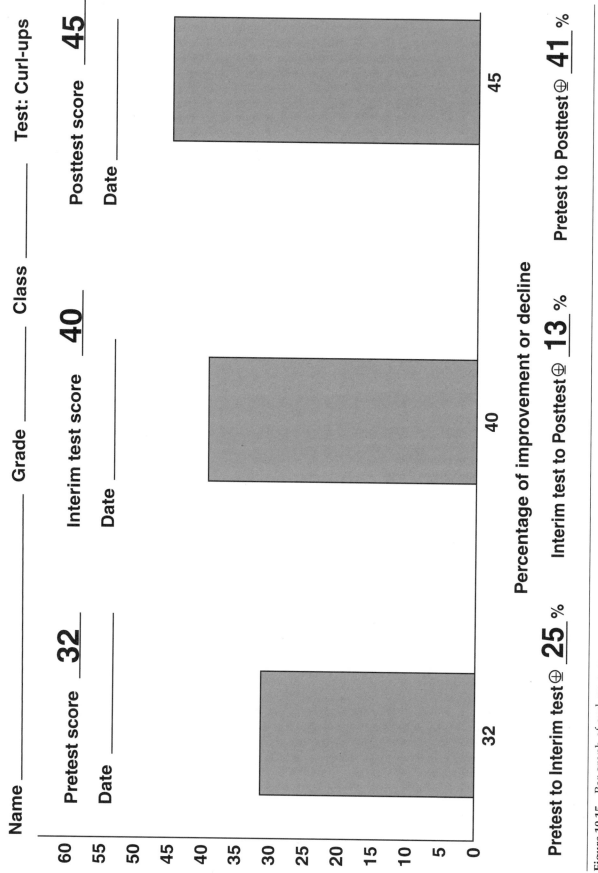

Figure 10.15   Bar graph of curl-up progress.

Art

Divide the class into five groups. Ask each group to look through the food magazines you have provided. Have them cut out the pictures of foods high in carbohydrates and paste the pictures on a large posterboard labeled "Carbo Collage." Allow each group to decide on poster colors as well as additional decorations. Display the posters in the room. You may want to give each group a name, such as, "Fitness Finders" or "Heart Smarties" or have each group invent their own name.

Summary

With so little time for physical education in most elementary schools, it seems appropriate to enlist the help of the classroom teacher to reach your program goals. To ensure the success of this process, first gain administrative support and the confidence of the faculty. Establish open communication channels throughout the school in order to properly implement your innovations.

After establishing a close working relationship with the faculty of your school, provide them with the sample cardiovascular health thematic unit for level II in this chapter to initiate your collaborative efforts. Then use the classroom learning experiences in this chapter as examples of health-related physical fitness concepts the classroom teacher can integrate into the curriculum at the three developmental levels. Work with the classroom teachers to coordinate the use of these materials to compliment the content you are covering in physical education. You may want to suggest going into the classroom to team teach some of the activities described. The extra time and effort you invest will be well worth it!

FITNESS ACTIVITIES

PART III

Developmental Exercises

> *What a disgrace it is for man to grow old without ever seeing the beauty and strength of which his body is capable.*
>
> —Socrates

As you well know, cardiorespiratory endurance, muscular strength and endurance, flexibility, and weight control are each critical to the health and well-being of children, indeed, to all of us. As you design your program, include a variety of developmental exercises from these health-related physical fitness components throughout the school year. I recommend that you review the background information of each component in chapter 5 as well as the specific exercise guidelines so that you can safely and effectively implement the activities in this chapter in your physical education curriculum.

The exercises I'll describe in this chapter serve only as examples of cardiorespiratory endurance, muscular strength and endurance, and flexibility from the number of developmentally appropriate fitness experiences that are suitable for children. For additional exercises refer to Corbin and Lindsay (1997).

Present these exercises in an open, personalized manner, allowing students to make decisions and assume individual responsibility for their progress. This gives children the decision-making practice they need in order to become lifelong fitness advocates. In contrast, emphasizing rigid class structure and regimentation may cause negative attitudes about exercise and therefore may have an adverse effect on long-term participation in physical activity. Moreover, as we discussed in chapter 5, exercise prescription recommendations and formal workout schedules often advised for adults may not be appropriate for school-aged children. Rather, children are better-suited to interval-type activities, spontaneity, and group play, which are all fun ways for them to increase their physical activity levels and therefore their overall fitness.

Tailor exercises and your activity recommendations to meet the individual needs of your students. Furthermore, be certain that every child in your class feels truly included and has an opportunity to become successful in each task. Let's start by examining specific exercises for developing cardiorespiratory endurance.

Cardiorespiratory Endurance

First, let's quickly review the four basic techniques used to enhance cardiorespiratory endurance: continuous activity, interval activity, fartlek course, and circuit course, along with specific related activities.

Continuous Activity

As the name implies, continuous activity refers to large muscle movements sustained for an extended period of time. The activity may vary in intensity but remains continual for several minutes. Activities appropriate for elementary students include jogging, walking, rope jumping, dancing, aerobic dancing, step aerobics, and basketball and soccer games. Table 11.1 illustrates physical activities that you may wish to recommend to children and parents outside of school. (See additional examples of continuous activity in chapters 12 and 13.)

Table 11.1   Outside-of-School Cardiorespiratory Endurance Activities
Biking
Swimming
Hiking
Skating (ice and in-line)
Rowing
Family walks
Exercising to videotapes
Jogging and walking

RANDOM RUN

Ask children to walk or jog in any direction for a specified period of time. At the signal, the class returns to the starting point.

BUDDY WALKS

Have students find a friend in class to walk with for a specified period of time. If both agree, allow them to also jog or run. Encourage students to stay together, interact with each other, and work as partners in this cooperative learning activity.

LINE CHANGE

Arrange students in straight lines of seven or eight, facing the same direction. Have them begin jogging or walking in any direction, staying in lines. At the signal, have the last student in line jog to the front to become the leader. Continue until everyone has had a chance to lead the line.

ESTIMATION

Inform students that they will be walking or jogging three times around the course you have outlined while you time them. Have students write down the times they estimate the course will take them on index cards before they start. Declare the student who comes the closest to guessing her final time as the winner. The bases around a softball infield work well as the route for this activity and moving around the bases is a nice warm-up activity before a softball class.

Interval Activities

Interval activities effectively enhance cardiorespiratory endurance in school-aged children. Children normally work hard, rest, and recover quickly during physical activity. As you may recall, this approach uses continuous large muscle movements alternated by lowering the intensity, varying the distance or recovery time, or modifying repetitions or number of sets. Choose from many appropriate activities to incorporate this technique. The following is an example of a jogging interval workout appropriate for level III:

JOGGING INTERVALS

Warm up.	5 minutes
Walk briskly.	50 yards
Jog at 75 percent speed.	150 yards
Walk briskly.	50 yards
Jog at 75 percent speed.	150 yards
Walk briskly.	50 yards
Jog at 75 percent speed.	150 yards
Walk briskly.	50 yards
Cool down.	5 minutes

JUMP ROPE INTERVALS

Rope jumping makes an extra fun interval routine. Provide a rope for each student (the plastic beaded ropes are the most common and appropriate for children since they are easy to control). The following example is appropriate for level II:

Warm up.	3 to 5 minutes
Ask students to design various letters with the ropes and imitate the different letter shapes with their body parts.	3 to 5 minutes
Ask students to place the rope in a straight line on the floor. Have them walk, jog, skip, and then hop once around the rope.	2 minutes

Play music during the next set of activities (124 beats per minute). When the music stops, have children pause and listen for the next direction.

With ropes still on the floor, jump back and forth over the ropes.	15 to 20 seconds
Jump with one foot back and forth.	15 to 20 seconds
Walk around the playing area as if legs are pieces of spaghetti.	15 to 20 seconds
Walk around the playing area as if legs are stiff as steel.	15 to 20 seconds
Do side swings: Hold the rope with both hands on left side of the body and swing the rope in rhythm.	15 to 20 seconds
Do two-footed basic step: Jump with two feet (include a rebound step while rope is overhead).	15 to 20 seconds
Do side swings: right side.	15 to 20 seconds
Do two-foot basic step.	15 to 20 seconds
Do side swings—left to right in crisscross motion.	15 to 20 seconds
Do two-footed basic step.	15 to 20 seconds
Cool down.	3 to 5 minutes

If students feel uncomfortable performing the two-footed basic step, allow them to hold the rope in one hand at one side and turn the rope while jumping in rhythm to the music.

Fartlek Course

This technique is similar to interval activity, however, the intensity and speed are not controlled. The activity course varies to place stress on dif-ferent muscle groups by changing the levels and the direction often. Figure 11.1 illustrates an example of a fartlek course adapted for elementary school levels II and III. The course includes eight different movements. Place task cards at each new movement to identify the activity as well as arrows to remind students of the direction to take next.

Circuit Course

A circuit course is a continuous activity that includes a general body workout, developing various components of health-related physical fitness, such as cardiorespiratory endurance, muscular strength, muscular endurance, and flexibility. Once again, place task cards at each station, describing the specific task and the proper techniques. Pictures may be helpful at some stations to remind students of proper form and body alignment (e.g., curl-ups). Separate the stations by 15 to 20 yards. Encourage students to move at their own paces but remind them that speed is not the major objective (see figure 11.2).

Muscular Strength and Muscular Endurance

As you know, muscular strength and muscular endurance are not the same thing. Muscular strength is the capacity of a muscle or muscle group to exert maximum force against a resistance. Muscular endurance is the capacity of a muscle or muscle group to exert force over a period of time against a resistance that is less than the maximum you can move.

School-aged children may improve strength levels before puberty (Bouchard et al. 1990); however, only students who are training for specific sport events, such as gymnastics, should work specifically on this component of health-related physical fitness. Because of the danger of overuse, injuries, stress to major joints, and muscle imbalance, carefully supervise elementary students who do engage in strength exercising.

You can choose from a broad range of exercises that may enhance strength and endurance. The activities I'll describe will broadly develop muscular strength and endurance, rather than specifically build muscular strength. To maintain

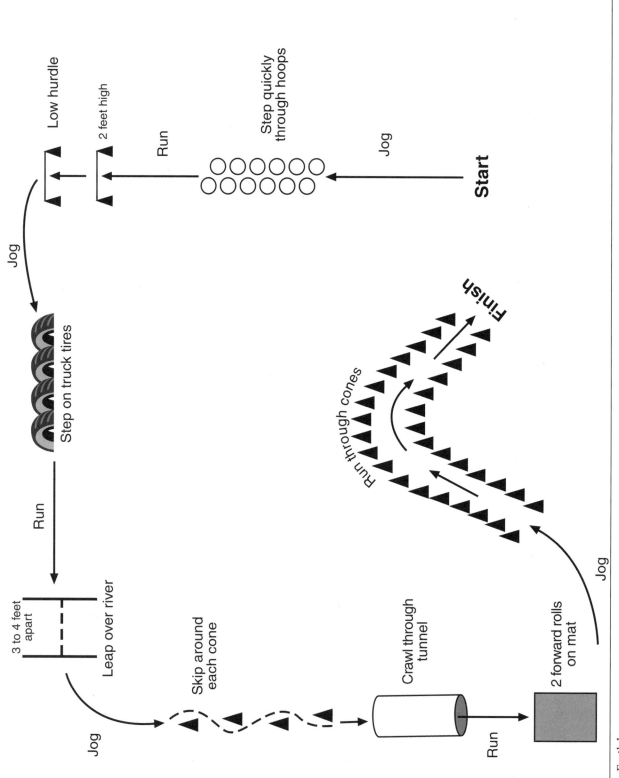

Figure 11.1   Fartlek course.

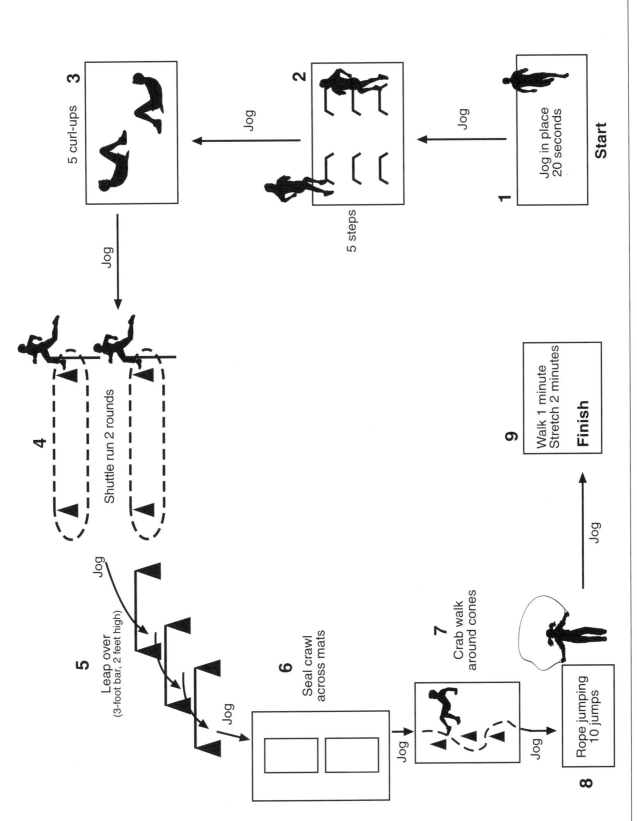

Figure 11.2   Cardiorespiratory endurance circuit course.

muscular balance, it's important to cover all the major muscle groups: shoulders, arms, chest, back, trunk, and legs. Furthermore, ensure that students perform exercises equally on each side of the body as well as properly align their bodies for each activity.

Exercises

Incorporate the following muscular strength and endurance exercises throughout your physical education program. Table 11.2 lists the appropriate developmental level for each activity. Where possible, I have written the instructions as you might speak them directly to the students, making them easy for you to begin using immediately. Study the illustrations carefully and demonstrate proper technique to ensure that your students perform the exercises safely.

SEAL CRAWL

Lie on your stomach with your hands directly under the shoulders, pointing slightly outward, and your arms straight, feet three to four inches apart. Move your hands left, right, left, right while dragging your legs along the floor. (Muscle groups: arms and shoulders; see figure 11.3.)

Figure 11.3   Seal crawl.

CRAB CRAWL

Lie on your back with your weight supported on your hands and feet. To begin, move your right hand and left foot forward at the same time, then your left hand and right foot forward. Move your body sideways, forward, or backward. (Muscle groups: arms and shoulders; see figure 11.4.)

Figure 11.4   Crab crawl.

ARM SAWS

In partners, stand 8 to 12 inches apart, facing each other. Clasp hands, keeping the wrists stable. Begin with each of you pushing your right hand and pulling with your left at a steady, controlled pace. Pretend to be sawing a tree. (Muscle groups: arms and shoulders; see figure 11.5.)

Figure 11.5   Arm saws.

TURTLE WALK

Lie face down with your hands flat on the floor, your arms straight and your knees off the floor. Keep your arms and legs slightly wider than shoulder-width apart. Move the right arm and leg together, then the left arm and leg. Move forward, backward, or sideways. Make small movements to reduce the stress on your muscles and joints. (Muscle groups: arms and shoulders; see figure 11.6.)

Table 11.2 Muscular Strength and Endurance by Developmental Level

Activity	Level I	Level II	Level III
Seal crawl	✓		
Crab crawl	✓		
Arm saws	✓		
Turtle walk	✓		
Push-ups		✓	✓
Inchworm	✓		
Problem-solvers	✓		
Stork stand	✓		
Treadmill	✓	✓	
Curl-ups	✓	✓	✓
Curl-up and twist			✓
Diagonal crunch			✓
Parachute curl-ups		✓	✓
Chute down		✓	✓
Wrist rolls		✓	✓
Parachute push-ups		✓	✓
Hurricane		✓	
Superdome		✓	✓
Bubble		✓	✓
Floating cloud		✓	✓
Popcorn		✓	✓
Parachute golf			✓
Tug-of-war		✓	✓
Medicine ball chest pass			✓
Curl-up and throw			✓
Overhead pass			✓
Half-twist pass			✓
Resistance tubes		✓	✓
Ball squeeze	✓	✓	✓
Heel raises	✓	✓	✓
Wall seat	✓	✓	✓

Figure 11.6 Turtle walk.

PUSH-UPS

Lie on your chest on the floor (or mat). Place your hands under your shoulders with your body in a straight line. To begin, raise your body by extending your arms, then go down until your chest is two inches from the floor. (Muscle groups: arms and shoulders; see figure 11.7.)

Figure 11.7 Push-up.

Use the modified bent-knee push-up to decrease difficulty (see figure 11.8).

Figure 11.8 Modified bent-knee push-up.

To increase difficulty, try these modifications:

1. Open-hands (wide-stance) push-ups
2. Closed-hands (four inches apart) push-ups
3. Hold in upright position for 10 seconds
4. Slow-motion push-ups
5. Only one foot on floor
6. Push up and clap hands
7. Box push-up (figure 11.9)
8. Chair push-ups (hand on each seat)
9. Wall push-ups (Stand two to three feet from the wall, hands flat, legs straight and back straight. Push away from the wall.)
10. Bar push-ups (figure 11.10)

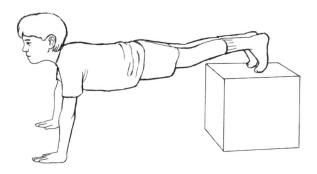

Figure 11.9 Box push-up.

Figure 11.10 Bar push-up.

INCHWORM

Sit on the floor with your arms folded across your chest. To move, pull your bottom and hips forward while pushing with your heels. (Muscle groups: hips and legs; see figure 11.11.)

PROBLEM-SOLVERS

Ask students a series of questions, such as, "From a supine position (demonstrate) with both knees bent can you raise your left leg, place it down, raise your right leg, place it down? Can you raise your left knee to your chest? Now can you raise your right knee to your chest? Can you raise both knees to your chest? With knees bent, can you raise your head while looking straight up? Can you raise your shoulders off the mat a few inches? Can you raise your head and bring your left knee to your chest?" (Muscle group: abdominals.)

STORK STAND

Stand straight and tall with your hands on your hips. Bend your right knee slightly. Place your left foot gently against the inside of your right knee. Hold for 5 to 10 seconds. This activity helps strengthen your legs and may also develop your balancing skills. (Muscle group: legs; see figure 11.12.)

TREADMILL

Begin in a crawling position. Bring one leg up to the chest and extend the other leg backward. Begin moving by alternating your legs in a steady rhyth-

Figure 11.12   Stork stand.

mic pattern. Keep your upper body still and your head up. I'll start by timing you for short intervals (20 to 30 seconds). (Muscle groups: legs and abdominals; see figure 11.13.)

CURL-UPS

Lie on your back with your knees bent to approximately 90 degrees with your feet flat on the floor (demonstrate). Place your arms alongside your body with your palms down. Lift your head and shoulders to a 45-degree angle (demonstrate; see figure 11.14). Slowly lower your head and shoulders until your shoulder blades touch the floor. (Muscle group: abdominals.)

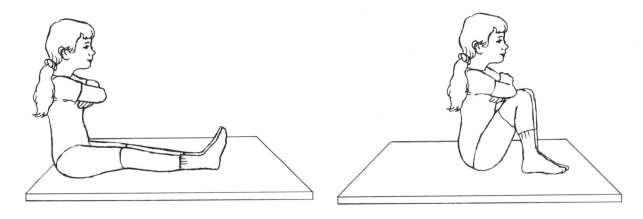

Figure 11.11   Inchworm.

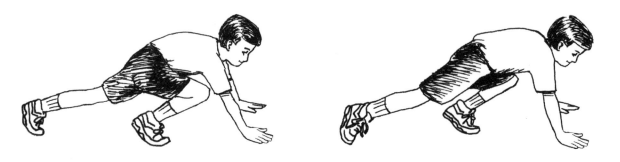

Figure 11.13   Treadmill.

Figure 11.14   Curl-up.

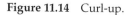

CURL-UP AND TWIST

Lie on your back with your knees bent and feet flat on the floor. Fold your arms across your chest. Begin with a curl-up, then twist to one side by rotating the upper torso, next go back to a straight position, and then down. Repeat, alternating sides. (Muscle groups: abdominals, obliques, and hip flexors; see figure 11.15.)

Figure 11.15   Curl-up and twist.

DIAGONAL CRUNCH

Lie on your side with one leg on top of the other, knees bent. Make sure your bottom shoulder blade is flat against the mat. Place one hand behind your head to support your neck. Crunch up by

raising the bottom shoulder blade off the mat. Repeat, alternating sides. (Muscle groups: upper abdominals and obliques; see figure 11.16.)

Figure 11.16   Diagonal crunch.

Parachute Activities

The parachute can be an excellent piece of equipment to promote muscular strength and endurance. Through teamwork and cooperation, the entire class will be able to participate in highly active games, locomotor movements, shape formations, and exercises.

CURL-UPS

Everyone sit with knees bent, holding the parachute at your waist with an overhand grip. (Divide the class in half.) This half, lie back to perform the curl-up. The other half, lean forward to give slack. Then do the opposite. (Muscle group: abdominals.)

CHUTE DOWN

Everyone hold the parachute at waist level with an overhand grip, feet at least shoulder-width apart. Everyone lift the chute overhead. At the signal, pull the chute back to your waist, using only your arms and shoulders. (Muscle groups: arms and shoulders.)

WRIST ROLLS

Everyone hold the chute straight out with an overhand grip. Now slowly roll the chute toward the center, keeping it tight by leaning slightly backward. (Muscle groups: wrist and forearms.)

PUSH-UPS

Everyone raise the chute overhead. Pull the chute down to the floor. Place your hands on the edge of the chute with your legs extended away from the chute. Perform as many push-ups as possible before the chute deflates. (Muscle group: arms.)

HURRICANE

Everyone grasp the parachute with an overhead grip. Begin by making moderate (medium-sized) waves, moving the chute up and down. (Describe an approaching storm as students move the chute in response to your description.) The sky gets black, the wind picks up, the waves get larger with deep swells. Now the wind is swirling, the waves get short and choppy. Oh no, the hurricane is here! Move the chute up and down as fast as you can. (Cool down by describing how the storm is passing and everything is safe and back to normal.) (Muscle groups: arms and shoulders.)

SUPERDOME

At the signal "Up" everyone lift the chute overhead. At the signal "Down" everyone bring the chute down to the floor. Watch the chute form a dome. (Muscle groups: arms and shoulders.)

BUBBLE

This activity begins with the parachute on the floor. Everyone squat down and grasp the chute with an overhand grip. At the signal, lift the chute overhead and at the same time walk quickly into the center forming a large bubble. (Muscle groups: arms and shoulders.)

FLOATING CLOUD

Everyone grasp the chute with an overhand grip. At the signal, raise the chute overhead. At the command "Release" let go of the chute. (Muscle groups: arms and shoulders.)

POPCORN

Place several types of balls in the parachute. Everyone grasp the parachute with an overhand grip. On the first signal "Simmer" shake the chute, creating small ripples. On the second signal "Cook" make the balls move more rapidly by shaking the chute harder. On the last signal "Popcorn" make large, fast ripples by waving your arms and jumping up and down to pop the balls straight up—but try to keep the popcorn in the pan. (To culminate the activity, ask students to pop the balls outside the parachute; muscle groups: arms and shoulders.)

PARACHUTE GOLF

Divide the class into a red and a yellow team around the parachute. Place all students of each team on one side of the parachute. Place a red and yellow ball inside of the parachute. At the signal, both teams try to move the parachute to get their ball in the center hole. Do not use your hands to move a ball. The first team to score three points wins. (Muscle groups: arms and shoulders.)

TUG-OF-WAR

Divide the class in half. At the signal "Pull" each side pulls straight back. The team that pulls across the curved line, marked three to four feet directly behind them, is the winner. The entire team need not cross the line—the teacher may use basic judgment. Take care not to damage the parachute. (Check for tears or holes before each use; muscle groups: arms and shoulders.)

Medicine Ball Activities

Medicine balls are back in various colors and sizes, weighted to develop hand, arm, and upper torso strength. The new and improved balls are soft, pliable, and stuffed with a special fiber padding. The three most appropriate medicine balls for the elementary school level are

- the 4-pound, 7-inch diameter medicine ball;
- the 2.2-pound, 6-inch diameter PVC plastic ball; and
- the 2-pound, 6-inch diameter powerball with handle.

The following exercises may be used as a medicine ball routine.

CHEST PASS

Stand, with feet shoulder-width apart, two steps from a partner. Push the ball slowly from the chest with palms facing outward. Keep your knees and back slightly bent. The catcher receives the ball with the palms facing upward, knees bent and hands shoulder-width apart. (Muscle groups: chest and arms; see figure 11.17.)

Figure 11.17   Chest pass with medicine ball.

CURL-UP AND THROW

Lie on your back with knees bent, holding ball at chest, arms slightly bent. Slowly perform a curl-up, lifting your head and shoulders off the mat, contracting (tightening) the abdominal muscles. Gently toss the medicine ball to your partner. The partner tosses it back in one smooth motion without losing the continuity of the curl-up movement. (Muscle groups: abdominals, shoulders, and arms; see figure 11.18.)

OVERHEAD PASS

Stand back-to-back about eight inches from a partner with knees slightly bent. The student with the ball passes it directly overhead. The partner accepts the ball with palms facing upward and hands shoulder-width apart. (Muscle groups: arms and shoulders; see figure 11.19.)

HALF-TWIST PASS

Stand back-to-back with your partner with your knees bent. The student with the ball holds it at waist level. At the signal, both of you perform a

Figure 11.18   Sequence for curl-up and throw with medicine ball.

Figure 11.19   Overhead pass with medicine ball.

gentle half-twist. The student with the ball twists to the right, the partner twists to the left to accept the ball at waist level. Repeat the exercise, alternating sides. (Muscle groups: abdominals and obliques; see figure 11.20.)

Exercises With Resistance Tubes and Bands

The use of rubberized resistance equipment is a new and creative way to increase muscular strength and endurance in the elementary school. The tubes and bands are light and durable and add variety to your program. The rubberized resistance equipment is color-coded to denote the various levels of resistance, allowing you to tailor specific exercises to individual fitness needs. In addition, this equipment provides moderate resistance without placing undue stress on the muscles and joints common in other weighted exercise products. Remind your students to

- never tie pieces of tubing together;
- inspect the tubes before each class;
- breathe normally—never hold your breath;
- when standing, exercise in slow, controlled movements with proper body alignment, with your knees slightly bent;
- perform an equal number of repetitions with each arm or leg to avoid muscle imbalance;

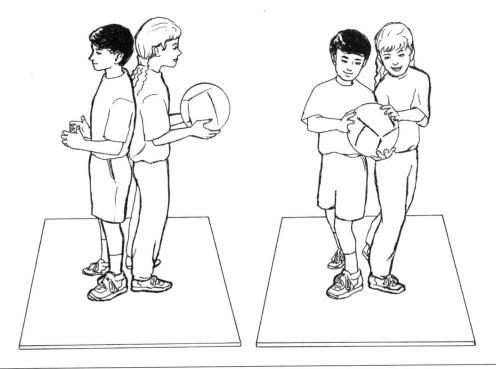

Figure 11.20   Half-twist pass with medicine ball.

- rest at least 10 seconds between sets of exercises; and

- when standing, step firmly on the tube with the middle of your foot to secure the tube, keeping knees slightly bent.

The following are examples of exercises performed with exercise tubing and bands. Remember to make sure students always anchor the tube under the instep of one foot or both feet (to increase resistance), slightly bending both knees.

ARM CURL

Grasp one handle in each hand with palms facing up, arms straight at the side and elbows against the sides of the body. Curl both arms toward the chest while keeping the elbows at the sides. Return slowly to starting position. (Muscle group: biceps; see figure 11.21.)

Figure 11.21 Arm curl with exercise tubing.

TRICEPS EXTENSION

Stand in a lunge stance (demonstrate) and place tubing under front foot. Cross the tubing and grasp the handle with hand of nonexercising arm and rest on upper leg. Bend forward at the waist, resting weight of upper body on nonexercising arm. Grasp the handle with the exercise arm next to your hip with your palm facing backward.

Keeping your wrist firm, slowly straighten exercise arm and end with your palm facing up. Return slowly to the starting position. (Muscle group: triceps; see figure 11.22.)

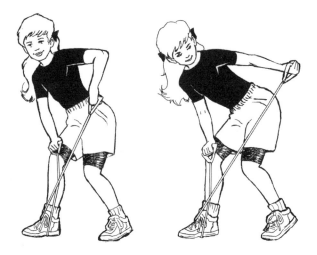

Figure 11.22 Triceps extension with exercise tubing.

LATERAL DELTOID RAISE

Grasp one handle in each hand. Keep your elbows slightly bent at the sides of your body. Raise your elbows away from your sides while keeping your wrists and forearms firm. Slowly return to starting position. (Muscle group: deltoids; see figure 11.23.)

Figure 11.23 Lateral deltoid raise with exercise tubing.

UPRIGHT SHOULDER ROW

Grasp handles with both hands and position your arms straight in front of your thighs. Bend your elbows and pull your hands up to chest height. Slowly return to starting position. (Muscle group: deltoids; see figure 11.24.)

Figure 11.24 Upright shoulder row with exercise tubing.

ARM EXTENSION

The arm extension and the chest press are illustrated using the toner rubberized resistance equipment from Quik-Fit for Kids (see appendix B), but you can use any type of resistance band.

Grasp the toner with your left hand and position it behind your back with your elbow bent and palm facing outward. Position the exercise arm over the shoulder with the palm facing up. Grasping the toner handle, slowly pull the exercise arm (right) away from the shoulder, and return. Do the same number of repetitions on each side. (Muscle groups: triceps and shoulders; see figure 11.25.)

CHEST PRESS

Stand with your feet slightly wider than shoulder-width apart with your knees bent. Position the toner behind your back with the rubber pad squarely in

the middle. Grasp the handles with the palms facing outward. Extend your arms outward. Keep a slight bend in your elbows. Slowly return to the starting position. (Muscle groups: chest and triceps; see figure 11.26.)

Figure 11.25 Arm extension with toner.

Figure 11.26 Chest press with toner.

BALL SQUEEZE

Provide each student with a dead rubber ball about the size of a tennis ball. Squeeze the ball with the right hand and hold for three seconds. Alternate hands. (Muscle groups: hands, wrists, and forearms.)

BIG BAND MARCH STEP

Position the resistance band around both ankles, with your knees slightly bent. Bend the leg you're exercising and lift it off the floor several inches. Place your hands on your hips, keeping the hip and trunk muscles tight. Slowly return to the start position. (Muscle groups: quadriceps and hip flexors; see figure 11.27.)

Figure 11.27 March step with exercise band.

KICKBACK

While standing, position the exercise band around both of your ankles. Balance on the leg you're not exercising, bending your knee slightly. Bend the leg you are exercising and lift that heel from the floor. Slowly lift and press the exercising leg backward, keeping the knee slightly bent. Point the toes and allow the hip to rotate outward slightly. Avoid overarching the low back. Return slowly to the starting position. Adaptation: Move the band up higher on the leg to increase the resistance. (Muscle group: hamstrings; see figure 11.28.)

Figure 11.28 Kickback with exercise band.

CROSSOVER LIFT

Position band around the lower leg. Balance on the leg you're not exercising, bending your knee slightly. Place your hands on your hips to keep them and your low back from moving too much. Keep your shoulders and hips stable (still). Slowly lift and sweep the leg you are exercising up and across the front of your body, keeping your knee slightly bent. Return slowly to the starting position. Rest your toes on the floor between each repetition. Adaptation: Move the band up higher on the leg to increase resistance. (Muscle groups: inside of thighs and hip flexors; see figure 11.29.)

Figure 11.29 Crossover lift with exercise band.

HEEL RAISES

Stand on a board or a book with your heels resting on the floor. If you need to, use a chair for support and to help keep your body aligned. Slowly rise onto the toes, hold for three seconds, and return to the starting position. (Muscle group: calf; see figure 11.30.)

Figure 11.30   Heel raises.

WALL SEAT

Stand with your back against the wall, feet slightly wider than shoulder-width apart, hands on your hips. Slowly bend your knees, sliding your back four to six inches down the wall. Keep your body lined up so that your hips and the rest of you face straight ahead. Hold for 10 to 15 seconds and slowly slide back up to the beginning position. Repeat. (Muscle group: quadriceps; see figure 11.31.)

Flexibility

Remember, flexibility is the ability to move the joints in an unrestricted fashion through a full range of motion. The best time to enhance flexibility is during the cool-down period following 15 or more minutes of continuous physical activity when the muscles are already warm.

Figure 11.31   Wall seat.

Keep in mind that flexibility is joint-specific, which simply means a student with flexible hamstrings may not have the same degree of flexibility in the shoulder region. For this reason, flexibility exercises in your program should cover a wide range of muscle groups.

The following exercises illustrate static stretching movements—the safer, more controlled approach to enhancing flexibility appropriate for all elementary school children. For safety reasons, avoid the bouncing, jerky movements of ballistic stretching.

According to Corbin and Lindsay (1997), the following six exercises can serve as baseline assessment measures of the neck, lower back, quadriceps, hip flexors, calf, and shoulder.

NECK

Bend your neck forward. (The chin should move to about two inches from the upper chest; see figure 11.32.)

Figure 11.32   Baseline assessment of neck flexibility.

LOW BACK

Using both hands, pull your thighs to your chest. (Thighs should gently touch chest; see figure 11.33.)

Figure 11.33   Baseline assessment of low back flexibility.

QUADRICEPS

Grasp your right foot with your right hand. Bend your right leg so that the heel touches your buttocks. Repeat with your left leg. (Heel should touch buttocks; see figure 11.34.)

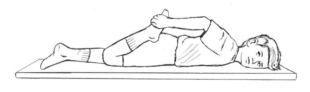

Figure 11.34   Baseline assessment of quadriceps flexibility.

HIP FLEXORS

Pull your left thigh into your body. (Your right leg should remain straight and flat on the floor.) Change legs and repeat. (See figure 11.35.)

Figure 11.35   Baseline assessment of hip flexor flexibility.

CALF

Place one heel on the floor. Raise the rest of your foot. Repeat with your other foot. (The ball of the foot should be at least two inches from the floor; see figure 11.36.)

Figure 11.36   Baseline assessment of calf flexibility.

SHOULDER

Place your right hand over the right shoulder as far as possible. Take your left hand and reach back and touch your right hand. The fingers of the right hand should at least touch the fingers of the left. (Reverse hands to assess the left shoulder; see figure 11.37.)

Figure 11.37   Baseline assessment of shoulder flexibility.

Flexibility Exercises

Have students perform the following exercises with a static stretching technique. Each stretch should be held for at least 15 seconds and should be done in a slow, deliberate fashion with the body in proper alignment. Never have children do full head circles or hyperextend the neck. For additional flexibility exercises see Alter (1990).

FORWARD HEAD DROP

To increase neck flexibility, drop your head, placing the center of your chin on your chest (see figure 11.38).

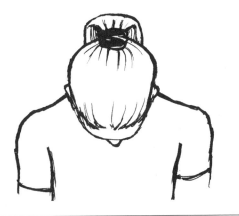

Figure 11.38   Head drop.

LOOK-OVER

This exercise stretches the neck muscles. Keeping your shoulders stable, turn to the left and look over your left shoulder and then turn to the right side and look over your right shoulder (see figure 11.39).

Figure 11.39   Look-over.

NECK TILT

Place your ear to your shoulder (see figure 11.40).

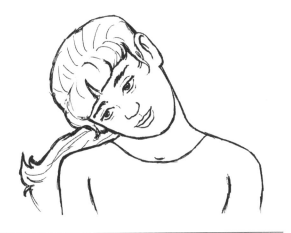

Figure 11.40   Neck tilt.

STRAIGHT-UP

To increase shoulder flexibility, extend your arms overhead and press your palms together. Stretch your arms straight up, then slightly backward (see figure 11.41).

Figure 11.41   Straight-up.

ARM-CROSS STRETCH

This exercise stretches the shoulders. Place your right arm across your chest while supporting your right elbow with your left hand. With your left hand, pull your right elbow gently across your chest (see figure 11.42). Repeat on the other side.

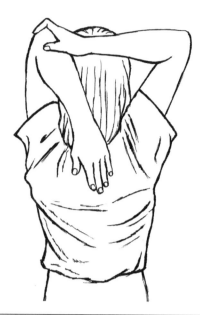

Figure 11.43   Overhead arm stretch.

Figure 11.42   Arm-cross stretch.

OVERHEAD ARM STRETCH

To stretch your shoulder and back of your arm, raise one arm overhead with the elbow bent. Hold the elbow in position with your opposite hand. Gently pull the elbow of the arm you're exercising behind your head. Hold, then repeat the stretch with your opposite arm (see figure 11.43).

SIT-AND-TWIST BACK STRETCH

This stretches the midback, the trunk, and outside of the hips. Sit with your right leg extended, knee slightly bent. Cross your left leg over your right knee, bending your left leg. Bring your right arm across your left leg, rotating your trunk. Push your right elbow against your right knee. Repeat on the opposite side (see figure 11.44).

Figure 11.44   Sit-and-twist back stretch.

CAT AND CAMEL STRETCH

This exercise helps make your back more flexible. Sit on the mats (or grass). To do the cat part, arch your back slightly by relaxing your low back muscles, lifting your chin, tucking your abdominal muscles, and expanding your chest. The camel part begins on your hands and knees in line with your hips. Gently round your upper back while tightening and tucking your abdominal and pelvic muscles. At the same time, lower your head, keeping your neck and shoulders relaxed. Hold (see figure 11.45).

Figure 11.45   Cat and camel stretch.

LEG HUG

To stretch your low back, pull your knees to your chest. Hold on behind your knees. Curl up into a ball, bending your chin slightly toward your chest (see figure 11.46).

Figure 11.46   Leg hug.

HAMSTRINGS STRETCH

Lie on your back with one foot flat on the floor, knee bent. Pull the other knee to your chest. Place one hand on the calf and the other hand on the thigh. Slowly straighten the knee until the hamstrings become tight. Never completely straighten and lock the knee. Repeat with the opposite leg (see figure 11.47). You may use a towel around the foot you're exercising to help keep your leg in place.

INSIDE LEG STRETCH

To stretch the muscles of the inside of your thighs, sit with the bottoms of your feet together. Press

your knees gently toward the floor and hold (see figure 11.48).

Figure 11.47   Hamstrings stretch.

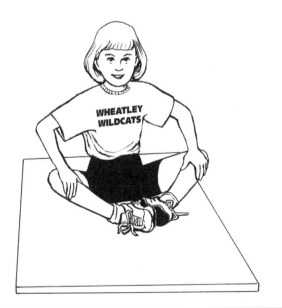

Figure 11.48   Inside leg stretch.

QUADRICEPS STRETCH

To stretch the quadriceps (front of thigh) stand upright with the top of one foot resting on a chair, bench, or low standing support behind you. Bend your front knee, keeping your hips and back stable and lined up with the support leg. Hold and repeat with the other leg (see figure 11.49).

Figure 11.49 Quadriceps stretch.

LUNGE

To stretch your hip flexors and quadriceps, bend your right leg, keeping your right knee directly above the right ankle. Stretch your left leg backward and touch your left knee to the floor. Press your hips forward and down and hold. Repeat with your other leg (see figure 11.50).

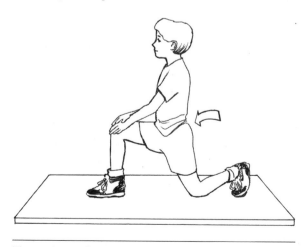

Figure 11.50 Lunge.

CALF STRETCH

To stretch the calf, face something sturdy to lean against for support such as a wall. Bend one knee and bring it toward the support. Keep your back leg straight with the foot flat and toes pointed straight ahead. Slowly move your hips forward while keeping your back leg straight and your heel down. Repeat for your other leg (see figure 11.51).

Figure 11.51 Calf stretch.

Exercises to Avoid

The following exercises are unsafe to perform. Many of the exercises place undue stress on the major joints and may have an adverse effect on a student's physical health.

PLOW

The plow may stress the nerves and disks in the neck and back area (see figure 11.52). Alternatives: leg hug and cat and camel stretch.

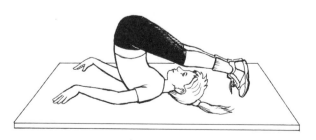

Figure 11.52 Plow.

TOE TOUCHES

Standing toe touches may cause severe low back strain (see figure 11.53). Alternative: hamstrings stretch.

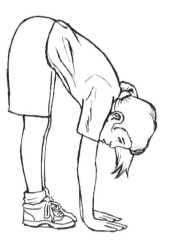

Figure 11.53 Toe touches.

FULL SQUATS

Full squats may place excessive strain on the knee ligaments (see figure 11.54). Alternative: wall seat.

Figure 11.54 Full squats.

LEG LIFTS

Leg lifts cause stress on the low back by compressing disks (see figure 11.55). Alternative: curl-ups.

Figure 11.55 Leg lifts.

NECK CIRCLES

Neck circles may pinch the nerves in the neck and irritate the disks (see figure 11.56). Alternatives: forward head drop, look-over, and neck tilt.

Figure 11.56 Neck circles.

ARM CIRCLES

Arm circles with palms down stresses the shoulder ligaments and joint (see figure 11.57). Alternative: use backward rotation with palms up.

WINDMILL

The windmill causes low back strain and irritates disks (see figure 11.58). Alternatives: hamstring stretch and sit-and-twist back stretch.

FULL SIT-UPS

Full sit-ups with hands locked behind the neck places stress on the back and the neck (see figure 11.59). Alternative: curl-ups.

Figure 11.57 Arm circles.

Figure 11.58 Windmill.

Figure 11.59 Full sit-ups.

Summary

Use the numerous examples of cardiorespiratory endurance, muscular strength and endurance, and flexibility exercises in this chapter to offer a wide, but well-balanced, variety of physical activity opportunities to your students, incorporating them into any skill- or sport-related unit in your curriculum to maintain fitness and physical activity levels throughout the school year. Moreover, use the illustrations in this chapter as visual reminders of proper form and body alignment. Finally, avoid the dangerous exercises I have listed and use the safer alternatives suggested to provide developmentally appropriate physical activity.

Active Games

CHAPTER 12

It should be noted that children's games are not merely games; one should regard them as their most serious activities.

—Michel de Montaigne

Games are an excellent way to increase physical activity levels in the elementary school. Most children view playing an active game as recreation, considering it fun and enjoyable. So use games to motivate children to become more physically active. But work to maintain the enthusiasm children feel for games without compromising sound educational principles. Therefore, avoid games that eliminate players, otherwise embarrass children, include low activity levels, or do little to develop objectives.

Characteristics of Developmental Games

To maximize learning experiences, match the game to the developmental level of the students. Thus, modify games by changing the boundaries, the formation of the game, the method of tagging, varying the rules, and so on. For example, to increase the level of physical activity, you can increase the distance children have to move within the game by expanding the boundaries. Or vary the locomotor movements to change the tempo and develop various muscle groups, for example, have students skip, then hop instead of always running. More-

over, change the rules of a game so that everyone feels included and has the opportunity to succeed. For example, awarding points for each successful task within a game encourages student participation. When choosing and modifying games, keep in mind the following characteristics of developmentally appropriate games.

Objective-Based

Each game should have an educational objective, providing you with an instructional focus instead of allowing the game itself to become the sole purpose of your class. For example, the primary objectives for a game may be to promote social interaction, to enhance a skill, to apply problem-solving techniques, to increase physical activity levels, or to accomplish a combination of objectives.

Humanistic

Choose games that develop positive feelings in students. Activities that foster cooperation and sportsmanship will help your students see the value of physical activity. For example, use physical education equipment such as balls, Frisbees, and beanbags to develop skills—not to kick or throw at other students as a condition of a game.

Inclusive

A game should include each child in the class at all times. Modify the rules, equipment, or procedures of the game to ensure that every child is an active participant capable of success. Never eliminate a student from the game because he or she was somehow unsuccessful.

Engaging

Students should spend most of their time on-task. Children who spend an inordinate amount of time waiting in lines or standing inactively cannot fully reach their physical potentials. Indeed, a high percentage of time off-task is a form of exclusion. Organize a game so that children truly benefit from the lesson because they are actively and continually involved in kicking, running, throwing, catching—whatever you have structured the game to accomplish.

Active

Don't forget to be inclusive when it comes to the activity level. Ask yourself "Do all of my students have the opportunity to continuously move throughout the game?" If a game is dominated by a few active students, change the procedures to allow others to more actively participate. For example, you may rotate positions or responsibilities of players to ensure activity for the entire class. Then, to help keep children interested in participating, vary the activity levels of the games you incorporate into your program as well as the health-related physical fitness components you focus on.

Success-Oriented

The best way to ensure that a game is humanistic, inclusive, engaging, and active is to structure it so that everyone can feel like a winner. Within the game, provide many opportunities for scoring points or completing a task that may assist the team. This approach will reassure each student that they have made a positive contribution to the team. For instance, in the game VBS (page 176), you may

award a point for each base successfully made rather than only a point if a student made it home. Beyond this, make certain that each student in class has the skill or the physical development to successfully participate in the game. If not, teach the skill or modify the game further.

Positive Competition

Most games require a certain amount of competition; however, you can structure this aspect of a game to provide a positive experience for children. First, don't focus on the team, group, or individual who is successful but on the skills learned and the enjoyment of the game. Teach children how to compete in the spirit of fair play by promoting cooperation, teamwork, and sensitivity to others in class. Furthermore, work to reinforce to your students the concept that we play active fitness games primarily for the health-related benefits. For example, ask students to monitor their heart rates before and after the game and discuss what muscles were most involved in the activity. Help your students view games as healthy and fun activities, rather than as competitive experiences between classmates.

Appropriate Equipment and Facilities

The equipment should match the developmental level of the learner. Provide the class with a range of equipment to match the sizes and strengths of your students. Adjust standard equipment, such as basketball goals, to a suitable height (seven to nine feet). Constantly assess playing areas and game boundaries for compatibility with the developmental level of each class.

Safe

Safety first! Always make the safety of your students the top priority in game situations. As a teacher, the first thing on my list every morning was to check the playground equipment and field area for hazards. It is important to arrange safe, wide-open spaces for highly active games. Specifically, in the gymnasium, leave at least an 8- to 10-foot buffer zone between the playing area and walls, stages, doors, and the like. Mark your field clearly with orange-colored cones. Make sure that any playing surface is level, dry, and free from debris. Check daily to ensure that children are wearing proper footwear (sneakers and sport socks) and are not wearing jewelry. Teach children to move in their own personal spaces, respecting the spaces of others, by reviewing the techniques of body management, such as how to stop, change direction, and accelerate.

Fun

To children a game isn't a game unless it's fun. We should never lose sight of this essential aspect. While children do not have to be yelling, cheering, and screaming to have fun, a well-developed, challenging game can be a positive and exciting addition to your curriculum.

Promoting Physical Activity Through Active Games

I have selected the games in this chapter to help you increase the activity levels of your students throughout the school year in humanistic and fun ways. Use them as warm-up activities or as a closing segment for a skill-oriented lesson, not as the core of a lesson to supplement your basic curriculum, thereby helping children recognize how games help promote healthy physical activity. To avoid unnecessary frustration, however, first teach any specialized manipulative skills the game requires.

The primary purpose of the games in this chapter is to promote physical activity levels. To make planning easier for you, I have divided the games by developmental levels and have used the following symbols to indicate the physical intensity level of each game:

Warm-up

Moderately active

Highly active

Developmental Level I Games

HOOPSCOTCH

Arrange 60 or more standard hula hoops in six configurations (three illustrated in figure 12.1). Ask children to each toss a beanbag into one of the hoops. Ask them to "hoopscotch" through the hoops, hopping on one leg, picking up their beanbags along the way. They should hop once in each hoop as they hop through the arrangement. Adaptation: Increase the difficulty by having students quickstep through the hoops.

Figure 12.1   Hoopscotch.

ZOOWILD

Arrange students in two parallel lines, 40 to 50 feet apart. Put two identical sets of pictures of different animals in two boxes, one for each team. Students in each line select a picture of an animal from their team's box. At the signal, have the students begin to walk slowly toward each other making the noises of the animals they selected (e.g., pig, cow, dog, horse, snake, monkey, cat, lamb, tiger), trying to find their matches. Once students find their partners, they must imitate the animal sounds and their physical movements. Repeat the procedure. This game also promotes expressive movement and creativity.

SHAPE UP

This game promotes flexibility as well as body awareness and creative movement. You'll need a box full of various pictures mounted on 3-by-5 index cards (e.g., chair, pencil, television, couch, washing machine, blender, ball, desk, car). Make sure you have at least 10 more picture cards than the number of students in the class. Ask each student to select a picture card from the box. Then have them try to shape their bodies to imitate the selected pictures in their personal spaces. Provide enough time for everyone to create the special formation selected. Then say "Shape up!" to signal small groups of children to come over to the box and exchange their cards for new ones.

HOPPING THE ISLANDS

Scatter hoops 10 feet apart throughout the playing area, making sure you have one hoop for every student. At the beginning of class, ask students to each find a home island by stepping inside a hoop. Ask students to perform one movement activity of their choice inside their hoops. Now ask them to perform a movement outside their hoops. Then have them hop back on their islands. Next, play a popular children's song. Ask them to walk, jog, or skip throughout the playing area without stepping inside the islands. When the music stops, tell the children to hop inside a different island. Then allow 10 to 15 seconds for them to perform an exercise, movement, or stretch of their choice. Play the music and repeat the procedure. To add variety, use music with different beats and ask the students to match the pace of their movements to the tempo of the music. Alternate the physical activities each turn or have a student decide for the class. For closure activities, ask the students to return to their original home islands. Because this game allows for plenty of personal choice, it also develops physical activity decision-making skills.

LIFELINE

Divide the students into groups of three or four. In each group, have one student hold the end of a standard jump rope (the "lifeline"). At the signal "Go!" he runs throughout the playing area dragging the rope along the ground and shaking it. The students in the group try to pick up the end of the jump rope. The student who picks up the lifeline then gets to run with the rope. Allow each student in the group to have a turn running with the lifeline. Remind the class "The reason the rope is called a 'lifeline' is that jumping rope is a good exercise for the heart and exercise will improve your life and keep you healthy." Remind children to keep the rope on the ground level.

THE WHEEL OF FITNESS

Use chalk or gym tape to design two large circles, one inside the other. Arrange an equal number of children around each circle. Say "At the signal 'Go!' the outside circle runs clockwise (point), the inside circle runs counterclockwise (point). At the signal 'Stop!' turn and face your partner." Have them greet their partners with "high fives." Now, allow 10 to 15 seconds for the children to choose and perform an additional exercise with their partners. Repeat the procedure. Adaptation: Vary the locomotor movements, e.g., walking, skipping, hopping.

BACK-TO-BACK

Have an uneven number of students scatter around the playing area. Say "On the signal 'Go!' find a partner and stand back-to-back. The student without a partner calls out the next class movement activity, such as hopping, skipping, or walking. The student claps twice to start the next round." If you have an even number of students, have students find a different partner each round and alternate the students who call out the next type of movement.

This is a great game to reinforce good standing posture. When students find their partner remind them to stand straight, with head and shoulders back, chest out, and feet pointing straight ahead. Demonstrate or illustrate a picture of good standing posture. Ask "What types of jobs require workers to stand most of the day?" (Police officers, waiters, cashiers, toll booth operators, teachers.) Remark "Good posture is especially important to these adults." As a closing activity have each student perform the twin walk: "Stand back-to-back with a partner and gently lock elbows and walk together forward and backward." Encourage cooperation and unity (see figure 12.2).

Figure 12.2   Twin walk.

VEINS AND ARTERIES

Review the basic concepts that veins carry blood to the heart and arteries carry blood away from the heart. Reinforce that exercise will keep the veins and arteries healthy. Design a heart with chalk or gym tape about 10 feet in diameter, including veins and the two main arteries. Mark an area inside the heart and a safe area outside the heart, each with four cones. Select two to four "its," designating them with red jerseys. Explain "Begin walking around the playing area. At the signal 'Veins!' everyone tries to run back to the inside of the heart (marked by the cones) without getting tagged by the its. At the signal 'Arteries!' run away from the heart to the safe area (marked with cones). Tagged students become its and get red jerseys." (This game may be more appropriate for advanced level I students.)

Developmental Level II Games

LAS VEGAS FITNESS

This is a motivating activity that works especially well as a five-minute warm-up routine. Have students form a large circle. Select a student to roll one large foam die. Each number (one through six) represents a different exercise.

1. Hopping around the gym
2. Push-ups
3. Vertical jumps
4. Toe raises
5. Seconds in the seal crawl position
6. Curl-ups

After the first roll chooses the exercise, have the student roll the dice (two die) for the number of repetitions or seconds to be performed by the class. After the repetitions of the first exercise are completed, select another student to roll for exercise and repetitions.

FITNESS GUESS

Replace the old squad formation calisthenics routine with this great warm-up activity. Have students form a large circle. First, select a fitness guesser and have her leave the gym or turn away from the circle and close her eyes. Now select a fitness leader who will change the exercise by miming a new one before the group every 10 to 15 seconds. Bring the guesser, with eyes opened, back to the middle of the circle. The class begins exercising and the guesser must try to name who the fitness leader is. Keep track of the students who did not get a turn as fitness guessers and leaders and reassure them that they will get a turn in the next few classes.

FIND A FRIEND

This is a great activity to do at the beginning of the school year. Have the students scatter throughout the playing area. Select two students as "its" and have them wear colored jerseys. Explain "On the signal 'Go!' the 'its' choose a number from one to five and call it out, telling you how many people should be in a group holding hands. If the number four is called, for example, form groups of four by holding hands. The 'its' try to tag any students who are not in groups. The 'its' may start chasing as soon as a number is called. The first two students who were tagged become the new taggers. Once you are in a group, shake hands and introduce yourselves to each other. This game is called 'Find a Friend' because everyone in class is a friend working and playing together."

ROMAN CANDLE

Make at least four Roman candles around the gym by placing four folding mats standing up on their sides to form each candle. Divide the children into groups of seven or eight and have three or four children stand inside their group's Roman candle. Place 10 to 15 foam balls inside each Roman candle. Say "At the signal 'Go!' begin tossing the balls outside the Roman candle. The students outside the mats chase or catch the balls and toss them back in." After two to three minutes stop and count the number of balls in the center of the mats.

At the end of the game, have students check their heart rates. Ask them to merely feel the pace of the beat. Explain to the class how something simple—such as retrieving and throwing balls—can elevate the heart rate, having a positive impact on their health. Reinforce to the class that physical activity may take many forms and still be quite beneficial, such as washing the car, raking leaves, taking a nature hike, or playing fun games in physical education.

CIRCLE CIRCULATION

Explain to students that this game will elevate the level of intensity in a manner similar to jogging. By increasing their heart rates, students are increasing their circulation. Ask the students to take their heart rates before, during, and after the game.

Have the class form a large circle around a plastic bowling pin. Divide the circle into two equal halves, called teams A and B. Have the students on each team count off starting with "one" so that every person shares a number with someone on the other team. Begin the game by asking everyone to walk around the circle. After a few seconds, call out a number. Explain "The two players with the same number run out and try to steal the plastic bowling pin and run back with it to any part of the circle without getting tagged by the other player. If a player succeeds, her team gets two points. If the player stealing the pin gets tagged by the other player before getting back to the circle, the player who successfully tagged the other gets one point for

his team. All the while, the other players continue to walk in a circle." To add variety, change the locomotor movement each round (e.g., walking, jogging, skipping, hopping, and so on). Or call out simple addition problems with the answer forming the number called (for example, 3 + 2 = 5, students with the number five must try to steal the pin). Ask students to check their heart rates halfway through the class period and also at the end of the class period and then compare these two heart rates. Point out that their moving around the circle is similar to the blood circulating in their bodies and that exercise improves circulation.

HEARTY HOOPLA

Discuss the fact that running helps decrease the bad cholesterol (LDL) and increase the good cholesterol (HDL). Divide the class in four equal groups and position one group in each corner of the playing area. Place a hoop in each corner with five beanbags and five tennis balls. Label the beanbags "LDL," (bad cholesterol), and label the tennis balls "HDL," (good cholesterol). Say "On the signal 'Go!' run to another team's corner to get as many tennis balls (good cholesterol) as possible and bring them back to your home. At the same time, try to clean out the beanbags (bad cholesterol) from your corner and place them in another team's hoop. But you can grab only one tennis ball or beanbag at a time. You may not guard your home or steal tennis balls from other students, and you may not interfere with someone placing beanbags in your home." After two to three minutes of playing time call out "Freeze!" The team with the most good cholesterol (HDL) and the least bad cholesterol (LDL) is the winner. Remark "Exercise helps build the amount of good cholesterol (HDL), and reduce the bad cholesterol (LDL) that can develop if you don't exercise and you eat too much fat."

TRIANGLE TAG

Divide the students into groups of four. Have three of the students in each group hold hands in the shape of a triangle. One of these three is an "it." The student outside of the group is also an "it." Explain, "The 'it' outside of the triangle tries to tag the 'it' in the triangle. Students in the triangle must stay together in the triangle formation as they are being chased." Rotate the "its" until each student has had a turn. You may vary the activity, for example, the triangle students may hop on one foot, walk briskly, run on toes, on heels, and so on. At the end of the activity, point out that everyone in class performed about 7 to 10 minutes of healthy, vigorous physical activity in this game. Remind them that a total of 30 minutes is recommended each day. Ask "What will you be doing for physical activity after school today?" (Allow a few minutes for this important discussion.)

FITNESS TAG

Have students scatter throughout the playing area. Select four "its." Each "it" wears a different-colored jersey and sign denoting a heart disease risk factor and an exercise name.

- Smoking: curl-ups (5 times)
- Inactivity: jog in place (10 seconds)
- Junk food: sit-and-reach (5 seconds each leg)
- Stress: vertical jumps (5 times)

When a student is tagged, she must stop and perform the exercise that is assigned to the risk factor, then continue to play. After three or four minutes change the taggers. If students have trouble remembering the exercise for each risk factor, tape a card on the jersey that has the name of the risk factor, the name of the exercise, and the number of repetitions or the duration of the exercise.

CATCH THE DRAGON'S TAIL

This is a great activity to help bring the class closer together. Divide students into groups of seven or eight and have each group stand in a straight line holding hands. The last person in line tucks a scarf behind him in his waistband. The scarf should fall at least 18 inches below the waist. Say "At the signal 'Go!' the student in the front of the line tries to catch the last student by grabbing the dragon's tail without the line breaking apart." Rotate positions and repeat activity. As a closing activity, try putting the entire class into one line. Emphasize the teamwork and cooperation needed to be successful in this game. (Have a few elastic belts for students wearing a dress without a waistband.)

CRAZY CONES

Take 10 more cones than you have students in class and scatter them throughout the playing area. Knock over half of the cones so they are lying on their sides. Divide the class into two even groups: lumberjacks and farmers. Explain "When the music begins, the lumberjacks try to knock over the standing cones while the farmers try to pick up the cones that are lying down. After one minute, we'll change roles and repeat the activity." Adaptation: Ask the lumberjacks to knock down cones with different body parts (e.g., knee, elbow, foot). Use plastic milk containers or two-liter soda bottles if you do not have enough cones.

SHAPE-A-ROUND

Try this interesting warm-up activity. Divide the class into circles of seven or eight students. In each circle, give each student a number, one through eight. Have students spend a few minutes deciding on an exercise or physical movement to perform as individuals. Then have students demonstrate their choices to the class, beginning with number one and so on. The other students should jog in place in their small group circles. When they hear their number called, they first perform the exercise just finished by a student in their own group followed by their own individual exercise. Everyone else continues to jog in place. The student who begins this game may copy an exercise you demonstrate first.

Developmental Level III Games

KNOTS OF PROBLEMS

This activity promotes group problem-solving skills and may enhance flexibility. Divide the class into circles of five to seven children standing shoulder-to-shoulder. Have each player reach forward and grasp the hands of other players in the circle as shown in figure 12.3. Students may not hold both hands of the same person or hold the hand of a student to the left or right of their positions. Have students work to unravel the hands into a circle. Remind students not to release their grips. In addition, caution them to be careful not to twist another student's wrist or shoulder.

SPORT LINEUP

Before class, set up a minicircuit course adjacent to the playing field. Divide the class into two teams. Have the defensive team play traditional softball fielding positions. Assign the offensive team a batting order. Say "Before playing offense each inning, the offensive team must complete the minicircuit course. To take a turn, you step up to home plate and

Figure 12.3   Knots of Problems.

either throw, punt, or placekick the Nerf football, then run all four bases without stopping. The defensive team's job is to line up behind the player who catches or retrieves the ball. The lead player then passes the ball overhead until it gets to the last player who must run to the front of the line so everyone can then sit down. The base runner scores one point for each base successfully passed before the defensive team completes the lineup." Change sides after each player on the first offensive team has had a turn. Adaptations: Use other sport skills such as soccer kicks, hitting a Wiffle or rubber ball off a tee, or serving a volleyball.

Circuit course:

1. Three curl-ups on mat

2. Three push-ups on mat

3. Five rope jumps

4. Jog to the tree and back in right field (total of 200 yards)

5. Three arm curls using an exercise tube

VBS (VOLLEYBALL, BASKETBALL, SOFTBALL)

For this game, you'll need six to eight volleyballs, six to eight tennis balls, six to eight basketballs, four bases, and one basketball goal. Set up the game as a softball field in the gymnasium with home plate directly in front of a basketball goal. Have the defensive team play traditional softball fielding positions. Assign the offensive team a batting order. Explain "To take a turn, you step up to home

plate and properly serve the volleyball, then run around all bases without stopping. The objective for the defensive team is to catch the ball, throw to any two bases—in any order—then back to the catcher at home plate. Then the catcher must try to score a basketball layup before the runner passes home. If the catcher is unsuccessful, the runner scores. A player is out if the catcher makes a layup in time, if the player serves the ball in foul territory, or if a defensive player catches a fly ball." Play two or three outs per inning. Each inning rotate the defensive positions to allow everyone a chance to practice fielding skills and lay-ups. To keep everyone active and involved, have players waiting their turns perform a series of different, but related, skill drills off to the side of the playing field, for example, volleyball (bump and set), softball (catch and throw with tennis balls), or basketball (chest and bounce passes). Adaptation: Score a point for each base a runner passes before the catcher makes the layup.

SOCCER GOLF CHALLENGE

For this game, you'll need two cones, three bowling pins, one large garbage pail, one hula hoop, one hockey goal, one cardboard box, and one index card and pencil for each student. Divide students into groups of three. Have one group, each student with a soccer ball, begin at station 1 as illustrated in figure 12.4. Say "Keep track of how many kicks it takes to complete the task at each hole (station). Record the number after each station on an index card. If you do not complete a task in five kicks, record a score of six and move on to the next station. Try to improve your personal bests." When the first group has completed station two, have the next set of players begin. You may even choose to have a small part of your class work on this activity while the rest of the class plays a soccer game on the adjacent field.

Here is a list of possible stations you should set up 30 yards apart:

1. Kick ball at a tree
2. Kick ball through cones set three feet apart
3. Kick ball to knock over bowling pins
4. Kick ball into large garbage pail lying on its side
5. Pass ball into the hula hoop
6. Score a point in the hockey goal
7. Lift ball with foot kick into a cardboard box

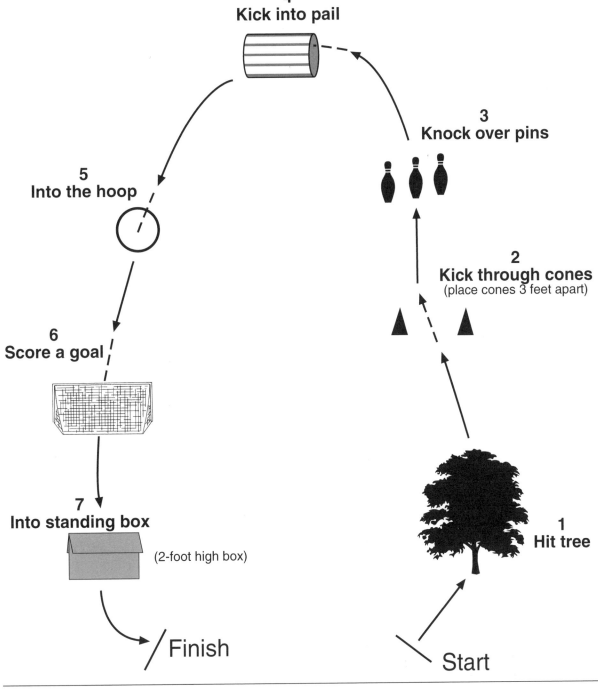

Figure 12.4   Soccer golf challenge.

CHUTE THE BALL

This game increases muscular endurance and promotes cooperation and teamwork. Divide the class into two teams and have them stand around a large parachute, with one team on one side and the other on the other side. Place a large inner tube and two different-colored balls on top of the chute near the center. Say "At the signal 'Go!' each team tries to shake the parachute to get their colored ball through the inner tube. The first team to score three points wins the game." Adaptation: Place more than one ball for each team inside the parachute.

ESTIMATION RUNNING

To help students become more aware of pacing skills during distance runs, design a route three-quarters to one mile in length throughout your school and playground area for students to jog around, positioning large cones with arrows pointing the way. Be certain the ground is level and clear of any obstacles. Before starting have each student estimate the time she will finish in and write it down on an index card. Walk them through the course so they understand how far it is. Send two groups of 10 to 15 students each, separated by 30 to 40 seconds to avoid route congestion. Time the students with a stopwatch. The student closest to her estimated time when she completes the course is the winner.

HEART SMART LOTTERY

Write different heart smart food items (e.g., carrots, yogurt, brown rice, chicken, turkey, low-fat milk) each on a piece of plain white paper. On two pieces of paper write a junk food item (e.g., candy, cookies, potato chips, cheeseburger). Crumple the pieces of paper into individual balls and place them in a box. Have each student select a paper ball and start jogging in the circle. Explain "At the signal 'Heart smart lottery!' unfold your paper balls and read the food item. The students with the junk food items are 'it' and try to tag the other students. If tagged, you freeze and yell 'I'm heart smart!' Another player comes over and performs 10 jumping jacks with you to release the junk food from your body. You're in a safe zone when you're performing the jumping jacks and cannot be tagged." Every two or three minutes, begin a new round of play. Reinforce the difference between heart smart foods and unhealthy food items at the beginning and end of the activity.

HOOP DRIBBLE

Have students scatter in pairs around the playing area. Fasten a standard jump rope securely to a hula hoop for each pair. Explain "One student drags the hoop around the court at a slow to moderate pace. The other partner tries to dribble or bounce a ball in the center of the hoop as it moves."

BUMP AND RUN

Divide students into groups of eight. Have seven students in each group form a circle, which is marked with small cones or gym tape. Direct the eighth student to stand in the middle. Say "To warm up, bump a volleyball around the circle playing 'Keep-It-Up.' Next, the students in the circle begin side-stepping around the circle, and the student in the middle with the volleyball calls 'Bump and run.' Each time a player on the outside of the circle bumps the ball back to the middle, he runs completely around the circle back to his original spot." Add more players to the circle to keep the drill continuous. Have students count how many times their group is able to successfully bump and run. Encourage each group to compete against themselves for their best score, not against the other groups.

Summary

Incorporating active games into your physical education curriculum can be an exciting way to promote higher levels of physical activity. Children love well-designed, dynamic games and often remark that they have great fun when they are playing with classmates. Take advantage of this natural enthusiasm for games to teach children about the benefits of physical activity as well as to prove that fitness *is* fun, cooperation *is* a team effort, and that we can include everyone in all physical education activities.

To maximize the learning experiences for your students, keep in mind the characteristics of developmentally appropriate games we discussed in this chapter. Avoid games that eliminate players, embarrass children, and have low activity levels. Instead, sensitively promote moderate to vigorous physical activity levels to reach class objectives. Use the active games described in this chapter to augment your lessons as you strive to increase the degree of physical activity in your physical education classes. For additional active games see Foster et al. (1992) and Hinson (1995).

Dance and Rhythmic Activities

> *Dancing is the loftiest, the most moving, the most beautiful of the arts, because it is no mere translation or abstraction from life; it is life itself.*
> —Havelock Ellis

Dance and rhythmic activities naturally contribute to the goals of a balanced physical education program in the elementary school. They are an excellent way to develop motor skills, self-expression, creativity, and aesthetic appreciation as well as to increase physical activity levels. Whether you are teaching creative dance, tinikling activities, parachute dances, or step aerobics, the purpose remains the same: children actively moving in rhythm.

Dance and rhythms inherently help children enhance their self-concepts, express their feelings, and understand their bodies' potential. Certainly, dance and rhythms can develop body awareness as children explore space through locomotor movements such as walking, hopping, skipping and through nonlocomotor movements such as bending, stretching, twisting, and swaying. Moreover, teaching a variety of dance and rhythmic activities is an excellent strategy for communicating cultural and ethnic awareness. For example, if you have students of Hispanic descent, teach a variety of Latin dances and rhythms. This will help these students feel more comfortable in class. As an additional benefit, you will foster a personal bond with these students that will carry over to the rest of the school year. But teach a number of American folkdances, too, so everyone—regardless of their cultural heritage—

will develop an understanding and appreciation of this country's rhythmic heritage. Indeed, provide a variety of experiences to encourage students to appreciate other cultures and ethnic groups, thereby promoting better communication and understanding among your students.

Safety Precautions

Be aware of the following safety precautions as you plan dance and rhythmic activities for school-aged children. First, include proper warm-up and cool-down activities in each dance and rhythmic class session. Then, allow for intermittent rest periods within the class activity, taking these opportunities to reinforce the benefits of dance as a healthy physical activity.

Next, avoid movements that result in hyperextension of any joint because this places a significant amount of stress on different areas of the body. Do not repeat a movement more than four consecutive times on one leg; instead, vary the movement at least every four counts. Avoid any quick, jerky movements of the arms, head, or legs, which may cause muscle strain in transitions between advanced steps and may require a movement sequence before changing direction. Moreover, it's important to avoid movements that include forward trunk flexion, which can place undue stress on the low back. Be cautious of dance moves that use a crossover step because this may be stressful on the pronators, the muscles causing the strain, during the weight bearing phase of the crossover. Ensure that students maintain proper posture and body alignment while performing the various dance movements to avoid structural imbalances. Initially, teach a dance at a slow tempo without music and gradually increase to the normal level, moving from the simple to the advanced. Advise children well in advance of each class about appropriate attire: Do not allow children to wear jewelry of any kind and insist that they wear a general cross-training sneaker to provide support with cotton socks to absorb sweat and provide support while reducing friction on the feet during dance and rhythmic activities. Don't allow children to wear running shoes because these can constrict lateral movements and may cause ankle or knee injury.

Planning Developmentally Appropriate Activities

One of the most important ways to ensure safety and enjoyment is to introduce dance and rhythms in a developmentally appropriate progression similar to how you approach the other areas of your program. Study the activities for the three developmental levels in this chapter to help you discern what types of dance and rhythmic activities are more appropriate and motivating for each level.

I have designed and field-tested the activities in this chapter to be "user-friendly" and developmentally appropriate. Use and adapt these simple instructions for your lessons. Keep in mind, you don't have to be a dance instructor to incorporate rhythmic activities into your physical activity program!

Developmental Level I Dance and Rhythmic Activities

Music and dance are not always necessary to enhance rhythmic development in your curriculum. Skipping, hopping, throwing a ball—most large muscle movements are inherently rhythmic, providing the foundation for the beginning experiences of rhythmic movement. At this level, empha-size children moving through space, exploring variations, and developing body awareness through locomotor and nonlocomotor movements. To demonstrate how enjoyable physical activity can be in a child's life, incorporate creative dance, singing games, and rhythmic activities using streamers, hoops, lummi sticks, wands, and balls at this level.

THE BEAT GOES ON

This activity enhances expressive movement related to rhythm, tempo, and basic locomotor skills. Explain to the class that they will be moving in time to the beat of a drum. Allow the students to decide how to move based on their interpretations of the beat (hard, soft, fast slow, even rhythm, or uneven rhythm). Here are some suggestions:

1. Beat the drum in an even four-count rhythm.
2. Tap the drum lightly four counts.
3. Beat the drum heavily four counts.
4. Combine light and heavy beats.
5. Move to the beat of the drum, one step for each beat (even four-count beat).
6. Uneven beat.
7. Fast beat (change tempo).
8. Slow beat.
9. Make different quick, angular movements with arms and legs on each beat in a four-count rhythm.
10. Move to the beat of the drum in various ways, e.g., heel walking, toe walking, sidestepping, march steps, crawl movement.

THE SUNDAY TRIP

This creative activity is a dramatization of a Sunday trip using physical activity to promote self-expression and locomotor skills. Tell the class they will be taking a Sunday trip through the countryside. Give each student a scarf for bad weather (ask them to tuck it in their pockets) and a hoop to use as a steering wheel for a car. Use the following dialogue or create something similar: "Walk briskly throughout the playing area using your hoop to turn your car. Now place your hoop on the floor. OK—that was a long trip. Let's stretch. Stand inside your hoop and get as tall as you can." Continue as follows:

Get as small as you can.

Get as wide as you can.

Let's park our cars here and go for a hike in the country.

Show me how you would walk up a hill . . . down a hill.

How would you walk if you were carrying a heavy backpack?

Let's take a break and have a snack and some water. What kind of snack are you eating? Nuts, a banana . . . good!

OK, let's get moving.

It's starting to get cold. Everyone place your scarf on your head.

How would you walk on a cold day?

Can you feel the wind blowing? How would you walk on a cold, windy day with the wind blowing hard in your face?

Stretch one hand out and check for raindrops. Yes! It's starting to rain. Let's go over to that cave (standing mats in corner of gym)!

Is everyone here? Good, let's wait until the rain stops.

Look, there's a rainbow! What colors do you see?

OK, the sun is out now. Let's continue.

Look at the trees gently blowing in the breeze.

Let's pretend we are trees. Our arms and fingers are branches swaying in the breeze.

Let's start back to the cars. Walk carefully.

Let's take a big leap over the puddles.

Look, there's a rabbit hopping in the grass.

Everyone try to imitate the rabbit hopping through the grass.

OK, we're back at our cars. Everyone find your own hoop.

Start your engines. Let's drive home! That was a great Sunday trip through the country!

RHYTHM STREAMERS

This rhythmic movement activity reinforces manipulative skills and shape formations while developing arm and shoulder muscle endurance. Give each student a streamer and have students scatter around the playing area, reminding them to stay in their personal spaces facing you. Encourage the students to keep time to the music as they twirl the streamers (see figure 13.1).

Figure 13.1 Rhythm streamers.

Four-count rhythm suggestions:

Left-side circles (four times).

Right-side circles (four times).

Lasso overhead with left hand (four times).

Lasso overhead with right hand (four times).

Front circle with left hand (four times).

Front circle with right hand (four times).

Figure eight (four times).

Repeat.

Once students are familiar with this routine, vary the movements. For music, use the record "Theme from Magnum P.I." (Mike Post, Elektra Records).

FREEZE DANCE

This activity develops decision-making skills and agility by encouraging continuous physical activity in short segments. Have students scatter around the playing area. Encourage students to move to the rhythm of the song "Turn the Beat Around" (Gloria Estefan, Epic Records) using any locomotor movements they select (walking, hopping, skipping, galloping) throughout the playing area. Explain "When you hear me beat the drum (with two quick beats), change direction. When the music stops, freeze like statues and hold the freeze for five seconds." Repeat.

OLD MACDONALD HAD A HEALTHY BODY

Try this old favorite with updated, active, healthy lyrics. Use it to help children identify body parts and as an interesting warm-up activity. Have students stand in a large circle facing the center. Use the traditional song "Old MacDonald" and develop lyrics such as the following:

Old MacDonald had a healthy body, E-I-E-I-O. And on his body he had healthy arms, E-I-E-I-O. With a bend, bend here and a bend, bend there, here a bend, there a bend, everywhere a bend, bend, Old MacDonald had healthy arms, E-I-E-I-O. Old MacDonald had a healthy body, E-I-E-I-O. And on his body he had healthy legs, E-I-E-I-O. With a march, march here and a march, march there, here a march, there a march, everywhere a march, march, Old MacDonald had healthy legs, E-I-E-I-O. Old MacDonald had a healthy body, E-I-E-I-O. And in his body he had a healthy

heart, E-I-E-I-O. With a jog, jog here and a jog, jog there . . . .

HOKEY POKEY

This singing activity is a motivating warm-up activity that will help students learn to identify body parts while enhancing their basic locomotor skills. Have students stand in a large circle facing the center. Practice chanting the lyrics to the song first before you begin.

Verse:

You put your right foot in;

You put your right foot out;

You put your right foot in;

And you shake it all about;

You do the Hokey Pokey;

And you turn yourself around;

That's what it's all about!

During lines five and six children place their hands overhead and shake their fingers while turning completely around. Do different body parts: left foot, right arm, left arm, right hip, left hip, head. Then do the final verse:

You do the Hokey Pokey;

You do the Hokey Pokey;

You do the Hokey Pokey;

That's what it's all about!

At the end of the song, have everyone clap their hands in time to the last words: "That's what it's all about!" Have everyone cheer!

Developmental Level II Dance and Rhythmic Activities

You can introduce simple combinations of locomotor and nonlocomotor movements at this level. Make sure, however, that the combinations include no more than three different motor skills. Introduce a variety of activities that utilize individual, partner, small group, and entire class experiences. Try activities such as tinikling, parachute dances, expressive dance movement, jump ropes, simple folkdances, and basic dance steps.

THE CHICKEN DANCE

Have students scatter around the playing area facing you. First, practice the movements to the song "The Chicken Dance." Describe and demonstrate the movements to the children: "Begin with four finger snaps with your hands up to shoulder height, then you do four wing flaps with arms up, elbows bent, and an up and down motion. Now you do four wiggles with knees bent and back bent, gently wiggling the waist and trunk area. Finally, you do four claps while standing in place. We'll repeat the four movements three times." After the third time through the sequence, have the students find a partner and hold hands and perform 16 walking steps or skips in a circle, moving counterclockwise.

CALIFORNIA DREAMIN'

This rhythmic activity includes walking, jogging, sidesteps, arm movements, and expressive movements. To begin have students form a single line.

California Strut (a single line dance to the song "California Dreamin'," Mamas and Papas, Capitol Records)

- Walk forward (4 counts); clap.
- Walk backward (4 counts); clap.
- Sidestep right (4 counts); clap.
- Sidestep left (4 counts); clap.
- Jog in place (16 counts); clap.
- Repeat sequence.

Surfin' Dudes (to the song "Surfin' U.S.A.," The Beach Boys, Capitol Records)

Have the students scatter around the playing area. Tell them to pretend they are each on a surfboard (see figure 13.2). Participate with the class by leading the actions:

- Wax down your imaginary surfboard.
- Hop on your boards.
- Bend your knees to go low.
- Lean to the right.
- Lean to the left.
- Surf on the right leg . . . now on the left.
- Move around the gym, pretending to surf.
- Hop off your surfboards and swim
  a. front crawl,

Figure 13.2   Surf movements.

  b. backstroke, and
  c. breaststroke.
- Repeat swimming motions.
- To finish, jump up and down and splash in the water!

EVERYBODY CONGA (LATIN AMERICA)

This activity emphasizes Latin rhythms as well as walking and changing directions. Have students form two lines, resting their hands on the shoulders of the student directly in front of them. Use the songs "Conga" and "Rhythm Is Gonna Get You" (Gloria Estefan, Epic Records). Explain the dance: "When the music begins, start on your right foot, and everyone walk together. Take three steps and kick with the left foot. Take three steps and kick with the right foot. Take three steps left, then three steps right. At the signal 'Change' everyone turn around and go in the opposite direction. The conga line continues and the last student in line now becomes the leader." End the activity with the entire class in one large line. Leave the gym and conga around the school campus, being careful not to disturb other classes.

MEXICAN HAT DANCE

In this dance, students learn to do the LaRapsa step in time to the music. Have students stand in a circle grasping a large parachute. Explain the LaRapsa step: "Hop on your left foot with your right heel pointed forward, toes up, heel on ground. Hop on your right foot with your left heel pointed forward, toes up, heel on ground. Hop on your left foot with right heel pointed forward toes up, heel on ground, and hold. So it was left-right-left and hold. The next LaRapsa step is right-left-right and hold." Have students perform eight LaRapsa steps while standing in place. During the chorus, have students jog around counterclockwise, grasping the parachute with their left hands. Repeat, changing the locomotor movements during each chorus (e.g., skipping, hopping, galloping). At the end of the song, have everyone raise the chute straight up and walk to the center to make a cloud.

TINIKLING

Years ago a rice bird from the Philippine Islands developed the strange habit of hopping and kicking its legs so as not to get tangled in the weeds of the swampy marshlands. The tinikling dance steps were created to replicate the tinikling bird's movements and improve agility and rhythmic timing. Divide students into groups of four (two dancers, two bangers) and have the students scatter around the playing area. Tell the bangers to kneel while holding two 7- to 8-foot bamboo poles (3 inches in diameter), about 15 inches apart, resting the poles on two wooden crossblocks, 2 inches by 2 feet long. If desired, play a waltz, in 3/4 time. Say "The pole movement is the same throughout the dance. The bangers hit the poles twice against the crossblocks, then slide the poles together and tap once." Demonstrate the action and allow bangers sufficient time to practice (see figure 13.3).

Explain and demonstrate: "With your left side to one pole, touch toes between the poles twice, then bend that leg up, and hold. Repeat this six times. Then leading with your left foot, hop into the middle of the poles on your left foot, hop into the middle of poles on your right foot, hop out of poles with your left foot to the opposite side. Repeat leading with the opposite foot."

With partners, have students move in opposite directions across the poles but jump together into the middle of poles. After practicing the partner dance, have dancers and bangers switch roles. Ad-

Figure 13.3 Tinikling dance.

aptation: You can modify the tinikling steps to be a 4/4 rhythm with the poles open for two counts and closed for two counts (close, close, tap, tap). You may also use jump bands to replicate similar dance step movements.

Developmental Level III Dance and Rhythmic Activities

Group activities characterize this level. Given enough time to practice, students at this level can learn advanced steps such as the grapevine or the two-step. Most students will be motivated to participate in up-to-date dance trends as well as more traditional activities such as aerobic dance, step aerobics, and line dancing (such as The Electric Slide and the Macarena).

LOW-IMPACT AEROBIC DANCE

The term "low-impact" simply means that one foot is always in contact with the floor, placing less stress on the joints and creating continuous physical activity through basic dance movements performed to music. Have students scatter throughout the playing area, facing you. For a successful lesson, select the tempo of the dance music carefully. If the music is too fast, students will become frustrated and give up; if it is too slow, you will not elicit a desirable level of activity, and students will become bored. The following guidelines will help you gauge the appropriate tempo:

- Warm-up (3 to 5 minutes): 120 to 125 beats per minute (BPM)

- Main event (15 to 20 minutes): 128 to 145 BPM

- Cool-down (3 to 5 minutes): 120 to 125 BPM

Choreograph the following basic dance steps to popular music. Keep the dance steps simple, building your routines throughout the school year as the students gain experience and confidence.

Warm-Up Dance Steps

1. Step touches: Begin with weight on right foot. Step to side with left foot. Close with right, touching the ball of the foot to the floor. Reverse. (See figure 13.4.)

2. Touchbacks: Begin with weight on right foot and left foot touching back on the ball of the foot. Step to the side with left foot. Bring the right foot back. Repeat. (See figure 13.5.)

3. Heel touches: Alternate heel touches in front of the body, keeping knees slightly bent. Repeat. (See figure 13.6.)

Dance Steps

1. March step: Raise knee up parallel to the floor with toes pointed down and swing arms in opposition to legs (left arm is up when right knee is up), keeping head up and shoulders back. (See figure 13.7.)

2. Jog step: Hold arms at waist level with elbows bent, hands in half-fist. Contact floor with heel, roll to outside of foot, push off with the ball of the foot last. (See figure 13.8.)

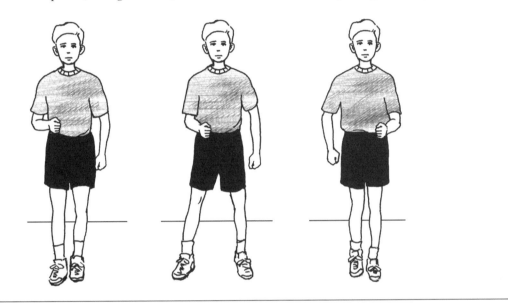

Figure 13.4   Step touches.

Figure 13.5   Touchbacks.

Figure 13.6 Heel touches.

Figure 13.7 March step.

Figure 13.8 Jog step.

3. Plié touches: Reach arms to right side while touching left foot out to side, bending both knees. Swing arms in front of body, then stretch them to the left side, touching right foot out to side. (See figure 13.9.)

Figure 13.9 Plié touches.

4. Simple grapevine step: Step to right on the right leg, arms bent to shoulders. Step behind with left leg while pushing arms above the head. Step to the right on the right leg, arms bent to shoulders. Touch to the left side with the left heel while pushing arms above the head. Then reverse and step to other side. (See figure 13.10.)

5. Cross-elbow touch: Step up on the right foot, lifting the left knee up and touching the left knee to the right elbow. Reverse. (See figure 13.11.)

6. Step-kicks: Step with the left foot, then kick the right foot with toes pointing downward, keeping a slight bend in both knees. Stretch arms out to the side, elbows slightly bent. Reverse. (See figure 13.12.)

7. Heel tap and snap. Bring the left leg behind the body and touch the right hand to the left lef. Now, stretch the leg outward and snap fingers of right hand. (See figure 13.13.) Reverse.

Figure 13.10   Simple grapevine step.

Figure 13.11   Cross-elbow touch.

Figure 13.12   Step-kicks.

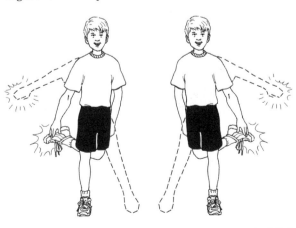

Figure 13.13   Heel tap and snap.

Cool-Down

You can use the warm-up steps for the cool-down.

STEP AEROBICS

Step aerobics is an adaptation of aerobic dance and is usually considered low-impact. The intensity levels may exceed aerobic dance, however, because the students are stepping up and down on and off a bench while performing various dance steps (see figure 13.14).

You may use popular or oldies music with tempos of 118 to 122 BPM. Select songs with a clear beat. The step bench should be six to eight inches in height. Teachers have been using alternatives to the step bench; however, for safety considerations, I

Figure 13.14   Technique for stepping on step bench.

Figure 13.15   Basic single lead on step bench.

only recommend a manufactured step from a reputable company.

Have students consider the following guidelines:

- Maintain good posture.

- Keep the knees "soft" (never locking the joint) and centered over the toes.

- Keep the buttocks tucked under the hips.

- Line up the shoulders over the hips.

- Step up lightly and with control.

- Stay close to the bench when stepping down.

- Do not twist or pivot the knee or the weight bearing leg.

- Do three to five minutes of both warm-up and cool-down.

Use this key when studying the following directions: R = right and L = left.

1. Basic single lead: Beginning from the front of the step, move R foot up, L foot up, R foot down, L foot down for four counts while arms extend, punching on up, and pull, punching on down (see figure 13.15); repeat, leading with the left foot.

2. Single lead tap up, tap down: Beginning from the front of the step, move R foot up, L foot tap up, L foot down, R foot tap down while snapping fingers with arms bent at elbows, hands just below shoulders for four counts; repeat, leading with the L foot.

3. V-step: Beginning from the front of the step, move R foot up wide step, L foot up wide step, R foot down center, L foot down center while curling biceps on same side as leading leg (see figure 13.16) for four counts; repeat, leading with the L foot.

Figure 13.16   V-step on step bench.

4. Kickback step: Beginning from the front of the step, move R foot up, L leg kicks back, L foot down on floor, R foot down on floor while doing bicep curls with both arms on the kickback movement (see figure 13.17) for four counts; repeat, leading with the L foot.

Figure 13.17 Kickback step with double-arm bicep curl.

Figure 13.18 Side leg lift step on step bench.

5. Side leg lift step: Beginning from the end of the step, move R foot up, L foot side leg lift, L foot down on floor, R foot down on floor for four counts; repeat with the L foot leading. (Raise both arms when lifting a leg to the side and lower arms when stepping down. See figure 13.18.)

6. Over the top: Beginning from the side of the step, move R foot up, L foot up, R foot down on the opposite side, L foot down for four counts. Arms move as follows: first beat—elbows up;

second beat—cross arms; third beat—elbows up; fourth beat—cross arms (see figure 13.19). Repeat, leading with the L foot.

THE ELECTRIC SLIDE

This is a line dance that includes moderate physical activity and simple dance steps. It is helpful to play the song "The Electric Slide." Divide students into three lines spaced about 3 yards apart facing you. Start with feet together, weight evenly distributed.

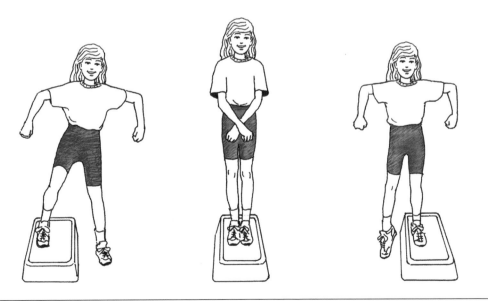

Figure 13.19 Over the top with step bench.

Measures

1 through 4:	Step sideways right, close left to right; Step sideways left, close left to right; Step-touch with left toe.
5 through 8:	Repeat same movements, beginning to left.
9 through 12:	Moving backward, lead with the right foot; Close left to right; Step right and click, left heel to right foot.
13 and 14:	Rock forward on left foot, touch right foot in place, making a digging movement (may swing right arm in arc); Bend over and touch floor in front of left foot on "dig" (knees bent).
15 and 16:	Rock backward on right foot.
17 and 18:	Step left (count one); pivot one-quarter turn left and brush right foot forward (count two).

Repeat measures 1 through 18.

HORA (ISRAEL)

This is a fun, highly active dance that will also bring more cultural awareness to your class. Have students form a single circle, facing the center and holding hands. Explain to the class that this is the national dance of Israel. It is a celebratory dance that includes kicks, arm movements, singing, and shouts of joy. The song "Hava Nagila," meaning "Let's Be Happy," is traditionally used with this dance.

Measures

1. Step left foot sideways to left.
2. Step right foot, crossing in back of left foot.
3. Step left foot sideways to left.
4. Hop left foot while swinging right foot toward the center of circle.

5. Step right foot sideways to right.
6. Hop right foot and swing left foot.

Repeat four times; circle left, then move to the right, using identical steps but beginning on the right foot. At the end of the dance, all raise hands and walk into the center of the circle and shout "Hey!"

MACARENA

This is a Latin line dance with its origin in Spain. A few years ago Miami, Florida, popularized this dance, which has migrated across the United States. Arrange students in three lines, shoulder to shoulder, facing the teacher. Have students dance to the song "Macarena Club Cutz," RCA Records (see figure 13.20).

Measures

1. Put out right hand, then left hand, palms down.
2. Turn up right palm, then left palm.
3. Place right hand on left arm, then left hand on right arm.
4. Place right hand behind the head.
5. Place left hand behind the head.
6. Put right hand on right hip, then put left hand on left hip.
7. Sway hips gently from side to side, repeating three times.
8. Jump up.
9. One-quarter turn to the right and start over.

Summary

Incorporating these developmentally appropriate dance and rhythmic activities into your fitness education program is an excellent way to promote higher physical activity levels. Use the brief overview for planning dance and rhythms activities in this chapter as well as the specific safety precautions to help you design productive lessons. Make dance and rhythmic movement an integral component of your physical education curriculum. But don't forget to teach children the joy of moving to music—for fun and fitness!

Figure 13.20   Macarena steps.

School-Wide Events

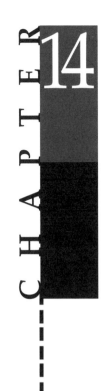

CHAPTER 14

*What its children become, that
will the community become.*
—Suzanne Lafollette

School-wide events will help bring additional attention to your efforts to promote physical activity at your school. When the entire school is involved in a well-organized physical education project, children's morale and spirits are heightened, which often permeates the entire school atmosphere. Classroom teachers usually report that students seem to be more alert and interested in learning when a physical education special event is conducted at their school. Successful school-wide events are often characterized by highly organized, well-planned projects that include the entire school community. Also, gaining administrative support and approval as well as securing a budget are all essential for the event to run smoothly. Furthermore, it would be important to communicate your project early in the school year and have it placed on the master calendar so all may plan accordingly. You and your colleagues can also use school-wide events to integrate classroom learning activities with physical fitness education (e.g., Geography Run; see later in this chapter). You might also choose to help classroom teachers coordinate a health-related thematic unit with a special school-wide event (see chapter 10). Whatever you choose to do, conducting various school-wide projects will provide you with many opportunities to communicate and network with

the faculty, staff, and administration at your elementary school. This will not only strengthen your physical education program itself, it will also make clear to your colleagues that you are truly willing to collaborate with them.

School-wide events are also excellent opportunities to enlist the help and support of parents and the community (see chapter 7). If your school organizes an event committee, be sure to ask at least one parent to serve. Seeing this parent on the committee will encourage other parents or community members to participate. And don't forget another wonderful resource: senior citizens. They are highly capable, eager, and available during the school day.

Study the brief descriptions in this chapter of school-wide events to help promote physical activity and maintain positive public relations for your physical education program. As you read, think about what you can use or modify the contents to suit your situation and needs. But don't limit yourself to only one school-wide event: Incorporate these exciting activities throughout the school year. Change the special school-wide events each year so they don't become monotonous or routine. The same events repeated each year simply will not be special after a while; they will certainly lose their impact and that vital sense of excitement.

Fitness Field Day

This school-wide activity is ideal for the spring or early fall. Promote the fitness field day with the central theme of physical activity for health and fun. It helps to identify the event with a special title, for example, "The Fun, Food, and Fitness Field Day!" Unlike traditional field days that focus on competition in various events, your field day should emphasize participation, physical development, and social interaction.

Form a field day committee to help organize this event. Include a few classroom teachers, special area teachers, and at least two parents. Contact the local university for student volunteers. Health, physical education, and elementary education majors at a nearby university make ideal personnel to help manage this event. Of course, parents, grandparents, and members of the community can also assist. In addition, ask the local school site committee from the American Heart Association or the American Cancer Society to help develop a display.

Ensure that each class has an opportunity to participate in each activity by using a station approach. Set up at least 10 stations throughout the outdoor physical education area (see figure 14.1).

Organize the field day into two phases: kindergarten through third grade and fourth through sixth grades. Consider this sample schedule: 8:30 to 9:00, set up; 9:00 to 11:00, kindergarten through third grade; 12:30 to 2:30, fourth through sixth grades; 2:30, clean up. Assign each class a station number to begin the field day. Then have classes move through the station in sequence. Use a loud horn to signal a change of station every 11 to 12 minutes. At the end of your fitness field day, give each participant a special "Fun, Food, and Fitness" certificate, pin, ribbon, headband, or button. Ask local businesses to donate incentives such as water bottles, key chains, or T-shirts with a health message to distribute to everyone.

Station 1: Step Aerobics

Ask a local health spa if you may speak to a qualified instructor to lead this station. Be sure you have observed a few classes that they are teaching before you invite them to your school. Meet with the instructor before the field day and visit a class he or she is teaching to get to know your volunteer.

Station 2: Cageball Fun

Set two cageballs in automobile tires approximately 30 yards from a starting line. Divide the class in half. At the signal, each team runs up to their ball and rolls it back by pushing it with their hands to the finish line, then back to the tires. The first team to place the cageball back in the tire is the winner. Change teams for the second round.

Station 3: Line Dancing

Using popular music, organize the class for a line dance. Line dancing is an ideal physical education activity because it requires no partners, the steps are easy, and everyone is moving together, which makes students feel more secure (see chapter 13 for details).

Station 4: Parachute Play

Take a group jog with everyone grasping a large parachute. Then play "Pop Out." Divide the class into two teams. Place one or two playballs in the center. Then have the teams try to pop the balls over the opposing team's heads to score a point. Three points wins the game.

Station 5: Exercise Tubes and Bands

Incorporate the use of exercise tubes and bands as illustrated in chapter 11. Design a large task card describing and, if possible, demonstrate the specific exercise you selected for this station. Be certain to provide a number of different exercises so everyone will be able to participate and feel successful. Remember to include a wide variety of tension levels for the tubes and bands so everyone will have an opportunity to participate. Incorporate music to add excitement.

Station 6: Jump for Health

Allow students to jump rope at their own paces or participate in groups. Provide long ropes for small groups of students to use with two turning the rope and two others taking turns jumping. If you wish, include standard individual ropes and heavy individual ropes to offer a variety of physical activities that will enhance arm muscle endurance.

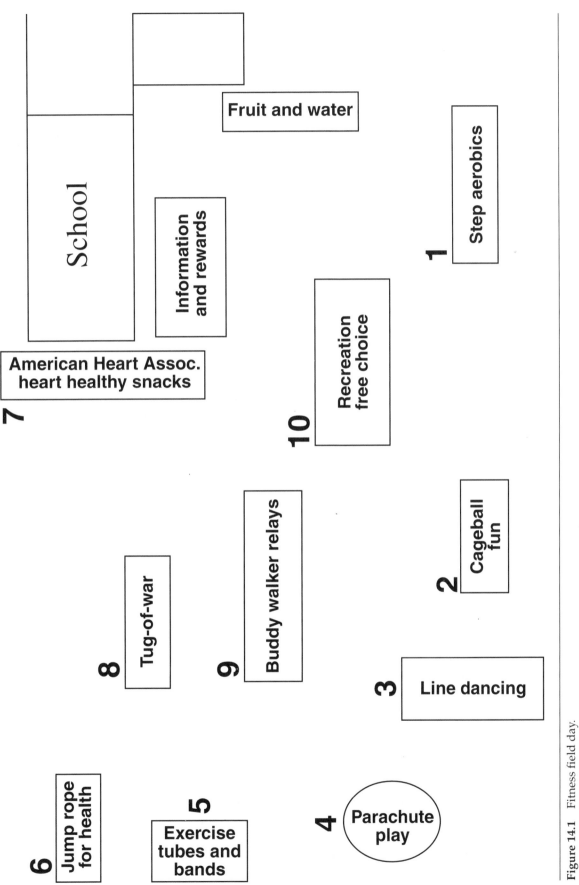

Figure 14.1   Fitness field day.

Station 7: American Heart Association Heart Healthy Snacks

This station will help teach children about healthy snacking. Ask a volunteer from the American Heart Association to set up a display and provide a brief explanation about heart healthy foods two to three minutes long. If you choose, distribute sample healthy snacks, such as yogurt, low-fat cookies, or rice cakes. Ask the American Heart Association to provide a handout or brochure with recipes for healthy snacks (see figure 14.2).

Station 8: Tug-of-War

This is a great way to encourage teamwork and cooperation. If possible, use the lightweight synthetic fiber webbing ropes to help prevent cuts and burns. (See Sportime, appendix B.)

Station 9: Buddy Walker Relays

Each walker consists of 2 seven-foot wooden runners with 12 nylon stretch cord handles (2 per player, 1 per side). Six students step on the runners, hold a strap in each hand, and move in unison (see figure 14.3; see also U.S. Games, appendix B.)

Station 10: Recreation Free Choice

Provide a number of recreation options: hopscotch, jump bands, balance sticks, horseshoes, paddle ball, individual balance boards, and the like.

In addition to the 10 basic stations, you may wish to organize a fruit and water station supervised by the PTA, perhaps setting it up as a chance for a break in the field day circuit, in addition to the healthy snacks at station 7. Use the information and incentives station as a central organizing and equipment

Figure 14.2   School health fair station for heart healthy snacks.

Figure 14.3 Buddy walker.

management location. At the end of the fitness field day, have each class walk by to receive their participation incentives.

Fit for Life Family Night

Hold this event on a weekday evening or on a Saturday morning for parents, grandparents, and children alike. Advertise at least six weeks in advance so that busy parents are able to fit in this event. In the initial announcement, recommend that parents obtain medical clearance before participating in this event. Enlist the help of university students majoring in physical education to assist you with the management and instruction of the family activities. The following is a sample program outline.

Facts About Fitness (10 minutes)

Give each parent a handout listing the health-related benefits of physical activity and printed materials such as brochures from NASPE, the American Heart Association, or the American College of Sports Medicine. Ask a professor of physical education from the local university or another guest to make a few opening remarks about physical activity and its health benefits. The speaker may make specific points about the benefits of physical activity and the importance of a well-balanced physical education program. The speaker also may instruct every-

one to take their resting heart rate to get the audience involved.

Warm-Up (5 minutes)

Have everyone perform march steps, double-arm reaches, and the like to music as well as a few static stretching exercises, such as the lunge, calf stretch, and arm crossovers.

Fit for Life Activities (45 minutes)

Divide the parents and students into three groups, doing three different activities in three different areas. Set up a circuit course in the gymnasium, including activities such as curl-ups, rope jumping, using exercise bands, and doing basketball activities. Organize aerobic dancing and line dancing in the cafeteria. Discuss heart healthy eating and provide snacks in the auditorium or a large classroom. Have groups rotate every 15 minutes.

Cool-Down (10 minutes)

Have everyone meet back in the gymnasium. Lead the entire group in exercises to music, gradually decreasing activity levels. Allow two to three minutes of rest, then ask everyone to take their heart rates once again. Remark how it is important to have a good heart rate recovery. It should be close to the resting heart rate they had at the beginning of the event.

Geography Run

This is an excellent school-wide walking and jogging program. Students may walk or jog in class, at home, or during recess and report the individual mileage to you on a "trip ticket." Insist that this ticket be signed by the student as well as either a parent or teacher. Plot the total mileage on a large map of the United States posted in the gym, hallway, or school cafeteria. For example, the school may run from New York to California (Disneyland) or plot the route of the Oregon Trail. Meet with classroom teachers about how to integrate math, science, art, and language arts into meaningful, related classroom activities. For example, classroom teachers could design math problems to calculate the miles traveled and the miles needed to reach the next state or the final destination. They could organize activities to teach the geography of the region your students are traveling through. Encourage the school cafeteria personnel to prepare special lunches or snacks to represent the next state or region the students will enter, e.g., low-fat pizza for New York, red beans and rice for Louisiana, taco salad for New Mexico, barbecued chicken for Texas. When the students have run or walked the miles necessary to reach the final destination, celebrate by sponsoring a school party. Choose a theme; for example, throw a "California Beach Party." Encourage teachers, staff, and students to come to school dressed in their California "cool" attire. Organize students to decorate the cafeteria with a beach theme and play surf music. Serve turkey club sandwiches with sprouts and vegetables. Present each student who participated in the Geography Run with a special reward for a job well done (e.g., frozen yogurt coupons, free play physical education pass, or a participation certificate commemorating the event).

School Health Fair

Hold this event in the gymnasium or school multipurpose room. Have each class be responsible for a specific health area and have them design a health fair display. Meet with classroom teachers and parents to set up the guidelines for the displays, schedules, and selected topics. Hold a health fair in the fall and the spring by having kindergarten through third grade develop the fall health fair and fourth through sixth grade develop the spring event. Give all grades, however, an opportunity to review the displays at both fairs. The following are possible topics for displays:

Cardiovascular health

No smoking, please

Back and neck care

Healthy snacking

Daily physical activity

Managing stress

Reading food labels

Say "No!" to drugs

Dancing for fun and fitness

Cancer prevention

Weight control

Muscle up

I'm OK—everyday!

Make it the responsibility of the class that designed the health station to explain its content to visitors. In the younger grades, have children display their individual projects, such as "Health Art" pictures or other creative experiences. Set aside the last hour of the school day for parents and community members to visit the health fair. And, if possible, schedule hours after school for working parents to attend. (See also chapter 7.)

Early Bird Stretch and Afternoon Perk-Up

Start the day right and perk up those slow afternoons with this fun idea. For a week in the fall and again in the spring, use this activity to bring attention to physical activity throughout the entire school. Directly following the morning announcements, have everyone in the school (teachers, students, parents, staff, custodians) stand up for an early bird stretch. Develop a voice-cued audiotape to music with a series of exercises to play on the school public address system. At approximately 1:30, use the same tape for an afternoon perk-up.

Jump Rope for Heart, Hoops for Heart, and Step for Heart

Recently, new events such as Hoops for Heart (basketball) and Step for Heart (step aerobics) have offered exciting activity alternatives to the traditional, yet still fun, Jump Rope for Heart. These school-wide events are sponsored by the American Heart Association and the American Alliance for Health, Physical Education, Recreation and Dance. You can obtain a complete package of information, materials, and pledge cards from your local American Heart Association. While waiting for your package, set aside a day for the entire school to participate in one of these activities. Next, have students obtain monetary pledges from the community for the exercise they will perform. The funds are divided among your school, AHA, and AAHPERD. Then, have fun!

ACES: All Children Exercising Simultaneously

This event was created by Len Saunders, a New Jersey physical educator. In May during National Physical Fitness and Sports Month, one day is set aside each year so millions of children throughout the world can exercise in unison at their schools—whether they are in physical education class, in the classroom, or having lunch in the cafeteria. To participate, each school organizes its own 15-minute activity, such as walking, jogging, dancing, or doing aerobics. The objectives are to promote fitness, nutrition, and world peace. Project ACES is supported by the President's Council on Physical Fitness and Sports (PCPFS). This special project comes as a package that includes support materials about National Physical Fitness and Sports Month and information about exercise. The package can be ordered from the PCPFS; for more information contact Len Saunders, Valley View School, Montville, NJ 07045.

Recess Workouts

Use recess for additional time for physical activity. Set up several activity stations with task cards around the playground. Don't make the stations a requirement, rather, let students volunteer to participate in this opportunity to be more physically active. Volunteer your time to help supervise the activities or enlist the help of a college student, parent, or senior citizen to support this effort. Take advantage of this extra time to interact with children who have special needs (e.g., obesity, spinal cord impairments, low activity levels). Recess workouts will also support those students interested in improving their fitness levels.

Fitness Clubs

Organize a fitness club for students who have a special interest in exercising. Meet before school, after school, or during recess. Give the club a clever name such as "The Physical Activators." Provide each student with a detailed portfolio, including information on exercise principles, practical exercises, and recommended training techniques along with log sheets to keep track of their efforts. Con-

sider taking the club on a field trip each year to an exercise physiology lab at the local university or to a health spa. In addition, you may wish to train the students in this club to help with fitness activities, assist with equipment set-up, or help other students enter data on eating and physical activity levels in the computer.

Principal Walks

Help your principal get to know the students in the school better. This activity works well in developmental levels I and II, but it may be appropriate in level III as well. For this event, every Friday the principal walks with two classes for about 20 minutes throughout the school building, the outside school campus area, or the neighborhood. If necessary, organize parent volunteers or other assistants to help supervise students during walks in the neighborhood. But stay in the background for this event. Let the students perceive the principal as the professional promoting physical activity for the health and social benefits.

Holiday Classics

This school-wide event, developed by Allen (1996), brings attention to physical activity during certain holidays throughout the year. Provide each classroom teacher with colored slips of paper denoting the holiday (e.g., orange for Halloween). Ask students to write on the slips their names and what, if any, physical activity they participated in outside of school for a total of 30 minutes. Make it clear that each day of adequate activity allows the student to submit additional entries. Then collect the slips of paper and place them in a large box for a drawing at the end of the month. The more days of physical activity, the more chances students have to win. But give each student who enters the drawing a sticker, certificate, or token to help encourage continued effort and participation. Explain your program objectives to local businesses and ask if they would donate the prizes in return for a little publicity. Examples of prizes are a large pumpkin for Halloween, a snowboard for Christmas, an American Heart Association cookbook and educational kit "Heart Power" for Valentine's Day, and a baseball glove for Easter.

Summary

Integrate school-wide events into your physical education program to benefit everyone by reinforcing the major goals of health-related physical fitness, by raising student spirit, by encouraging positive morale, and by creating more interest in your physical education program. Moreover, these events create effective public relations opportunities to help you build support for your curriculum as well as any innovative program reforms you may have in mind. Indeed, parents and other community members who volunteer to help you run events will see first-hand how exciting your program is and how important increasing physical activity is. School-wide events may also help you network with the faculty, staff, and administration, thereby helping you to develop positive, long-term professional relationships as you strive to integrate physical education goals throughout the school curriculum. Study and adapt the examples of school-wide events in this chapter to your situation and you'll be off and running!

Sample Personal Fitness Education Portfolio

My Physical Activity Pledge

I, _____, pledge that today, _____,
I am determined to change my lifestyle and become more physically active.

I acknowledge that I need improvement in the various components of physical fitness and promise to devote _____ minutes, most days of the week or every day, toward making positive changes in my fitness level and physical activity habits. I will do this in school or at home.

The best time of day for me to work on this change is _____ A.M./P.M.

I will try my best to fulfill this pledge as I work toward my personal fitness goals to the best of my ability.

Signed _____
                        Student

This pledge was witnessed by _____
                                  Parent or guardian

Name _____   Grade _____

Age _____   Sex _____

Class _____

My Health and Fitness Profile

Measurement	Date:	Date:	Date:	Comments
Body weight				
Body height				
Body composition (percent fat)				
Resting heart rate				
Target heart rate zone				
Flexibility (sit-and-reach)				
One-mile run				
Curl-ups				
Push-ups				
Posture				

FITNESS GRAPHS

Name _____

Grade _____

Class _____

Sex _____

Age _____

Plot your fitness scores on the correct line on the graph each time you measure a component of physical fitness. Use dots to plot your results. Connect the dots with a straight line to see your progress.

One-mile run

Minutes

I m p r o v i n g

15				
14				
13				
12				
11				
10				
9				
8				
7				
6				
5				
4				
3				
2				
1				
0				

Pretest date   Interim test date   Posttest date

_____   _____   _____

Curl-ups

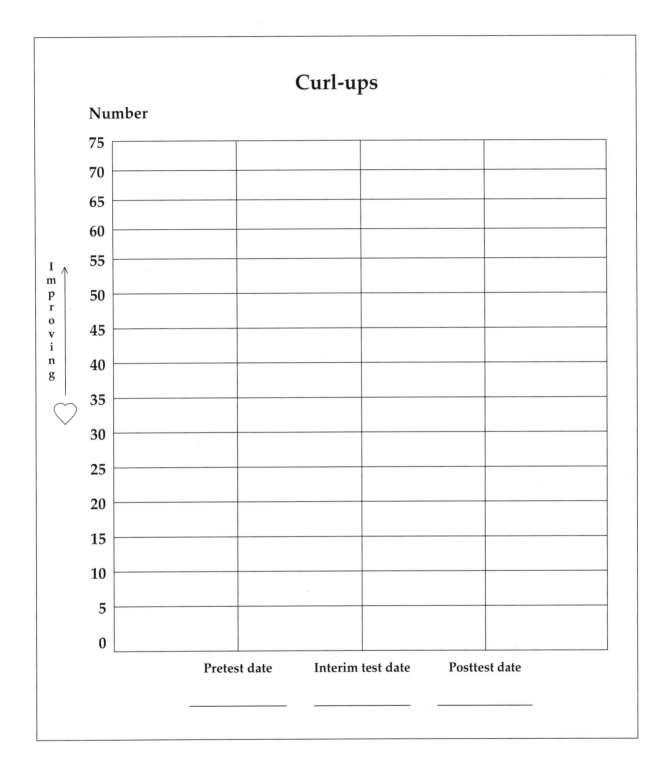

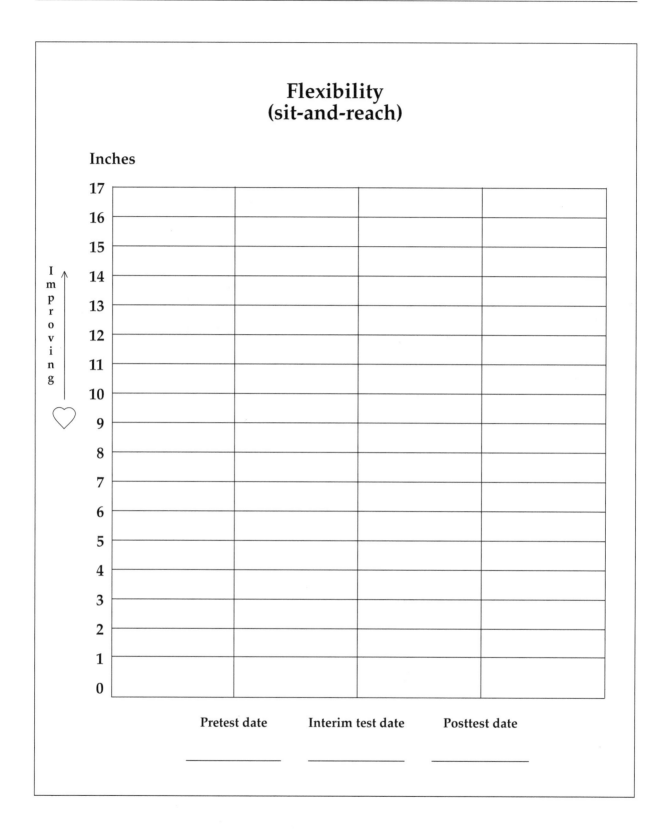

Flexibility
(sit-and-reach)

Inches

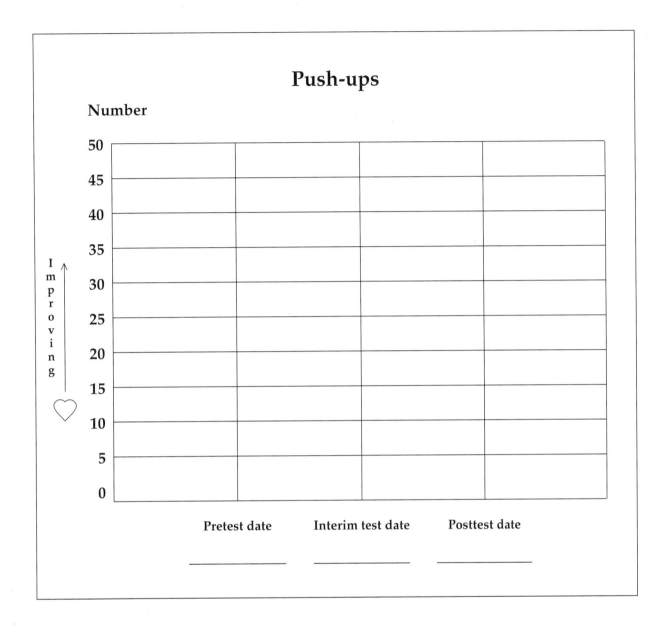

My Fitness Program

Name _____   Grade _____

                                          Class _____

I. **My fitness goal is**

II. **Activities I enjoy to help accomplish my goal are**

Warm-up activities	Cool-down activities
1. _____	1. _____
2. _____	2. _____
3. _____	3. _____
4. _____	4. _____

III. **My planned physical activity schedule**
   (Plan physical activity for at least four days per week.)

Date		Activity	Time of day
_____	Monday	_____	_____
_____	Tuesday	_____	_____
_____	Wednesday	_____	_____
_____	Thursday	_____	_____
_____	Friday	_____	_____
_____	Saturday	_____	_____
_____	Sunday	_____	_____

My Physical Activity Log

Name _____   Grade _____

Class _____

Date	Physical activity	Minutes of activity	Time of day	How I felt

My Daily Nutrition Log

Name _____

Grade _____

Class _____

Date	Breakfast	Lunch	Dinner	Snacks
Mon.				
Tues.				
Wed.				
Thurs.				
Fri.				
Sat.				
Sun.				

My Favorites

My favorite physical activity to do in school physical education is

_____

Because:

My favorite physical activity to do at home with my friends is

_____

Because:

My favorite physical activity to do with my family is

_____

Because:

My favorite physical activity to do by myself is

_____

Because:

Additional Resources

Curriculum Guides and Resource Materials

Aerobics With Fun—Fitness Finders
P.O. Box 160
Spring Arbor, MI 49283-0160
(517) 750-1500

Hundreds of fitness-related activities.

American Health Foundation—Know Your Body
320 E. 42nd St.
New York, NY 10017-5900
(212) 953-1900

General health education. Includes separate curriculum modules for different grade levels. "Juno's Journey."

American Heart Association
7272 Greenville Ave.
Dallas, TX 75231-4596
(214) 373-6300

Education kits: Heart Treasure Chest (3-5 years); Getting to Know Your Heart (K-6); Jump Rope and Hoops for Heart; Heart Trivia Challenge; and Heart Power.

Canadian Active Living Challenge
c/o CAHPER/CIRA
1600 James Naismith Dr.
Glouster, Ontario KIB5N4
(613) 748-5737

Curriculum modules for ages 6 to 8 and 9 to 11.

The Cooper Institute for Aerobics Research
12330 Preston Rd.
Dallas, TX 75230-2290
(214) 701-8001

A recognition system encouraging regular physical activity. Fitnessgram test described.

The Chrysler Fund-Amateur Union Physical Fitness Program
Chrysler Corporation Fund
Poplars Building
Bloomington, IN 47405
(800) 258-5497

Dine Systems, Inc.
586 N. French Rd., Suite 2
Amherst, NY 14228-2103
(716) 688-2492

Software for Macintosh and IBM. Diet analysis and computer activities.

Fit to Achieve
NASPE
NASPE/AAHPERD Publications
P.O. Box 704
Waldorf, MD 20604-0704
(800) 321-0789

Cardiovascular educational materials with teacher's guide.

Fitastic Kids, Inc.
P.O. Box 26311
Minneapolis, MN 55426-0311

Nutrition and fitness activities for lower elementary grades.

Go-For-Health
Center for Health Promotion, Research and Development
School of Public Health
University of Texas, Health Science Center
Houston, TX 70036

Comprehensive health education program at the elementary school level.

Growing Healthy
National Center for Health Education
30 E. 29th St.
New York, NY 10016-7925

Comprehensive health curriculum. Different module themes for each grade level.

Health Skills for Life
Eugene 4-J School District
Eugene, OR 97402

Comprehensive kindergarten through 12th grade health skills curriculum.

Healthy Growing Up
McDonald's Education Resource Center
P.O. Box 8002
St. Charles, IL 60174-8002
(800) 627-7646

Lessons in nutrition and exercise, grades K through 3.

Heart Smart Program
National Center for Cardiovascular Health
School of Public Health, Dept. of Applied Health Sciences
Tulane University
1500 Canal St.
New Orleans, LA 70112-2818
(504) 585-7197

Comprehensive school-based program for K through 6.

Hershey's National Track and Field Youth Program
100 Crystal A Dr.
Hershey, PA 17033-9529
(717) 534-7636

Track and field, fitness, and sportsmanship program for children ages 9 to 14.

Physical Best
American Alliance for Health, Physical Education, Recreation and Dance
1900 Association Dr.
Reston, VA 20191-1598
(800) 321-0789

Recognition system for fitness as well as activities.

Quik-Fit for Kids
138 High St.
East Williston, NY 11596-1418
(516) 739-2713

Muscle endurance program includes rubberized resistance toners in four color-coded levels, curriculum guide, muscle posters, wheelchair workouts, and ready-to-use task cards.

Rollerblade, Inc.
5101 Shady Oak Rd.
Minnetonka, MN 55343
(612) 930-7917

National skate in school program with NASPE.

Slim Goodbody Presents All Fit
Human Kinetics
P.O. Box 5076
Champaign, IL 61825-5076

Video program and teacher's guide with lesson plans.

SPARK (Sports, Play, and Active Recreation for Kids)
San Diego State University
6363 Alvarado Ct.
Suite 250
San Diego, CA 92120
(800) SPARK-PE

Instructional units for health-related fitness and sport skills.

Sunflower Project
Shawnee Mission Public Schools
6649 Lamar
Shawnee Mission, KS 66202

Cardiovascular health education materials.

You Stay Active
American Alliance for Health, Physical Education, Recreation and Dance
1900 Association Dr.
Reston, VA 20191-1502
(703) 476-3455

Fitnessgram and Physical Best programs described.

Fitness Equipment and Music Sources

Aerobic Beat Music Company
8350 Melrose Ave.
Los Angeles, CA 90069
(800) 536-6060

Cambridge Scientific Industries
P.O. Box 265
Cambridge, MD 21613
(800) 638-9566

Children's Music Center
5373 W. Pico Blvd.
Los Angeles, CA 90019

Creative Health Products
5148 Saddle Ridge Rd.
Plymouth, MI 48170
(800) 742-4478

Dance Record Center
1161 Broad St.
Newark, NJ 07714

Dynamix Music Service
711 W. 40th St.
Baltimore, MD 21211

Educational Activities, Inc.
P.O. Box 392
Freeport, NY 11520
(800) 645-3739

Fitness First
P.O. Box 251
Shawnee Mission, KS 66201
(913) 384-6262

Fitness Wholesale
895A Hampshire Rd.
Stow, OH 44224
(800) 537-5512

Flaghouse, Inc.
150 N. MacQuesten Pkwy.
Mt. Vernon, NY 10550
(800) 739-7900

Futrex, Inc.
Body Fat Analysis
P.O. Box 2398
Gaithersburg, MD 20886
(800) 255-4206

Kimbo Educational Records
P.O. Box 477
Long Branch, NJ 07740
(800) 631-2187

Lafayette Instrument Company, Inc.
P.O. Box 5729
Lafayette, IN 47903
(800) 428-7545

Passon's Sports
P.O. Box 49
Jenkintown, PA 19046
(800) 445-9446

Polar Electro, Inc.
Heart Rate Monitors
99 Seaview Blvd.
Port Washington, NY 11050
(800) 227-1314

PRO FIT
12012 156th Ave. SE
Renton, WA 98059
(206) 255-3817

Project Adventure, Inc.
P.O. Box 100
Hamilton, MA 01936
(508) 468-7981

Sportime
One Sportime Way
Atlanta, GA 30340
(800) 444-5700

SPRI Products, Inc.
1554 Barclay Blvd.
Buffalo Grove, IL 60089
(800) 222-7774

The Step Company
400 Interstate N. Pkwy.
Suite 1500
Atlanta, GA 30339

U.S. Games
1901 Diplomat Dr.
Dallas, TX 75234
(800) 327-0484

Youth Fitness, Inc.
8304 Chapel Hill Pl.
Fort Wayne, IN 46825

Web Sites

American Alliance for Health, Physical Education, Recreation and Dance (AAHPERD)

http://www.aahperd.org/

General information including conferences, events, resources, and membership.

American Heart Association

http://www.amhrt.org/

Heart healthy materials including the new "Heart Power" program for schools.

American Association of School Administrators

http://www.aasa.org/

A group dedicated to supporting educational leaders.

Centers for Disease Control and Prevention

http://www.cdc.gov/

Information related to research studies, including national reports such as the Surgeon General's statement on physical activity and health.

Dole 5 A Day

http://www.dole5aday.com/

Nutrition information describing the National 5 A Day For Better Health Program, which encourages regular consumption of fruits and vegetables.

Human Kinetics

http://www.humankinetics.com/

The information leader in physical activity produces books, journals, videos, and conferences.

Mark Manross's Physical Education Home Page

http://infoserver.etl.vt.edu/COE/COE_STUDENTS/dfour/marks_p.html/

View the Kids' Art Gallery and learn about the physical education program at Virginia Tech University.

MedAccess Health Quizzes

http://www.medaccess.com/entertain/enter_toc.htm/

Test your knowledge about health and fitness.

National Association for Sport and Physical Education (NASPE)

http://www.aahperd.org/naspe.html/

NASPE projects, materials, standards, and events.

PE Central

http://infoserver.etl.vt.edu/COE/COE_ADMIN/programs/hpe/PE.Central/PEC2.html/

Activities, lesson plans, and practical techniques for physical educators.

Sports Illustrated for Kids

http://pathfinder.com/SIFK/

Sport-related word games and news about a variety of sports.

REFERENCES

Allen, V.L. 1996. The out-of-school fitness connection. *Teaching Elementary Physical Education* 7(1):15-17.

Alter, M.J. 1990. *Sport stretch*. Champaign, IL: Human Kinetics.

American Alliance for Health, Physical Education, Recreation and Dance. 1995. *Physical best and nutrition*. Reston, VA: Author.

American Alliance for Health, Physical Education, Recreation and Dance and the Cooper Institute for Aerobics Research. 1995. *You stay active handbook*. Reston, VA: AAHPERD Publications and Dallas: Cooper Institute for Aerobics Research.

American College of Sports Medicine. 1993. News release. Experts release new recommendation to fight America's epidemic of physical inactivity. Indianapolis: Author.

Anderson, K.C., and S. Cumbaa. 1993. *The bones game book*. New York: Workman.

Bandura, A. 1986. *Social foundations of thought and action*. Englewood Cliffs, NJ: Prentice-Hall.

Berenson, G.S., ed. 1986. *Causation of cardiovascular risk factors in children: Perspectives on causation of cardiovascular risk in early life*. New York: Raven Press.

Berlin, J.A., and G.A. Colditz. 1990. A meta-analysis of physical education activity in the prevention of coronary heart disease. *American Journal of Epidemiology* 132(4):612-628.

Blair, S.N., H.W. Kohl, R.S. Paffenbarger, D.G. Clark, K.H. Cooper, and L.W. Gibbons. 1989. Physical fitness and all-cause mortality: A prospective study in healthy men and women. *Journal of the American Medical Association* 262(17):2395-2399.

Bouchard, C., R.J. Shephard, T. Stephens, J.R. Sutton, and B.D. McPherson, eds. 1990. *Exercise, fitness and health: A consensus of current knowledge*. Champaign, IL: Human Kinetics.

Centers for Disease Control and Prevention and American College of Sports Medicine. 1993. Summary statement: Workshop on physical activity and public health. *Sports Medicine Bulletin* 28:7.

Cole, J. 1991. *The magic school bus: Inside the human body*. New York: Scholastic, Inc.

Cooper Institute for Aerobics Research. 1992. *The Prudential Fitnessgram test administration manual*. Dallas: Author.

Corbin, C.B. 1987. Physical fitness in the K-12 curriculum: Some defensible solutions to perennial problems. *Journal of Physical Education, Recreation and Dance* 58(7):49-54.

Corbin, C.B., and R. Lindsay. 1997. *Concepts of physical fitness with laboratories*. 9th ed. Dubuque, IA: Brown and Benchmark.

Corbin, C.B., R.P. Pangrazi, and G.J. Welk. 1994. Toward an understanding of appropriate physical activity levels for youth. *Physical Activity Fitness Research Digest* 18:1-8.

Council on Physical Education for Children. 1992. *Guidelines for elementary physical education*. Reston, VA: National Association for Sport and Physical Education.

Dotson, C.O. 1989. *Dino∗Fit software system*. Burtonsville, MD: ARA/Human Factors.

Downey, A.M., G.C. Frank, L.S. Webber, S.J. Virgilio, D.W. Harsha, F.A. Franklin, and G.S. Berenson. 1987. Implementation of "Heart Smart": A cardiovascular school health promotion program. *Journal of School Health* 57(3):98-104.

Downey, A.M., J. Greenberg, S.J. Virgilio, and G.S. Berenson. 1989. A health promotion model: The university, the medical school, and the public health department. *Health Values* 13(6):31-46.

Downey, A.M., S.J. Virgilio, D.C. Serpas, T.A. Nicklas, and G.S. Berenson. 1988. A comprehensive staff development program model for a school-based cardiovascular health intervention: Heart Smart. *Health Education* 19(2):12-20.

Eichstaedt, C.B., and L.H. Kalakian. 1987. *Developmental adapted physical education*. New York: Macmillan.

Eichstaedt, C.B., and B.W. Lavay. 1992. *Physical activity for individuals with mental retardation*. Champaign, IL: Human Kinetics.

Elliott, E., and M. Manross. 1996. Physical educators and the Internet. *Teaching Elementary Physical Education* 7(5):12-15.

Foster, E.R., K. Hartinger, and K.A. Smith. 1992. *Fitness fun*. Champaign, IL: Human Kinetics.

Franck, M., G. Graham, H. Lawson, T. Loughrey, R. Ritson, M. Sanborn, and V. Seefeldt. 1991. *Physical education outcomes: A project of the National Association for Sport and Physical Education*. Reston, VA: National Association for Sport and Physical Education (NASPE).

Graham, G. 1992. *Teaching children physical education*. Champaign, IL: Human Kinetics.

Grossman, H. 1983. *Manual on terminology and classification in mental retardation*. Washington, DC: American Association on Mental Deficiency.

Hellison, D.R., and T.J. Templin. 1991. *A reflective approach to teaching physical education*. Champaign, IL: Human Kinetics.

Hinson, C. 1995. *Teaching children fitness*. Champaign, IL: Human Kinetics.

Kasser, S.L. 1995. *Inclusive games*. Champaign, IL: Human Kinetics.

Kelly, L.E. 1995. Spinal cord impairments. In *Adapted physical education and sport*, ed. J.P. Winnick. Champaign, IL: Human Kinetics.

Kern, K. 1987. Teaching circulation in elementary physical education classes. *Journal of Physical Education, Recreation and Dance* 58(1):62-63.

Kusinitz, I., and M. Fine. 1995. *Your guide to getting fit*. 3rd ed. Mountain View, CA: Mayfield.

Lockette, K.F., and A.M. Keyes. 1995. *Conditioning with physical disabilities*. Champaign, IL: Human Kinetics.

Mazzeo, K., and L. Mangili. 1993. *Step training plus*. Englewood, CO: Morton.

McArdle, W.D., F.I. Katch, and V.L. Katch. 1996. *Exercise physiology: Energy, nutrition, and human performance*. Philadelphia: Lea and Febiger.

McKenzie, T., P. Nader, P.K. Strikmiller, M. Yang, E.J. Stone, C.L. Perry, et al. 1996. School physical education: Effects of the child and adolescent trial for cardiovascular health. *Preventive Medicine* 25:423-431.

McKenzie, T.L., J.F. Sallis, N. Faucette, J. Roby, and B. Kolody. 1993. Effects of a curriculum and in-service program on the quality and quantity of elementary physical education classes. *Research Quarterly for Exercise and Sport* 64(2):178-187.

Meeks, L., and P. Heit. 1992. *Comprehensive school health education: Totally awesome strategies for teaching health*. Blacklick, OH: Meeks Heit.

Meinbach, A., L. Rothlein, and A. Fredericks. 1995. *The complete guide to thematic units: Creating the integrated curriculum*. Norwood, MA: Christopher Gordon Publishers.

Miller, D.K., and T.E. Allen. 1995. *Fitness: A lifetime commitment*. Boston: Allyn and Bacon.

Miller, P.D., ed. 1995. *Fitness programming and physical disability*. Champaign, IL: Human Kinetics.

Mosston, M., and S. Ashworth. 1994. *Teaching physical education*. 4th ed. New York: Merrill/Macmillan.

National Association of Sport and Physical Education. 1995. *Moving into the future: National standards for physical education*. St. Louis: Mosby.

Nichols, B. 1994. *Moving and learning: The elementary school physical education experience*. St. Louis: Mosby.

Ormrod, J.E. 1995. *Educational psychology principles and applications*. Columbus, OH: Merrill.

Pangrazi, R.P., and C.B. Corbin. 1994. *Teaching strategies for improving youth fitness*. Reston, VA: American Alliance for Health, Physical Education, Recreation and Dance.

Pangrazi, R.P., and V.P. Dauer. 1995. *Dynamic physical education for elementary school children*. 11th ed. Boston: Allyn and Bacon.

Pate, R.R., and R.C. Hohn, ed. 1994. *Health and fitness through physical education*. Champaign, IL: Human Kinetics.

Pate, R.R., M. Pratt, S.N. Blair, W.L. Haskell, et al. 1995. Physical activity and public health: A recommendation of changes from the Centers for Disease Control and Prevention and the American College of Sports Medicine. *Journal of the American Medical Association* 273(5):402-407.

Powers, S.K., and S.L. Dodd. 1996. *Total fitness*. Boston: Allyn and Bacon.

Prentice, W.E. 1996. *Get fit stay fit*. St. Louis: Mosby.

Ratliffe, T., and L.M. Ratliffe. 1994. *Teaching children fitness*. Champaign, IL: Human Kinetics.

Rimmer, J.H. 1994. *Fitness and rehabilitation programs for special populations*. Dubuque, IA: Brown and Benchmark.

Rink, J.E. 1993. *Teaching physical education for learning*. St. Louis: Mosby.

Rodgers, C.R. 1994. *Freedom to learn*. 3rd ed. New York: Macmillan.

Ross, J.G., and G.G. Gilbert. 1985. The national children and youth fitness study I: A summary of findings. *Journal of Physical Education, Recreation and Dance* 56(1):45-50.

Ross, J.G., and R.R. Pate. 1987. The national children and youth fitness study II: A summary of findings. *Journal of Physical Education, Recreation and Dance* 58(9):51-56.

Safrit, M.J., and C. Pemberton. 1994. *Complete guide to youth fitness testing*. Champaign, IL: Human Kinetics.

Sallis, J.F., and T.L. McKenzie. 1991. Physical education's role in public health. *Research Quarterly for Exercise and Sport* 62(2):124-137.

Seaman, J.A., ed. 1995. *Physical best and individuals with disabilities: A handbook for inclusion in fitness programs*. Reston, VA: American Alliance for Health, Physical Education, Recreation and Dance.

Seiger, L., K. Vanderpool, and D. Barners. 1995. *Fitness and wellness strategies*. Dubuque, IA: Brown & Benchmark.

Shear, C.L., D.S. Freedman, G.L. Burke, D.W. Harsha, L.S. Webber, and G.S. Berenson. 1988. Secular trends of obesity in early life: The Bogalusa heart study. *American Journal of Public Health* 78(1):75-77.

Sherrill, C. 1996. *Adapted physical activity, recreation and sport*. 4th ed. Madison, WI: Brown & Benchmark.

Simons-Morton, B.G. 1994. Implementing health-related physical education. In *Health and fitness through physical education*, ed. R.R. Pate and R.C. Hohn. Champaign, IL: Human Kinetics.

Thomas, T.R. 1993. *Fitness and health promotion*. Dubuque, IA: Eddie Bowers.

Tillman, K.G., and P.R. Toner. 1990. *How to survive teaching health*. West Nyack, NY: Park.

U.S. Department of Health and Human Services. 1989. *Asthma statistics*. Washington, DC: U.S. Government Printing Office.

———. 1991a. *Healthy children 2000*. DHHS publication no. HRSA-M CH 91-2. Boston: Jones and Bartlett.

———. 1991b. *Healthy people 2000: National health promotion and disease prevention objectives*. DHHS publication no. 91-50213. Washington, DC: U.S. Government Printing Office.

———. 1995. *Healthy people 2000 mid-course review*. Boston: Jones and Bartlett.

———. 1996. A report of the Surgeon General: Physical activity and health at a glance.

Vacca, R.T., and J.A. Vacca. 1996. *Content area reading*. New York: HarperCollins.

Virgilio, S.J. 1990. A model for parental involvement in physical education. *Journal of Physical Education, Recreation and Dance* 69(18):66-70.

Virgilio, S.J. 1996. A home, school, and community model for promoting healthy lifestyles. *Teaching Elementary Physical Education* 7(1):4-7.

Virgilio, S.J., and G.S. Berenson. 1988. Superkids-Superfit: A comprehensive fitness intervention model for elementary schools. *Journal of Physical Education, Recreation and Dance* 59(8):19-25.

Virgilio, S.J., G.S. Berenson, R. Feingold, and E. Kowalski. 1993. Fitness education: A comprehensive approach in Healthy From the Start. In *New perspectives on childhood fitness*, Teacher Education Monograph, no. 15, 95-102. Washington, DC: ERIC Clearinghouse on Teacher Education.

Virgilio, S.J., D. Serpas, D. Harsha, G.S. Berenson. 1987. *Superkids-Superfit exercise log book*. Unpublished manuscript. New Orleans: LSU Medical School.

Welkart, P.S. 1989. *Teaching movement and dance*. 3rd ed. Ypsilanti, MI: High-Scope Press.

Williams, M. 1996. *Lifetime fitness and wellness*. Dubuque, IA: Brown.

Winnick, J.P. 2d ed. 1995. *Adapted physical education and sport*. Champaign, IL: Human Kinetics.

A

Abdominal strength and endurance, assessment of, 15
ACES (All Children Exercising Simultaneously), 199
Adapted Physical Activity, Recreation and Sport, 47
Adapted Physical Education and Sport, 47
Administrative support, 116
Aerobic activity, defined, 43
Aerobic dance, 184-187
Affective learning, 29
Afternoon Perk-Up, 198
Agility, sport-related physical fitness, 8
American Alliance for Health, Physical Education,
    Recreation and Dance, 11
American Heart Association, 196
Anaerobic activity, defined, 43
Arm Circles exercise, 167-168
Arm-Cross Stretch, 164
Arm Curl exercise, 158
Arm Extension exercise, 159
Arm Saws exercise, 150-151
Art
    classroom fitness education and, 124-125
    Developmental Level I activities and, 129-132
    Developmental Level II activities and, 134-138
    Developmental Level III activities and, 139-141
Assessment. *See* Testing and assessment
Asthma, fitness education and, 51-52
Attitude, fitness education and, 21

B

Back-Saver Sit-and-Reach, 16
Back Stretcher, spinal cord impairments (SCI) and, 53
Back-to-Back game, 172-173
Back to the Basics (Level II) fitness lesson plan, 86-87
Back to the Basics learning activity, 107-108
Balance, sport-related physical fitness, 8
Ballistic stretching, 45
Ball Squeeze exercise, 160
Bar Push-up exercise, 152
Basic skills, motivation through, 23
Basketball Cats (Level III) fitness integration lesson, 92-95
Beat Goes On activity, 180
Behavioral change, fitness programs and, 18-26
Bent-Knee Push-up exercise, 152
Big Band March Step exercise, 160
Big buddy system, fitness motivation with, 26
Body composition
    health-related physical fitness, 8, 45-46
    testing and assessment, 14

Body Part Addition handout, 129, 131
Body Part Identification learning activity, 101
Body Systems learning activity, 108
Bow and Arrow Stretcher for Shoulders, spinal cord
    impairments and, 54-55
Box Push-up exercise, 152
Bubble exercise, 155
Buddy Walks activity, 146, 196-197
Bump and Run game, 178

C

Cageball fun, 194
Calf flexibility assessment exercise, 162
Calf Stretch, 166
    spinal cord impairments (SCI) and, 54
California Dreamin' activity, 183
Calipers, skinfold measurements, 8
Calorie chart, 125
Canned food drives, fitness education and, 77
Cardiorespiratory endurance (CRE)
    circuit course, 43, 147, 148
    continuous activity and, 43
    developmentally appropriate exercises, 145-149
    fartlek training, 43, 147, 148
    health-related physical fitness, 6, 43
    interval activity, 43
    spinal cord impairment (SCI) and, 56
    testing and assessment, 14-15
Cardiovascular health, thematic units on, 118-120
Cat and Camel stretch, 164-165
Catch the Dragon's Tail game, 175
Cereal Alert project, 120, 123
Cereal searching classroom project, 123
Chest Pass exercise, 156
Chest Press for Chest and Back of Arms, and spinal
    cord impairment (SCI), 55-56
Chest Press exercise, 159
Chicken Dance, 183
Children, coronary heart disease risk factors in, 4
Choices
    in fitness education, 21
    in thematic units, 118
Chute Down exercise, 154
Chute the Ball game, 178
Chute the Works! (Level II) fitness integration lesson,
    90-92
Circle Circulation game, 174
Circuit course
    defined, 43
    developmentally appropriate exercises, 147, 149

Classroom activities, fitness education and, 12, 98-128, 99, 117
  Developmental Level I activities, 129-132
  Developmental Level II activities, 132-138
  Developmental Level III activities, 138-141
  teachers, collaboration with, 115-128
Class structure, fitness education and, 38
Class tutors, disabled children's fitness education and, 49
Closure, fitness education and, 38
Closure, in fitness education, 98
Cognitive learning, 29, 118
Command teaching style, 30
Communication strategies
  classroom fitness programs, 116-117
  parental involvement in fitness education, 60-68
Community involvement
  fitness education and, 13, 74-77
  mental retardation and fitness education, 58
Competition, positive, 170
Components of Health-Related Physical Fitness Principles learning activity, 109
Computer learning, fitness education through, 38
Continuous activity
  developmentally appropriate exercises, 146-149
  health-related fitness with, 43
Cool-down activities, 42, 197
Cooperative learning groups, 26, 118
Coordination, 8
Coronary heart disease (CHD)
  Physical activity and, 4
  Risk factors in children, 4
Crab Crawl exercise, 150-151
Crazy Cones game, 175
Creative equipment, fitness motivation through, 23-24
Cross-elbow touch, 186-187
Crossover Lift exercise, 160
Curl-up exercise, 153-154
  health-related muscular endurance, 7
  with parachute, 154
  progress bar graph, 139-140
Curl- up and Throw exercise, 156
Curl-up and Twist exercise, 154
Curl-up test, 15
Curriculum development, 12, 117

D
Dance and rhythmic activities, 179-191
  Developmental Level I, 180-182
  Developmental Level II, 182-184
  Developmental Level III, 184-190
  safety and, 179-180
Developmental levels
  Level I classroom activities, 129-132
  Level I dance and rhythmic activities, 180-182
  Level I fitness concepts, 99-102
  Level I games, 172-173
  Level II classroom activities, 132-138
  Level II dance and rhythmic activities, 182-184
  Level II fitness concepts, 103-108
  Level II games, 173-177
  Level III classroom activities, 138-141
  Level III dance and rhythmic activities, 184-190
  Level III fitness concepts, 108-113

  Level III games, 178
  physical education curriculum and, x
  scope and sequence of fitness concepts and, 99-100
  yearly fitness plans for, 81-82
Developmentally appropriate exercises, 145-168
  cardiorespiratory endurance, 145-149
  circuit course, 147
  continuous activity exercises, 146
  exercises to avoid, 166-168
  fartlek course, 147-148
  interval activities, 146-147
  muscular strength and endurance, 147, 150-166
Diagonal Crunch exercise, 154
Diet, children and, 3-4
Dino*Fit software, 38
Disabled children, fitness education for, 47-58
  asthma, 51-52
  Individualized Education Plan (IEP), 47-48
  mental retardation, 56-58
  obesity, 49-51
  spinal cord impairments (SCI), 52-56
Dynamic muscle contraction, defined, 44

E
Early Bird Stretch, 198
Education for All Handicapped Children Act, 47
Education for teachers, 117
Electric Slide dance, 189-190
Elementary physical education, 3-10
E-mail messages, 116-117
Empathy, humanistic teaching model and, 29
Encouragement, words and gestures for, 24
Engaging games, 170
Environment
  disabled children's fitness education and, 49
  motivation through, 24
Equipment
  creativity through, 24-26
  for games, 170
Estimating techniques for exercise, 146
Estimation running game, 178
Evening's End workout, 70
Everybody Conga activity, 183
Exercise-induced asthma (EIA), 51-52
Exercise Science: Overload Principle lesson plan, 111-112
Exercises to avoid, 166-168
Extrinsic motivation, 22-23

F
Facts About Fitness activity, 197
Faculty meetings, and classroom fitness program, 116
Family fitness activities, 69-73, 120, 197
Family Fitness Contract, 70-71
Fartlek training
  defined, 43
  developmentally appropriate exercises, 147-148
Feedback, obesity management and, 50
Find a Friend game, 173-174
Fit for Life Family Night, 197
Fit Is Fun learning activity, 101
Fitness clubs, 199
Fitness concepts teaching model, 28, 97-99

Fitness education
    defined, ix-x, 9
    for disabled children, 47-58
    health assessment and, 13-17
    mixed messages regarding, 11-12
    motivation and, 21-26
    multidisciplinary approach to, 12-13
    program characteristics, 9
    team approach to, 11-17
Fitness Education Lessons, 83-88
Fitness Field Day, 194-197
Fitness Flash for parent-teacher conferences, 66-67
Fitness Fortune (family game), 69-70
Fitness fun, promotion of, 20
Fitness Integration Lessons, 89-95
Fitness Is for Everybody learning activity, 102
Fitness Is Fun (Level I) lesson plans, 99-104
Fitness minute, 70
Fitness Tag, 175
Fitness unit teaching approach, 28
FITT guidelines
    application of, 41
    health-related physical fitness and, 40-41
Five-minute warm-up, 28
Flexed-arm hang test, 16
Flexibility exercises, 161-166
    assessment tests, 16
    health-related physical fitness, 8, 44-45
    obesity management and, 51
    spinal cord impairments (SCI) and, 53-56
    Superstretch, 103
Floating Cloud exercise, 155
Food for Fitness learning activity, 112-113, 139-141
Food Guide Pyramid, 45-46, 112-113, 123, 125-127
Food labeling, 120, 122
Forearm and Shoulder Stretcher, spinal cord impair-
    ments (SCI) and, 53
Forward Head Drop exercise, 163
Freeze Dance activity, 182
Frequency, as health-related physical fitness principle,
    40
Front Butterfly for Chest and Back, spinal cord impair-
    ments (SCI) and, 54-55
Full Squats exercise, 167
Fun, fitness motivation through, 23
Fund-raising, fitness education and, 77
Fun Run, 75-76

G
Games and sports teaching model, 28
    developmental games, 168-171
    Developmental Level I games, 172-173
    Developmental Level II games, 173-177
    Developmental Level III games, 178
    physical activity through, 171-172
Genuineness, humanistic teaching model and, 28
Geography Run, 197-198
Grapevine step, 186-187
Graphing activities, classroom fitness programs, 123
Grocery store tour, 75-76
Guest speakers
    for classroom teachers, 117
    fitness motivation with, 26

Guided discovery learning, 34

H
Half-Twist Pass exercise, 156-157
Hamstring Stretch, 165
    flexibility and, 8
    self-check criteria checklist for, 30, 33-34
    spinal cord impairments (SCI) and, 54
Hand push, 7
Health assessment, fitness education and, 13-17
Health clubs, fitness motivation through, 24
Health fairs
    Community Health Fair, 75
    Health-Fitness Fair, 69
    School-Wide Health Fair, 117, 198
Health-related physical fitness
    classroom activities, 125
    components of, 6-8, 42-46, 109, 138-139
    exercise intensity, 109-110
    heart rate recovery, 110-111
    principles of, 39-46
    teaching plan for, 97-114
    testing and assessment, 13-14
Health status, physical activity and, 4
Healthy People 2000, 5
Heart Facts learning activities, 104-107
Heart healthy recipes, 120
Heart healthy snacks, 196
Heart Healthy Wordsearch, 121
Heart Jump (Level I) fitness integration lesson, 89-90
Heart Rate Recovery learning activity, 110-111
Heart Smart Lottery, 178
Heart Thump homework activity, 70, 72
Hearty Hoopla game, 174
Heel Raises exercise, 161
Heel tap and snap, 186-187
Heel touches, 185-186
Hip flexors flexibility assessment exercise, 162
Hokey Pokey, 182
Holiday Classics event, 199
Home-based physical activity programs, 69-73
Homework helpers, 70, 72
Hoop Dribble, 178
Hoopscotch game, 171
Hoops for Heart, 198
Hopping the Islands game, 172
Hora dance, 190
Humanistic games, 169-170
Humanistic teaching model, 28-29
Hurricane exercise, 155

I
I Can Take My Pulse! classroom program, 123, 128
I'm Important—Inside and Out learning activity, 101
Incentives
    motivation through, 24-25
    sample fitness reward certificate, 25
Inchworm exercise, 153
Inclusion guidelines, disabled children's fitness
    education and, 48-49
Inclusion teaching style, 34, 36
Inclusive games, 170
Individualism, humanistic teaching model and, 28

Individualized Education Plan (IEP), disabled
    children's fitness education and, 47-48
Infant mortality statistics, 3
Inservice workshops for teachers, 117
Inside Leg Stretch, 165
Instructional guidelines for fitness education, 29
Integrated learning approach, fitness education, 117-118
Intensity, as health-related physical fitness principle,
    40-41
Intensity of Exercise learning activity, 109-110
Interval activity
    defined, 43
    developmentally appropriate exercises, 146-149
Intervention, obesity management and, 49-50
Intrinsic motivation, 22-23
Isometric exercise, defined, 44
Isotonic exercise, defined, 44

J
Jogging
    as interval activity, 146
    reciprocal checklist for, 32
Jog step, 185-186
Jump for Health activity, 194
Jump Rope for Heart, 198
Jump rope interval activity, 146-147

K
Kickback exercise, 160
Kickback step, 188-189
Knots of Problems game, 175-176
Knowledge, fitness education and, 20-21

L
Language arts
    classroom fitness education and, 120-123
    Developmental Level I activities, 129-132
    Developmental Level II activities, 132-138
    Developmental Level III activities, 138-141
La Rapsa step, 184
Las Vegas Fitness game, 173
Lateral Deltoid Raise exercise, 157
Lateral Torso Stretcher, spinal cord impairments (SCI)
    and, 53
Leg Hug exercise, 165
Leg Lifts exercise, 167
Leg stretches, 165-166
Lesson focus, fitness education and, 38
Lesson plans, fitness education, 83-95
Let's Get Heart Smart (Level III) lesson plans, 108-113
Letter to parents, fitness education and, 61
Level leader meetings, classroom fitness program, 116
Lifeline game, 172
Lifestyle management, fitness education and, 21
Line Change exercise, 146
Line dancing, 194
Look-over exercise, 163
Low back flexibility assessment exercise, 162
Low-impact aerobic dancing, 184-187
Lunch Bunch project, 120
Lunge exercise, 166

M
Macarena, 190-191

Magic School Bus: Inside the Human Body, 120
Main event, of physical activity session, 42
Mainstreaming, disabled children's fitness education
    and, 47-48
Manley, Audrey F. (Dr.), 6
March step, 185-186
Math and science
    classroom fitness education and, 123-124
    Developmental Level I activities, 129-132
    Developmental Level II activities, 133-138
    Developmental Level III activities, 139-141
Measuring Madness handout, 133, 135
Medicine ball activities, 155-157
Memos, classroom fitness programs, 116-117
Mental retardation, fitness education and, 56-58
Me Tree handout, 129-130
Mexican Hat Dance, 184
Military style teaching, 227
Moderate to vigorous physical activity (MVPA), 4
Mortality, physical activity and, 4
Motivation
    fitness education and, 21-26
    strategies for, 23-26
    types of, 22-23
Motivational strategies, fitness programs and, 18-26
Mousercise video, 29
Muscle Mania learning activity, 103-104
Muscular endurance
    developmentally appropriate exercises, 147-168
    health-related physical fitness, 7, 43-44
    spinal cord impairments (SCI) and, 54-55
Muscular strength. See Strength training

N
National Association of Sport and Physical Education
    (NASPE), 9
National Children and Youth Fitness Study II, 11
Neck circles, 167
Neck flexibility assessment exercise, 161
Neck Tilt exercise, 163
Neighborhood fitness trail, 70, 73
Newsletters
    in classroom fitness program, 116, 120
    parental involvement in fitness education, 60, 64-65
Nutrition and fitness, 120. See also Food Guide Pyramid

O
Obesity, ix
    fitness education and, 49-51
Objective-based games, 169
Old MacDonald Had a Health Body activity, 182
One-Mile Run-Walk, 14
Open-ended contracts, 34, 37
Overhead Arm Stretch, 164
Overhead Butterfly for Back and Back of Arms, spinal
    cord impairments (SCI) and, 55-56
Overhead Pass exercise, 156-157
Overload principle, 40
    learning activity, 111-112

P
PACER (Progressive Aerobic Cardiovascular Endur-
    ance Run), 15
Parachute activities, 154-155, 194

Parachute golf, 155
Parental involvement
    action plan for, 59-60
    communication guidelines, 60-68
    disabled children's fitness education and, 48
    education programs and, 68-69
    fitness education and, 13, 26, 59-73
    home-based activities, 69-73
    newsletters, 60, 64-65
    obesity management and, 50
    parent-teacher conferences, 60, 66, 68
    participation in school hours, 69
Parent physical activity survey, 60, 62-63
Parent-teacher conferences, 60, 66, 68
Parent-teacher wellness room, 69
Personalized learning contract, 34-35
Physical activity
    in elementary school children, 3-4
    for exercise-induced asthma (EIA), 51-52
    games as promotion of, 171-172
    health and mortality and, 4
    mental retardation and, 57-58
    mixed messages regarding, 11-12
    obesity management and, 50-51
    parent physical activity survey, 60, 62-63
    session of, stages, 42
    spinal cord impairments (SCI) and, 52
    Surgeon General's report on, 6
Physical Best and Individuals With Disabilities, 48
Physical competence, 22
Physical education
    curriculum reform in, ix-x, 10
    elementary physical education, 3-10
    fitness education curriculum and, 13
Planning guidelines for fitness education, 81-95
Play, fitness education and, 22
Playacting, family fitness program and, 70
Plié touches, 186
Plow exercise, 166
Popcorn exercise, 155
Positive reinforcement, 24
Posture exercises, 133-134
Power, sport-related physical fitness, 8
Practical Body Composition Kit, 14
Practice, fitness education and, 20
Practice teaching style, 30-31
Present level of performance (PLP) assessment, 47-48
Pretest/posttest teaching model, 27-28
Principal Walks activity, 199
Problem Solver exercise, 153
Problem solving teaching style, 34, 37
Progression, health-related physical fitness and, 40
Prudential Fitnessgram Test Administration Manual, 14
Psychomotor learning, 29
PTA fitness demonstrations, 68
Pull-ups, health-related muscular strength, 7
Pull-up test, 15-16
Push-ups exercise, 151-152
    inclusion style task card for, 34, 36
    with parachute, 155
Push-up test, 15-16
Pyramid Power, 113

Q
Quadriceps flexibility assessment exercise, 162
Quadriceps stretch, 166

R
Rainbow to Youth Fitness and Active Lifestyles, 19-20, 97
Random Run exercise, 146
Reading materials, classroom fitness education, 117
Recess workouts, 199
Reciprocal teaching style, 30, 32
Recreation Free Choice activity, 196-197
Resistance exercises
    obesity management and, 51
    Resistance Walking, 111-112
    tube and band exercises, 157-161
Reversibility principle, 40
Rhythm streamers, 181-182
Risk factors in children, 4
Role identification, fitness education specialists, 116
Role models, motivation through, 24
Roman Candle game, 174

S
Safety
    active games, 170-171
    dance and rhythmic activities, 179-180
    disabled children's fitness education and, 48
Safety First learning activity, 102
Sample yearly fitness plans, 81-82
School-community fitness programs, 74
School health services, 13
School lunch, 12-13
School-wide fitness events, 193-200
    ACES (All Children Exercising Simultaneously), 199
    Early Bird Stretch and Afternoon Perk-Up, 198
    Fit for Life Family Night, 197
    Fitness clubs, 199
    Fitness Field Day, 194-197
    Geography Run, 197-198
    Health Fair, 198
    Holiday Classics, 199
    Jump Rope for Heart, Hoops for Heart, Step for Heart, 198
    Principal Walks, 199
    Recess workouts, 199
School-wide health committee, 116
Science. See also Math and Science
Seal Crawl exercise, 150-151
Self-check teaching style, 30, 33
Self-direction, motivation and, 24
Self-expression, fitness education and, 22
Self-monitoring
    in fitness education, 21
    obesity management and, 51
Seminars for parents, 68
Senior citizens, fitness education and, 77
Sensitivity, disabled children's fitness education and, 49
Set induction
    fitness education and, 38
    teaching plan, 97-98
Shape-a-Round game, 175
Shape Up game, 172
Short-term objectives (STOs), 48

Shoulder and Chest Stretcher, spinal cord impairments (SCI) and, 53-54
Shoulder flexibility assessment exercise, 162
Shoulder Stretch, 16
Sit-and-Twist Back Stretch, 164
Sit-ups, 167-168
Skeletal system exercise, 136-138
Skinfold measurements
    body composition, 8
    in fitness assessment programs, 14
Smart Heart (Level III) fitness lesson plan, 87-88
Soccer Golf Challenge, 176-177
Social interaction, fitness education and, 22
Special events, fitness motivation through, 26
Specificity, health-related physical fitness and, 39-40
Speed, sport-related physical fitness, 8
Spinal cord impairments (SCI), 52-56
SPORT-FITT principles of physical fitness, 39-46
Sport lineup game, 175-176
Sport-related physical fitness, 8-9
"Stairway to Lifetime Fitness," 19-20
Static stretching, 45
Step aerobics, 187-189, 194
Step for Heart, 198
Step-kicks, 186-187
Step touches, 185
Stork Stand exercise, 153
Straight-up exercise, 163
Strength training
    developmentally appropriate exercises, 147-168
    health-related physical fitness, 6-7, 43-44
    spinal cord impairments (SCI) and, 53-54
Success-oriented activities, 23
Success-oriented games, 170
Sunday Trip activity, 180-181
Superdome exercise, 155
Superpump (Level I) fitness lesson plan, 83-85
Superstretch learning activity, 103
Surgeon General's Report on Physical Activity and Health, 6

T
Task cards, practice teaching style and, 30-31
Teachable moments, 97-98
Teachers' fitness class, 117
Teaching strategies
    classroom collaboration guidelines, 115-128
    class structure, 38
    computer learning, 38
    disabled children's fitness education and, 49
    faculty meetings, 116
    for fitness education, 27-38, 97-114
    fitness motivation with, 26
    humanistic approach to fitness, 28-29
    teaching styles, 29-38

traditional models, 27
Team approach to fitness education, 11-17
    disabled children's fitness education and, 48
    multidisciplinary aspects of, 12-13
    obesity management and, 50
Television time-out, 70
Testing and assessment
    authenticity in, 17, 24, 26
    health-related physical fitness, 13-14
    present level of performance (PLP) assessment, 48
    youth fitness tests, 14
The Best I Can Be (Level II) lesson plans, 103-108
Thematic units, 117-120
Throwing exercises, 7
Time principle, 41
Tinikling dance, 184
Toe Touches exercise, 167
Touchbacks, 185
Train and maintain principle, 40
Treadmill exercise, 153-154
Triangle Tag game, 174-175
Triceps Extension exercise, 158
Tube and band exercises, 157-161, 194
Tug-of-War game, 155, 196
Turtle Walk exercise, 150-152
Twin Walk game, 173
Type principle, 41

U
Upper body ergometry, 56-57
Upper body strength
    assessment of, 15-16
    individual task card for, 31
Upright Shoulder Row exercise, 159

V
VBS (volleyball, basketball, softball) game, 176
Veins and Arteries game, 173
V-step, 188

W
Wake-up workout, 70
Wall Seat exercise, 161
Warm-up exercises, 197
Warm-ups, 28, 42
Watch Those Calories! classroom program, 123-125
Wellness learning activity, 108-109
Wheel of Fitness game, 172
Windmill exercise, 167-168
Wordsearches, in classroom fitness education, 120-121
Wrist Rolls exercise, 155

Y
Youth fitness tests, 14

Z
Zoowild game, 172

ABOUT THE AUTHOR

Stephen J. Virgilio is an associate professor of physical education at Adelphi University, Garden City, New York. He was an elementary physical educator for six years before earning his PhD from Florida State University in 1979. He is the coauthor of the Heart Smart Program, a comprehensive cardiovascular health education model for elementary schools, and the principal author of *SuperKids-SuperFit*, a physical activity curriculum designed for the Heart Smart Program.

Dr. Virgilio has published extensively throughout his career and has provided presentations for major conferences at the national, international, regional, and state levels. He is also a popular consultant and workshop presenter to school districts throughout the United States. He serves on the Board of Directors of the American Heart Association, Long Island, and on the editorial board for *Teaching Elementary Physical Education*. He is a member of the American Alliance for Health, Physical Education, Recreation and Dance; the Association for Supervision and Curriculum Development; and Phi Delta Kappa.

In his spare time, Steve coaches Little League and enjoys jogging, tennis, mountain biking, world economics, and family activities. He lives in East Williston, Long Island, New York, with

his wife, Irene, and their two sons, Stephen and Joseph.

If you'd like to contact Dr. Virgilio about his workshops, he may be reached at Adelphi University, Department of Physical Education, Woodruff Hall, Garden City, NY 11530.